the tree book

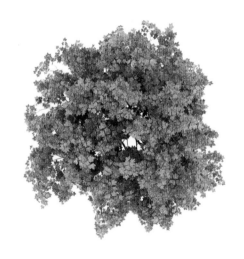

DK

◉ Smithsonian

the tree book

Penguin Random House

DK LONDON

Senior Editors Hugo Wilkinson, Gill Pitts	**Senior Art Editor** Sharon Spencer
US Senior Editor Kayla Dugger	**Project Art Editor** Steve Woosnam-Savage
Production Editor Jacqueline Street-Elkayam	**Senior Jackets Designer** Surabhi Wadhwa-Gandhi
Senior Production Controller Meskerem Berhane	**Jackets Design Development Manager** Sophia MTT
Managing Editor Angeles Gavira Guerrero	**Managing Art Editor** Michael Duffy
Associate Publishing Director Liz Wheeler	**Art Director** Karen Self
Publishing Director Jonathan Metcalf	**Design Director** Phil Ormerod

DK DELHI

Senior Editor Anita Kakar	**Senior Art Editor** Vaibhav Rastogi
Editor Sonali Jindal	**Project Art Editor** Anjali Sachar
Senior Jackets Editorial Coordinator Priyanka Sharma	**Art Editors** Debjyoti Mukherjee, Arshti Narang
Senior Picture Researcher Surya Sankash Sarangi	**Senior DTP Designers** Harish Aggarwal, Neeraj Bhatia, Vishal Bhatia
Project Picture Researcher Nishwan Rasool	**Illustrators** Mohd Zishan, Priyal Mote
Picture Research Manager Taiyaba Khatoon	**Managing Art Editor** Sudakshina Basu
Senior Managing Editor Rohan Sinha	**Production Manager** Pankaj Sharma
Pre-production Manager Balwant Singh	**Design Head** Malavika Talukder
Editorial Head Glenda R. Fernandes	

First American Edition, 2022
Published in the United States by DK Publishing
1450 Broadway, Suite 801, New York, NY 10018

Copyright © 2022 Dorling Kindersley Limited DK,
a Division of Penguin Random House LLC
21 22 23 24 25 10 9 8 7 6 5 4 3 2 1
001–323146–May/2022

A catalog record for this book is available from the Library of Congress.
ISBN 978-0-7440-2746-4

DK books are available at special discounts when purchased in bulk for sales promotions, premiums, fund-raising, or educational use. For details, contact: DK Publishing Special Markets, 1450 Broadway, New York, NY 10018 or SpecialSales@dk.com

Printed in China

For the curious
www.dk.com

This book was made with Forest Stewardship Council ™ certified paper—one small step in DK's commitment to a sustainable future. For more information go to www.dk.com/our-green-pledge

Contributors

Michael Scott OBE (lead author) has a degree in botany and is a natural history writer, broadcaster, and conservationist. Now largely retired, he is traveling the world as a natural history speaker on cruise ships. His books include *Scottish Wild Flowers* and *Mountain Flowers*.

Dr. Ross Bayton is Assistant Director of the Heronswood Garden, Washington. Trained in plant taxonomy at the Royal Botanic Gardens, Kew, he is author of several books on botany and horticulture, including *The Gardener's Botanical*. He also contributed to DK's *Flora*.

Andrew Mikolajski is the author of 40 gardening titles, including *World Encyclopedia of Apples* and books on pruning and permaculture, and was a contributor to DK's *Flora*. He has also contributed to several Royal Horticultural Society (RHS) reference works and to the RHS website, and is an RHS judge.

Keith Rushforth is a Chartered Arboriculturist who developed his passion for "anything temperate, woody and (at least) knee high" while reading Forestry at Aberdeen University, Scotland. He has since visited various rainforests, concentrating on South, Southeast, and East Asia. He has written around a dozen books and has contributed to others.

Consultants

Chris Clennett is the former Garden Manager for Kew Gardens and has been a professional horticulturist for over 40 years, having trained at Oxford Botanic Garden. While at Kew, Chris completed his Master of Horticulture, an MSc, and a PhD. His PhD study of Erythronium was published as the Kew Monograph in 2014, and he went on to write *Flowers of the High Weald* for Kew.

Fiona Stafford is Professor of English Language and Literature and Fellow of Somerville College at the University of Oxford. She is also a Fellow of the British Academy and of the Royal Society of Edinburgh. Her work includes an interest in nature writing and trees, flowers, and their cultural history. She is the author of *The Long, Long Life of Trees* and *The Brief Life of Flowers*.

Smithsonian curator: Cynthia A. Brown, Manager, Collections, Education & Access, Smithsonian Gardens

 S M I T H S O N I A N

Established in 1846, the Smithsonian Institution—the world's largest museum and research complex—includes 19 museums and galleries and the National Zoological Park. The total number of artifacts, works of art, and specimens in the Smithsonian's collections is estimated at 156 million, the bulk of which is contained in the National Museum of Natural History, which holds more than 126 million specimens and objects. The Smithsonian is a renowned research center, dedicated to public education, national service, and scholarship in the arts, sciences, and history.

contents

Ancient woodland
Wistman's Wood in Dartmoor National Park, UK, is the remnant of an ancient forest comprised mostly of oaks— sessile and English (*Quercus petraea* and *Quercus robur*)—but also trees such as mountain ash and hollies. Peppered with granite boulders, this woodland supports a variety of mosses and lichens that take years to form.

CHAPTER 1

How Trees Work

Trees are large, woody plants that reproduce via seeds
and are deeply connected with human history. This
chapter gives an outline of how they evolved, where
and how they live, and more.

What Is a Tree?

Botanically, plants are divided between shrubs (plants with woody stems) and herbs (with nonwood stems). A tree is therefore a shrub that typically grows taller than a variously defined height, usually with a single, columnar main stem (trunk) that does not die back in winter.

Humans have a clear image of what a tree looks like, but the somewhat imprecise definition above is needed because trees are highly adaptable species. A conifer such as a black spruce (*Picea mariana*) or Scots pine (*Pinus sylvestris*), which in good conditions can grow as tall as 100 or 150 ft (30 or 45 m), can live for 50 years yet grow no

taller than 6½ ft (2 m) if it is situated with waterlogged roots in a peat bog, in the taiga forest of the arctic north, or high up above the timberline on an exposed northern mountain. Different authorities adopt different definitions for the minimum height that constitutes a tree, but usually it is set at 16 or 20 ft (5 or 6 m).

▶ Parts of a tree

In most societies, even young children know and can draw the parts of a tree. Yet it is easy to overlook just how complex and sophisticated a tree is—a living organism, with every part playing a role.

DWARF TREES

Plants such as dwarf willow (*Salix herbacea*) further confuse the definition of a tree. It is a shrub that rarely rises more than 2½ in (6 cm) above the ground, but it forms large mats with gnarled, finger-thick, treelike branches that spread over mountain rocks or arctic tundra.

DWARF WILLOW

Crown comprises the branches extending from the trunk, together with the leaves, flowers, and fruit they support

Fruits

Conifers release seeds into the wind from their fruiting cones. Broadleaved trees often rely on animals to disperse seeds encased within fleshy, edible fruits.

Cone scale

CONE

Seed

DRUPE

Protective skin

Fleshy fruit with one or more seeds

FRUITS

Cones produce pollen and seeds

FLOWERS

Petal

BLOSSOM

CONIFER

Flowers

Like all higher plants, trees reproduce by seeds. Flowers allow pollen exchange by wind or animals, which enables fertilization and seed formation.

LEAVES

Vein

Petiole (stalk)

BROADLEAVED

Needles

Lobe

Leaves

Leaves are the tree's solar panels and chemical factories. Water loss from leaves sets up a vacuum pump system that draws in water through the roots.

CONIFEROUS

BRANCHES

Branches serve to spread the crown widely, maximizing the surface area of leaves exposed to sunlight

Branches
Branches and twigs are the scaffolding of the tree. Leaves and flowers develop from buds on twigs, accessible to sunlight and wind or pollinating animals.

TERMINAL BUD

Leaf bud beginning to burst

Bud scale

Multiple leaf buds

CLUSTERED BUDS

At up to 82 ft (25 m) long and 10 ft (3 m) wide, the raffia palm (*Raphia regalis*) has the largest leaves of any tree

TRUNK

CROSS-SECTION

Growth rings (usually annual)

Heartwood

Side branch

Sapwood

LONGITUDINAL SECTION

Trunk
The trunk is the tree's strength and lifts its crown above competition. It contains a plumbing system for transporting water and the products of photosynthesis.

Trunk typically is branched only in the upper portion (crown), but a few tree species have multiple trunks

BARK

Bark
Bark is the dead outer layer of the trunk and branches that protects the living wood from harm by weather, animals, and fire. It wears and cracks with age.

Ridges on outer bark

RIDGED

Peeling outer bark

Inner bark

PEELING

ROOTS

Roots often contain as much biomass (living matter) underground as the total tree growth above ground

AERIAL ROOTS

Absorb oxygen from water

BUTTRESS ROOTS

Act as props

Roots
Roots anchor the tree in the ground and spread through the soil to seek water and nutrients, in partnership with a fungus living in or around them.

Classification of Trees

With just over 60,000 species of tree worldwide, a system of classification allows for identification of individual trees. The system currently in use evolved over time as science progressed, with DNA techniques refining its accuracy.

▲ Botanical illustrations
Before the advent of photography, botanists relied on illustrations to record new plants. They are often highly detailed and drawn to scale, though also objects of beauty.

Botanical classification

Over the centuries, people have named and classified trees and other living things around them. The system used today originated in the 18th century, when specimens of trees from around the world flooded into Europe. Faced with an ever-increasing diversity, philosophers and scientists began to name and sort specimens, bringing together those that looked similar. The Swedish scientist Carl Linnaeus (1707–1778) is the best-known early taxonomist and his naming system, known as the Linnaean binomial, is still in use today, although his classification system has largely been superseded. Continued scientific discoveries provided a better understanding of how trees are related to one another, and a burgeoning fossil flora and the theory of evolution demonstrated how plants have changed and developed over time. Today, taxonomists also utilize DNA, the genetic instructions for life, to improve classification.

► Major tree groups

All trees alive today are spermatophytes. The fossil record shows that tree-sized club mosses and ferns existed in the past and, while some tree ferns survive today, they are not true trees. The classification shown here is the one used in this book.

SEED-PRODUCING TREES

Spermatophytes
All modern trees reproduce using seeds, unlike ferns and mosses, which produce spores.

Gymnosperms
The seeds of these trees develop within female cones, and male cones produce pollen.

NON-FLOWERING TREES

Angiosperms
The seeds of angiosperms develop enclosed within fruits. Most trees are in this group.

FLOWERING TREES

Cycads
These tropical trees and shrubs have separate male and female plants.

Ginkgoes
Only one species remains in this group, a deciduous tree with fan-shaped leaves.

Conifers
Conifers have narrow, waxy leaves and are evergreen or deciduous.

Magnoliids
The earliest branches of the angiosperm lineage include magnolias and their relatives.

Monocots
Most monocots lack a woody stem and so are not trees; palms are exceptions.

Eudicots
Most modern trees are eudicots. They are extremely variable and widespread.

Monocots and eudicots

Most modern trees are flowering plants, also known as angiosperms. The oldest flowering trees are known as Magnoliids and include magnolias, avocados, and nutmeg. The rest are split between monocotyledons (or monocots) and eudicotyledons (or eudicots). Monocot trees do not produce true wood, and are often not considered "real" trees. They include palms, yuccas, and aloes. Their flowers tend to have parts in threes, their leaves have parallel veins, and their seeds have a single cotyledon. Eudicot trees produce true wood, with rings. Examples include oaks and maples. Their flowers have parts in fives or fours, their leaves have branched veins, and their seeds each contain two cotyledons.

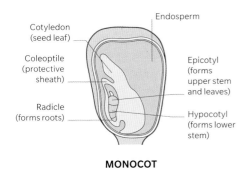

MONOCOT

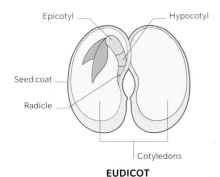

EUDICOT

▲ Monocot and eudicot seeds

Named for the differences between their seeds, monocots contain one embryonic leaf (or cotyledon), while eudicot seeds contain two. In eudicots, cotyledons contain food to fuel seedling growth, while in monocots, there is a separate store of nutritious endosperm.

Ornamental trees such as *Magnolia × soulangeana* are selected because they display useful characteristics, such as this large bloom

Hybrid bloom has white from one parent and pink from another

▲ Artificially bred hybrid

Hybrid trees usually exhibit characteristics from both parents, but often increased vigor. This means they are usually more productive, faster growing, and less prone to disease.

Hybrids and cultivars

Since the early days of agriculture, humans have improved their crop plants by selecting those with the best traits and crossbreeding them. Hybrids are the products of crosses between different species, and they do occur in nature. The gray poplar (*Populus × canescens*) is the result of natural hybridization between white poplar (*Populus alba*) and European aspen (*Populus tremula*). However, trees such as lemon (*Citrus × limon*) are the product of hybridization for horticulture and do not occur in the wild. Cultivars (or cultivated varieties) are selected forms of trees and other plants. Apple varieties such as 'Golden Delicious' are examples of cultivars.

TREE CLASSIFICATION

As with all members of the plant kingdom, botanists classify trees in a hierarchy according to the extent of their shared characteristics. The classification of the 'Golden Delicious' apple is shown below, from division to the lowest level (cultivar).

▼ **DIVISION or CLADE** Separates trees according to key features, such as flowering (angiosperms) rather than nonflowering (gymnosperms)

▼ **CLASS or CLADE** Divides trees according to fundamental differences, such as having two seed leaves (eudicots) rather than one seed leaf (monocots)

▼ **ORDER** A major subdivision of a class containing one or more families: in this example, the order Rosales

▼ **FAMILY** A group of several genera that share a set of underlying natural characteristics: in this case, the rose family Rosaceae

▼ **GENUS** A group of species that share a range of distinctive characteristics, such as the apple genus *Malus*

▼ **SPECIES** A group of individuals that interbreed naturally to produce offspring with similar characteristics, such as the domesticated apple species *Malus domestica*

▼ **CULTIVAR** An artificially bred distinct variant of a species, such as the 'Golden Delicious' cultivar *Malus domestica* 'Golden Delicious'

▼ How trees evolved

The rings in a tree trunk reveal the passage of time over the life of the tree, with the oldest rings at the center. This chart does likewise, showing the course of evolution for many familiar tree groups. As fossil evidence is often fragmentary, many of the dates are approximate.

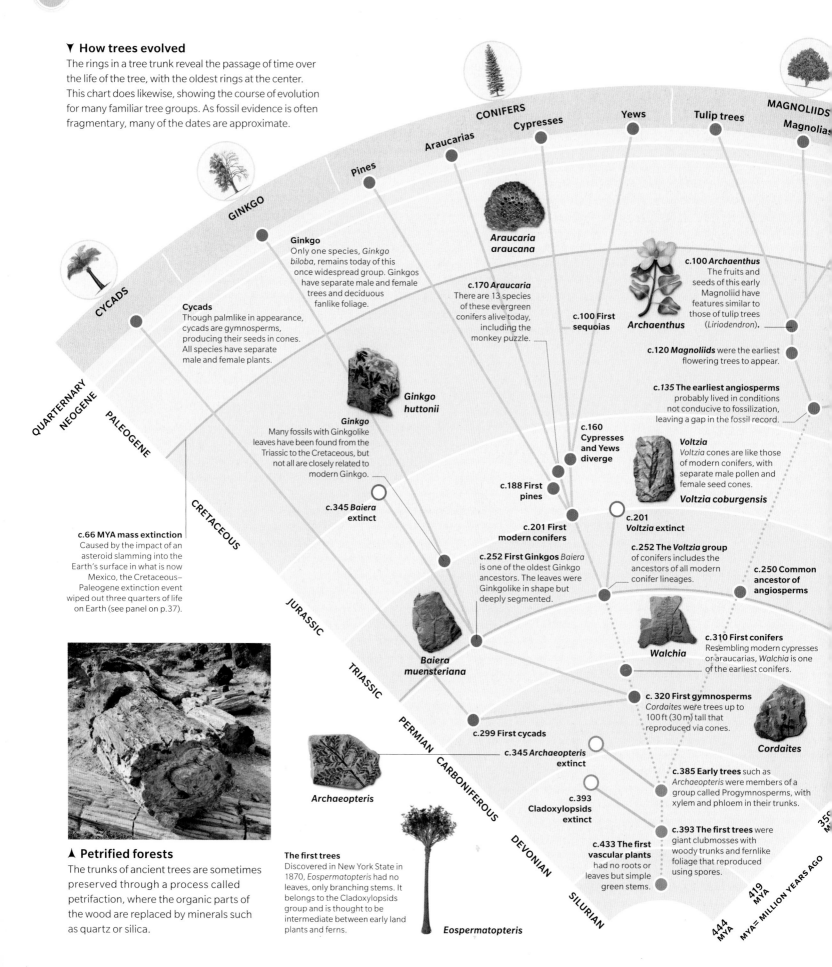

CONIFERS Araucarias Cypresses Yews Tulip trees **MAGNOLIIDS** Magnolias

Pines

GINKGO

Ginkgo
Only one species, *Ginkgo biloba*, remains today of this once widespread group. Ginkgos have separate male and female trees and deciduous fanlike foliage.

CYCADS

Cycads
Though palmlike in appearance, cycads are gymnosperms, producing their seeds in cones. All species have separate male and female plants.

Araucaria araucana

c.170 Araucaria
There are 13 species of these evergreen conifers alive today, including the monkey puzzle.

c.100 First sequoias

Archaenthus

c.100 Archaenthus
The fruits and seeds of this early Magnoliid have features similar to those of tulip trees (*Liriodendron*).

c.120 Magnoliids were the earliest flowering trees to appear.

c.135 The earliest angiosperms probably lived in conditions not conducive to fossilization, leaving a gap in the fossil record.

Ginkgo
Many fossils with Ginkgolike leaves have been found from the Triassic to the Cretaceous, but not all are closely related to modern Ginkgo.

Ginkgo huttonii

QUARTERNARY
NEOGENE
PALEOGENE

c.160 Cypresses and Yews diverge

Voltzia
Voltzia cones are like those of modern conifers, with separate male pollen and female seed cones.

Voltzia coburgensis

CRETACEOUS

c.66 MYA mass extinction
Caused by the impact of an asteroid slamming into the Earth's surface in what is now Mexico, the Cretaceous–Paleogene extinction event wiped out three quarters of life on Earth (see panel on p.37).

c.345 Baiera extinct

c.188 First pines

c.201 First modern conifers

c.201 Voltzia extinct

c.252 First Ginkgos *Baiera* is one of the oldest Ginkgo ancestors. The leaves were Ginkgolike in shape but deeply segmented.

c.252 The *Voltzia* group of conifers includes the ancestors of all modern conifer lineages.

c.250 Common ancestor of angiosperms

JURASSIC

c.310 First conifers Resembling modern cypresses or araucarias, *Walchia* is one of the earliest conifers.

Walchia

Baiera muensteriana

TRIASSIC

c.299 First cycads

PERMIAN

c. 320 First gymnosperms *Cordaites* were trees up to 100 ft (30 m) tall that reproduced via cones.

Cordaites

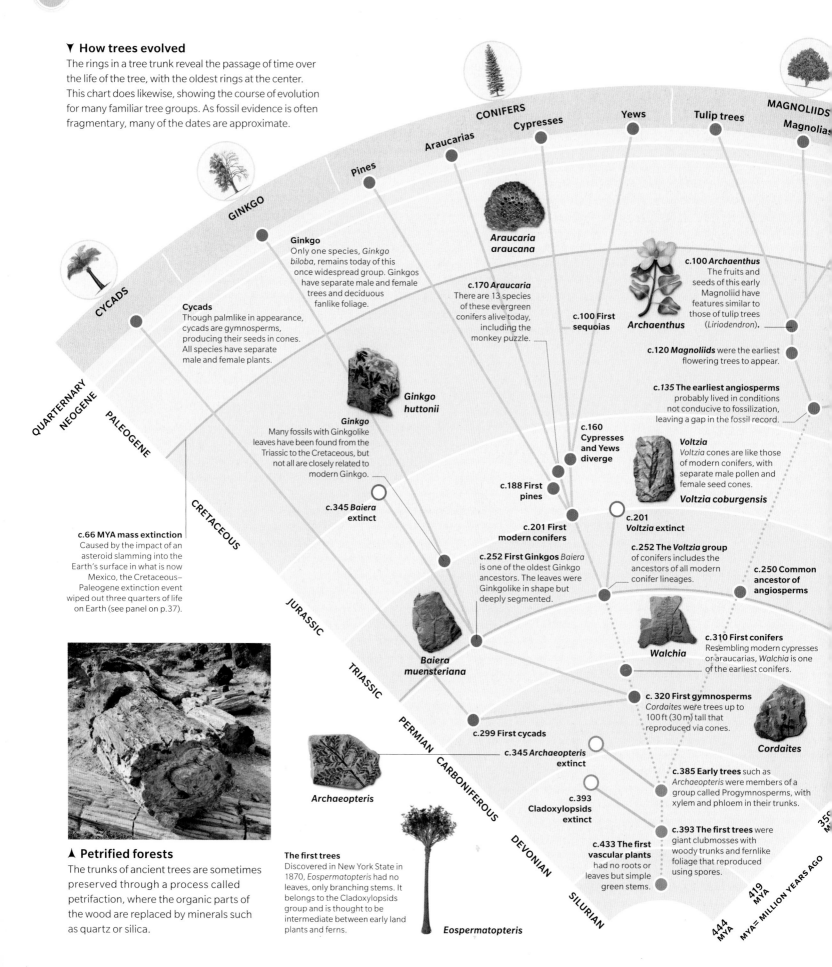

▲ **Petrified forests**
The trunks of ancient trees are sometimes preserved through a process called petrifaction, where the organic parts of the wood are replaced by minerals such as quartz or silica.

CARBONIFEROUS

c.345 Archaeopteris extinct

Archaeopteris

c.393 Cladoxylopsids extinct

The first trees
Discovered in New York State in 1870, *Eospermatopteris* had no leaves, only branching stems. It belongs to the Cladoxylopsids group and is thought to be intermediate between early land plants and ferns.

Eospermatopteris

DEVONIAN

c.433 The first vascular plants had no roots or leaves but simple green stems.

c.385 Early trees such as *Archaeopteris* were members of a group called Progymnosperms, with xylem and phloem in their trunks.

c.393 The first trees were giant clubmosses with woody trunks and fernlike foliage that reproduced using spores.

SILURIAN

350 MYA

419 MYA

444 MYA

MYA= MILLION YEARS AGO

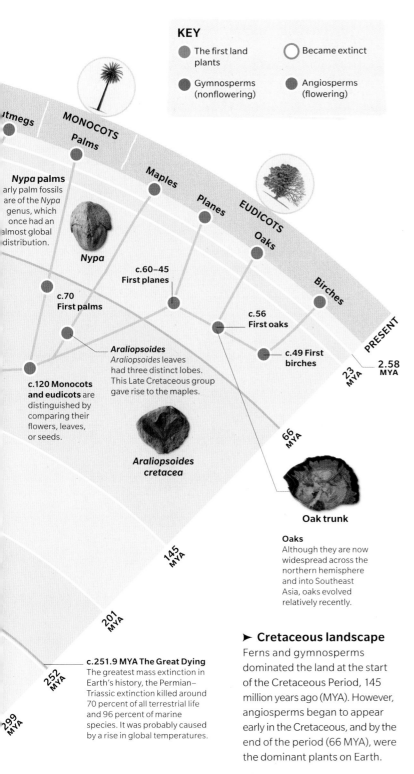

KEY
- ● The first land plants
- ○ Became extinct
- ● Gymnosperms (nonflowering)
- ● Angiosperms (flowering)

MONOCOTS

Palms

utmegs

EUDICOTS

Maples

Planes

Oaks

Birches

Nypa palms
arly palm fossils are of the *Nypa* genus, which once had an almost global distribution.

Nypa

c.70 First palms

c.60–45 First planes

c.56 First oaks

c.49 First birches

PRESENT

2.58 MYA

23 MYA

c.120 Monocots and eudicots are distinguished by comparing their flowers, leaves, or seeds.

Araliopsoides
Araliopsoides leaves had three distinct lobes. This Late Cretaceous group gave rise to the maples.

Araliopsoides cretacea

66 MYA

Oak trunk

Oaks
Although they are now widespread across the northern hemisphere and into Southeast Asia, oaks evolved relatively recently.

145 MYA

201 MYA

c.251.9 MYA The Great Dying
The greatest mass extinction in Earth's history, the Permian–Triassic extinction killed around 70 percent of all terrestrial life and 96 percent of marine species. It was probably caused by a rise in global temperatures.

252 MYA

299 MYA

► **Cretaceous landscape**
Ferns and gymnosperms dominated the land at the start of the Cretaceous Period, 145 million years ago (MYA). However, angiosperms began to appear early in the Cretaceous, and by the end of the period (66 MYA), were the dominant plants on Earth.

In 2005, a petrified tree trunk 237 ft (72 m) long was found in Thailand—the world's largest single fossil

Evolution of Trees

Trees have evolved many times. They are not one group of related plants; instead, numerous species with treelike forms and heights have appeared (and disappeared) in many distantly related groups of plants over millions of years.

Tree groups

From tree ferns to oak trees, many different plant groups have produced treelike species. Being treelike has advantages. Great height prevents many animals from feeding on the plant's foliage; allows the scattering of seeds farther away; and, importantly, dominates the competition for light. Attaining great height requires many engineering obstacles be overcome. Trees need a rigid structure to hold their weight yet also the flexibility to endure windy weather. A vascular system is vital to transport water from the ground up to the crown, against the pull of gravity. These requirements were not achieved overnight, but through the evolution of countless new species, accumulating and refining the structures that enable treelike life. The chart opposite follows the development of trees over time, based on fossil evidence and dating from DNA studies. Not all modern tree groups are included.

How Trees Live

Trees sustain themselves with sugars produced in the leaves and water absorbed through the roots, which are transported via a system of conductive tissues.

Energy for life

All life on Earth depends on plants—including trees—which manufacture sugars using only water and carbon dioxide. A byproduct of this process is oxygen, which plants and animals depend on for survival. This vital chemical reaction is called photosynthesis and can occur only in the presence of light from the sun, which provides energy to fuel the process. Sugars are the food that sustains the lives of plants and of the animals that feed upon them. Trees consume sugars through a process of cellular respiration, which provides them with the energy to grow.

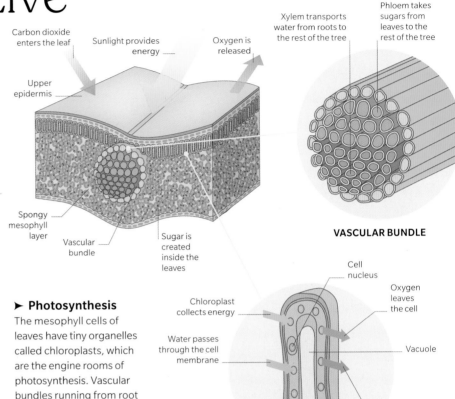

Carbon dioxide enters the leaf

Sunlight provides energy

Oxygen is released

Upper epidermis

Xylem transports water from roots to the rest of the tree

Phloem takes sugars from leaves to the rest of the tree

Spongy mesophyll layer

Vascular bundle

Sugar is created inside the leaves

VASCULAR BUNDLE

▶ Photosynthesis

The mesophyll cells of leaves have tiny organelles called chloroplasts, which are the engine rooms of photosynthesis. Vascular bundles running from root to leaf carry water to the leaves for photosynthesis and deliver the resulting sugars to the rest of the tree.

Cell nucleus

Chloroplast collects energy

Oxygen leaves the cell

Water passes through the cell membrane

Vacuole

Carbon dioxide enters the cell

Glucose transported to rest of plant

MESOPHYLL CELL

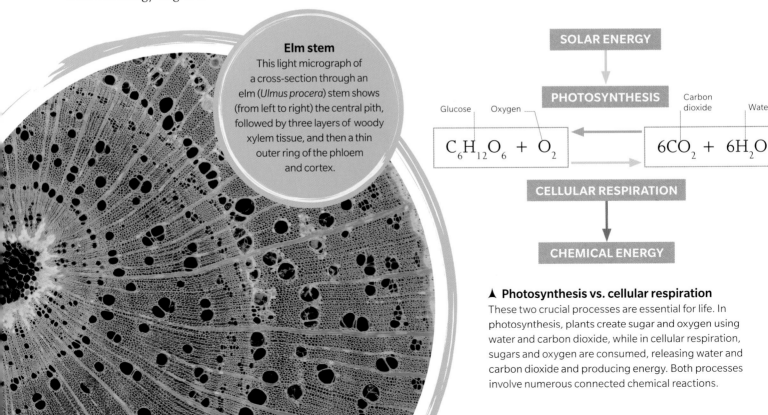

Elm stem
This light micrograph of a cross-section through an elm (*Ulmus procera*) stem shows (from left to right) the central pith, followed by three layers of woody xylem tissue, and then a thin outer ring of the phloem and cortex.

SOLAR ENERGY

↓

PHOTOSYNTHESIS

Glucose Oxygen Carbon dioxide Water

$$C_6H_{12}O_6 + O_2 \qquad 6CO_2 + 6H_2O$$

CELLULAR RESPIRATION

↓

CHEMICAL ENERGY

▲ Photosynthesis vs. cellular respiration

These two crucial processes are essential for life. In photosynthesis, plants create sugar and oxygen using water and carbon dioxide, while in cellular respiration, sugars and oxygen are consumed, releasing water and carbon dioxide and producing energy. Both processes involve numerous connected chemical reactions.

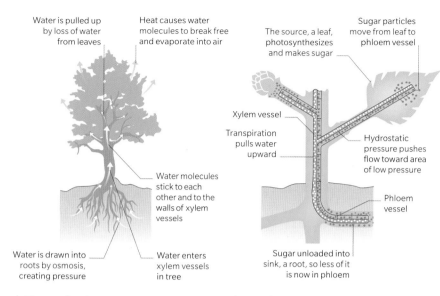

Water is pulled up by loss of water from leaves

Heat causes water molecules to break free and evaporate into air

Water molecules stick to each other and to the walls of xylem vessels

Water is drawn into roots by osmosis, creating pressure

Water enters xylem vessels in tree

▲ Transpiration

Evaporation of water from the pores of the leaves drives the flow of water up from the roots in a process called transpiration. Rates of transpiration increase on hot or windy days.

Sugar particles move from leaf to phloem vessel

The source, a leaf, photosynthesizes and makes sugar

Xylem vessel

Transpiration pulls water upward

Hydrostatic pressure pushes flow toward area of low pressure

Phloem vessel

Sugar unloaded into sink, a root, so less of it is now in phloem

▲ Moving sugar

Roots are unable to make their own sugars and rely on the leaves to produce them. Phloem transports sugars from areas of high concentration (sources) to areas of low concentration (sinks) via osmosis.

Circulation systems

The human circulatory system uses veins and arteries to move blood around the body. Trees also have a circulation system, and its function is to transport water from the roots throughout the tree and deliver sugars produced in the leaves to the roots and other organs. A tree's circulatory system is composed of specialized tissues called xylem and phloem, which are found together in vascular bundles. Xylem, which makes up the wood of a tree trunk, carries water upward from the roots, while phloem transports sugars and other organic compounds from the leaves. Vascular bundles contain numerous xylem and phloem cells, which sit end to end, forming extended tubes. They also include cambium cells, which produce new xylem and phloem, causing the trunk to expand.

> Trees cannot grow taller than 394 ft (120 m) because that is the maximum height to which the columns of water inside a tree can be lifted

Waste disposal

In the center of each plant cell is a large structure called a vacuole. Filled with water, the vacuole pushes outward, holding the cell rigid. In drought conditions, as water is lost from the vacuole, cells begin to contract and the plant wilts. Vacuoles store sugars; proteins; and, in some cases, as in flower petals, colorful pigments. Waste products are moved into the vacuole, so they do not damage the cell cytoplasm; toxins such as nicotine, which repel herbivorous animals, are stored there, too. Some trees store waste products in their leaves. In winter, these leaves are shed, taking the waste products with them.

▶ Why leaves are usually green

Photosynthesis depends on sunlight, and the pigment chlorophyll , inside chloroplasts, provides the means by which plants capture and utilize this energy. Chlorophyll absorbs light energy—particularly blue and red light—but reflects green wavelengths, making leaves appear green.

▶ Pigment change

As light levels decline in fall, leaves cease the production of chlorophyll, causing them to change color. Cooler temperatures also cause purple and red anthocyanin pigments to develop.

Sunlight

Chloroplast

Chlorophyll in pouches

Reflected light

Blue and red absorbed

Fall leaves change color as chlorophyll production diminishes and existing yellow pigments (carotenoids) become visible

How Trees Reproduce

Producing the next generation is crucial for the survival of
tree species. Unlike animals, which can seek out a mate, trees
are rooted to the ground and must therefore rely on other
ways to procreate and spread.

Pollination

Pollen contains genetic information from the
male reproductive organs of its parent tree.
Once transferred to another tree, it comes into
contact with an ovule, which contains female
genetic material, and together they form
a seed. In conifers, pollen and ovules
develop in separate cones and the
pollen is transferred by wind. The
word "conifer" means "cone bearer."
In flowering plants, pollen and ovules
can form within the same flower
(hermaphrodite), separate flowers on the
same tree (monoecious), or separate flowers
on separate trees (dioecious). Flowering trees
mostly rely on animals or wind to transfer
their pollen from one bloom to another, in
a process known as pollination.

Male cones produce
copious quantities
of winged pollen
and are then shed

Female cones contain
ovules, which form
seeds. These are
released when the
mature cone opens

▶ Male and female cones
Conifers reproduce using cones, with male
cones producing pollen and female cones
producing ovules. Male and female cones
may occur on the same tree, as in pines, or
separate trees, as in yews.

Leaves are
needle-shaped

CROSS-POLLINATION

Once pollen is transferred from one flower
to another, fertilization occurs. Pollen grains
adhere to the sticky stigma and germinate,
producing a pollen tube. This grows down
through the style to reach the ovary, where
the genetic information from the pollen is
transferred. Once fertilized, the ovules
develop into seeds, while the surrounding
ovary becomes the fruit. Fruits ensure that
the new seeds are dispersed.

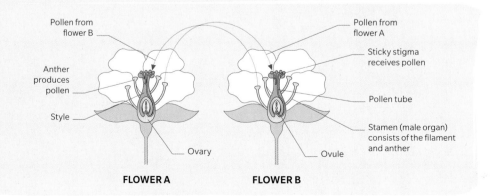

Pollen from
flower B

Pollen from
flower A

Anther
produces
pollen

Sticky stigma
receives pollen

Style

Pollen tube

Stamen (male organ)
consists of the filament
and anther

Ovary

Ovule

FLOWER A   **FLOWER B**

Wind pollination

Pollen grains are small and readily transported by wind. Wind pollination, or anemophily, is utilized by all conifers and many flowering trees, including oaks, alders, and birches. Wind-pollinated trees do not need to attract animals and therefore do not produce colorful or fragrant flowers, nor do they generate rewards such as nectar. Of course, wind does not guarantee delivery of pollen to the correct flower or cone, as an insect might, so these trees must produce pollen in great quantity to ensure that some reaches its target. Pollen from wind-pollinated trees is a common cause of allergies in humans.

Releasing pollen
Wind-pollinated trees often shed their pollen before their leaves appear in spring so that the foliage does not impede air flow around their flowers, as seen with these alder catkins.

A mature Monterey pine (*Pinus radiata*) tree can produce almost 2 pounds (1 kg) of pollen every spring

▲ Insect
Insects are the most common animal pollinators, and many different types of insect take on this role. Bees, butterflies, and moths are frequent pollinators, but beetles can also pollinate certain flowers, such as this magnolia.

▲ Bird
Pollination by birds is most common in the tropics, and several families participate, including hummingbirds, sunbirds, and honeyeaters. Bird-pollinated plants tend to have tubular flowers, with no scent and mostly red colors.

▲ Mammal
Many tropical bats act as pollinators. The flowers they visit tend to be white and have pungent aromas, so they can be easily located by the bats at night. Other mammal pollinators include possums and lemurs.

Animal pollination

Wind pollination is imprecise, and therefore inefficient. Pollen contains genetic material and is costly to produce, especially when most of it never reaches the intended target. Animal pollination, or zoophily, is more precise, so plants can save resources and produce less pollen. To attract animals, plants must offer them a reward, most often sugary nectar or protein-rich pollen. They also need to draw the attention of animals: colorful petals and fragrance act as lures and are readily modified to attract specific animals. Specialization, where a single type of animal pollinates one tree species, is a risky strategy. If the animal becomes extinct, the tree may follow. However, it does guarantee that pollen will be transferred to the correct tree and not be wasted. Some trees instead employ generalist blooms that welcome an assortment of animals, and many kinds of animals act as pollinators for them.

Seed dispersal

The soil directly under a tree is thick with roots, while the ground is dark and shady, creating unfavorable conditions for a tree seed to germinate. Saplings in this area would have to compete with their parent for crucial resources such as light, water, and soil nutrients. Instead, trees spread their seeds far away, reducing competition while also allowing them to expand into new territory. Because trees are largely static organisms, their reproduction relies on natural forces (such as wind, fire, and water) and animals to disperse their seeds far and wide.

Developing embryos are sustained through their long sea journey through the nutrition contained in the large seeds

Buoyant husks keep coconut seeds afloat for months, enabling their spread from island to island

▲ Wind
Conifers such as Douglas fir (*Pseudotsuga menziesii*) have wings on their seeds, which allow them to be carried by wind. Birch seeds are small and papery.

▲ Gravity
Heavy seeds such as conkers simply drop to the ground. Squirrels and other rodents collect and hoard them, and forgotten seeds germinate.

▲ Explosion
The mature fruits of sandbox tree (*Hura crepitans*) explode with a loud bang, scattering seeds widely, at speeds of up to 149 mph (240 kph).

▲ Fire
Some conifer cones and fruits, like these of *Banksia*, only open when burned. The seeds can then grow in areas cleared of competing trees.

◄ Water
Water provides a means of transport for seeds of plants growing alongside rivers and lakes. Saltwater can kill seeds, but those of coconuts are specially adapted to survive in the ocean.

▲ Animals
Many plants lure animals with fleshy fruits. Seeds of cassowary plum (*Cerbera floribunda*) only germinate after passing through the digestive tract of a cassowary.

MILLENNIUM SEED BANK, KEW, UK

▼ Suckering

By sending up shoots, known as suckers, from the roots spreading out from the original trunk, this stag's horn sumac (*Rhus typhina*) produces identical versions of itself.

Natural and artificial propagation

Seed production is a form of sexual reproduction where the offspring have different characteristics from the parents. However, this is not the only way in which trees procreate. Some can create genetically identical offspring by suckering from the roots (see pp.130–133), by stems rooting into the soil (layering), or by developing seeds via apomixis (see pp.164–165). Humans have taken advantage of these asexual processes to produce genetically identical trees for horticulture.

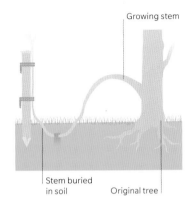

Growing stem

Stem buried in soil

Original tree

▲ Layering

Pegging a low branch to the soil stimulates root development along its lower surface. Once rooted, the branch can be removed and grown separately.

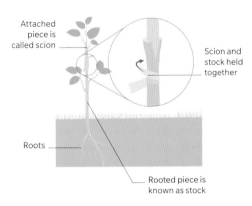

Attached piece is called scion

Scion and stock held together

Roots

Rooted piece is known as stock

▲ Grafting

Grafting combines parts from two different plants, such as a fruit tree branch and a trunk of a vigorous variety, so the resulting tree will have both qualities.

The double coconut (*Lodoicea maldivica*) produces the heaviest and largest seeds in the world, weighing up to 55 lb (25 kg) and reaching 20 in (50 cm) in length

Trees as an Ecosystem

Every tree is a miniature ecosystem, even a solitary tree clinging to a mountain crag or struggling to survive in a desert. Where trees cluster together, in the communities known as woods or forests, they support some of the most diverse ecosystems on Earth.

Tree life

The productivity of trees results in a huge amount of organic matter from which other species can benefit: leaves, flowers, fruits, and even the tough wood are consumed by various animals. Bacteria and fungi parasitize the living and rot the dead parts of the tree. Its trunk and branches provide a perch on which lichens and mosses and other plants can live as epiphytes (plants that grow on other plants). Fungi, parasitic plants such as mistletoes, and wood-boring insects extract nutrition from it. And birds and mammals feed on fruits, cones or seeds, and insects that feed in the tree.

◄ Roe deer
Roe deer are the most wood-adapted of deer in Europe, like white-tailed deer in North America. They can reach 4 ft (1.2 m) up to eat buds, shoots, and leaves of deciduous trees.

► Diversity in an oak
Because they grow close to many English universities, woodlands of English oak (see pp.184–189) are some of the best-studied in the world. Long-term datasets record the many species that depend on, or take advantage of, oak trees for survival.

FLOWERS

Flowers
Oak-mining bees feed mainly on pollen from oak catkins. Honey bees also eat the pollen. Dormice and squirrels devour the whole, protein-rich catkins.

Adults live in canopy, feeding on aphid honeydew and tree sap

PURPLE EMPEROR BUTTERFLY

OAK CATKINS

HONEY BEE

Honey bee with full pollen sac

BRANCHES

OAKMOSS LICHEN

Branches
More than 700 species of lichen grow on oak trunks and branches. Birds and squirrels build nests on the branches or shelter on them to rest.

Specialist oak tree species

Bird perches, sleeps, and nests on branches

Built by squirrel for breeding and shelter

SQUIRREL DREY

WOOD PIGEONS

Ground
Fungi; worms; and invertebrates, such as woodlice, feed on fallen leaves and dead wood. Jays bury acorns—any they do not find later grow into new oak trees.

Feeds on leaf litter, helping recycle nutrients

Buries excess acorns as a winter food store

COMMON WOODLOUSE

MOSS AND FUNGI

EURASIAN JAY

GROUND

Fruits

GROWING ACORNS

In a bumper year, one oak can produce 50,000 acorns. Rooks, nuthatches, and jays eat them and badgers, wild boar, deer, and mice feed on fallen acorns.

Young acorns cannot be digested by many animals

FRUITS

Buries acorns as a food store for winter

GRAY SQUIRREL

LEAVES

Leaves

New leaves attract aphids. The green oak roller moth lays its eggs near leaf buds. Its larvae can defoliate a tree, but blue and great tits reduce their numbers.

Larva feeds on oak leaves

Hunts tits and other small birds in oak tree food chain

ROLLER MOTH LARVAE

BLUE TIT

SPARROWHAWK

Trunk

PIPISTRELLE LEAVING ROOST

More than 1,100 invertebrate species live on oaks. Many wood-boring beetles live in the trunk, hunted by woodpeckers. Bats roost in tree hollows.

Bats roost in hollows in the bark

Tunnels eaten by beetle larvae

LESSER SPOTTED WOODPECKER

BEETLE BURROWS IN WOOD

TRUNK

A mature oak tree supports around 2,300 species, 326 of which are entirely dependent on it

▲ **Dormant English oak in winter**
Deciduous trees still support life when leafless in winter. Insect eggs and larvae survive in their roots or beneath their bark, where woodpeckers feed on them, and epiphytes grow on the branches. Squirrels may have winter dreys, and birds find sheltered roosts.

Forest life

As part of a forest, trees create a more sheltered microclimate for other plants and animals. Their dead leaves rot to create a rich woodland soil in which other species flourish. The boreal forests of northern Asia, Europe, and North America are dominated by a few conifer species, with a more varied understory and a relatively small group of specialist animals, from woodpeckers to lynx. The deciduous forests of temperate countries have a richer flora, which in turn supports a more diverse fauna. Where high rainfall combines with high temperatures, close to the equator, tropical rainforests are the world's richest ecosystems. Two and a half acres (1 hectare) of rainforest can be home to 480 species of tree—20 times the number in a deciduous wood—and 42,000 insect species.

How Forests Work

Trees form communities known as woods or forests, which create their own microclimate and form their own soils. These communities are dynamic and change over time, sometimes helped by external factors such as fire; the trees rely on hidden partners to provide the nutrients they need to survive.

How a forest forms

Most trees have mechanisms to disperse their seeds widely, in the wind or helped by animals. When temperatures are right, the seeds germinate. If the ground is too rocky, wet, or dry or the soil chemistry is unsuitable, the seedling soon dies, or it might quickly be eaten by passing animals. Sometimes a new habitat is opened up by a landslip, a fire, a wetland drying out, human activity, or grazing animals moving away. Then many seedlings can start growing together. These provide shelter to each other, and their falling leaves begin to alter and enrich the soil. In time, so many seedlings appear that the grazers are overwhelmed and a forest begins to spread.

◄ Young beech sapling

Decomposing dead leaves add humus to the soil in this beech wood, creating better conditions for beech seeds to germinate and grow. The two seed leaves on the beech seedling help it begin photosynthesis quickly.

▼ Woodland succession

Tough-leaved or spiny shrubs provide some protection for short-lived, pioneering tree species to grow. These begin to create a richer woodland environment in which slow-growing, longer-lived trees can establish.

In a typical temperate wood, around 2,700 lb of leaves fall on every acre in a year (3,000 kg per hectare)

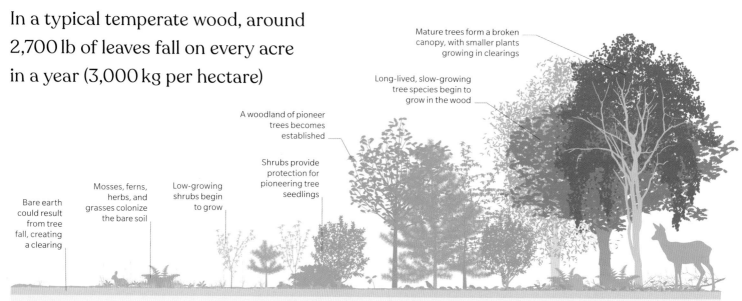

Mature trees form a broken canopy, with smaller plants growing in clearings

Long-lived, slow-growing tree species begin to grow in the wood

A woodland of pioneer trees becomes established

Shrubs provide protection for pioneering tree seedlings

Low-growing shrubs begin to grow

Mosses, ferns, herbs, and grasses colonize the bare soil

Bare earth could result from tree fall, creating a clearing

The role of fire

Wildfires play a key role in forest regeneration, especially around the Mediterranean and places with a similar climate, such as Australia and California. Fire removes competing vegetation and creates a productive seedbed for new trees. Some trees, such as giant sequoia (see pp.70–71) and cork oak (see pp.192–193), have fireproof bark that allows them to survive fires and sprout again quickly. Giant sequoia also relies on fire to release its seeds. To protect buildings near woodland, humans try to suppress forest fires, but this allows deadwood and brush to build up, making subsequent fires hotter and more damaging.

◄ **Resurrection**
Passing fires remove vegetation and leave behind a bare seedbed of soil and ash. Toxic chemicals in the ash are quickly washed out by rain. Tree seeds, with their large food stores, are often first to begin regrowth.

Life after death

All trees regularly shed their leaves or needles. Even evergreen trees lose their leaves progressively over several years, so they are never leafless. Dead leaves are soon broken down by bacteria and fungi, in the process adding humus to the soil and releasing nutrients that the trees need for growth. In time, this creates a fertile "brown earth" soil in deciduous, broadleaved woodlands.

In rainforests, most of the goodness is absorbed rapidly back into the growing trees, leaving a nutrient-poor soil beneath. To sustain the towering growth of trees, everything must be recycled. Up to a quarter of species in forest communities are "saprophytes." These feed on dead leaves and fallen timber, breaking them down and recycling nutrients back into the soil; the nutrients then support further tree growth.

▼ **A feast of timber**
Trees may form woodlands, but fungi make up at least 10 percent by weight of the living matter in a typical wood. Many, like this soft slipper toadstool (*Crepidotus mollis*) live by rotting the timber of stumps or fallen branches.

◄ **The web revealed**
The mycelial network in the soil is only evident when the fungus produces its fruiting bodies (mushrooms and toadstools). The hyphae of a typical woodland fungus can spread over an area of 37 acres (15 hectares).

How trees communicate

Although individual trees have a species name, every tree is in fact a community of species. All trees have fungi in their roots, with the fungal threads (hyphae) wrapped around, or in, the tree roots in a partnership called mycorrhizae. The web of mycorrhizae absorbs nutrients from the soil and in return imposes a levy on the tree, absorbing some of the sugars that the tree produces through photosynthesis. At least 16 fungi species commonly live in the roots of oak trees, for example, and, without those fungi, the trees would die.

In 1997, Canadian scientist Suzanne Simard showed that forest trees use these interlinked mycorrhizal networks to share and trade food, in what she called "the wood wide web." Later research showed that the trees communicate chemically throughout the entire forest. This allows trees to recognize and preferentially nurture their own offspring and to pass on to the young trees beneficial chemicals gained during past events, helping ensure the success of their shared genetic line.

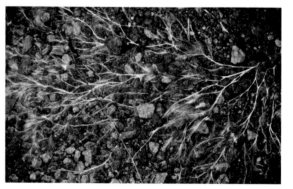

◄ **Fungal mycelium**
The working part of a fungus is this network of threads (hyphae) in the substrate, called the mycelium, which dissolves and absorbs food. Just 2¼ lb (1 kg) of woodland soil can contain at least 124 miles (200 km) of these hyphae, all interlinked.

Fungi consume about 30 percent of the sugar that trees make through photosynthesis

► **Wood Wide Web**
The mycorrhizal network of tree roots, bound with fungal hyphae, spreads through the forest floor. Chemical and possibly electrical signals can be sent through the network. As a result, a tree can recognize its own offspring and send nutrients to support their growth.

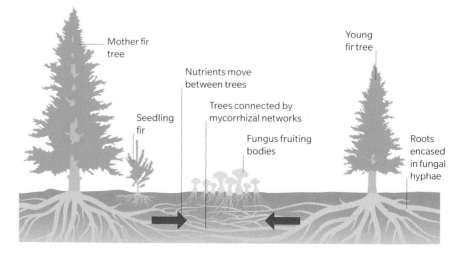

Mother fir tree

Young fir tree

Nutrients move between trees

Seedling fir

Trees connected by mycorrhizal networks

Fungus fruiting bodies

Roots encased in fungal hyphae

How trees defend themselves

Woodlands are places of fierce competition as trees fight for space and sunlight and battle to protect themselves from grazing animals. Prickly leaves, spiny branches, and impenetrable foliage help repel grazers; many species also have toxic chemicals in their tissues to discourage pathogens and wood-boring insects. The future of a species depends on reproduction, so trees divert lots of energy into producing seeds and fruits, with mechanisms to ensure wide distribution and even sweet bribes to encourage animals to eat their fruits and spread the seeds. Trees are known to pump water, sugars, and nutrients through their mycorrhizal networks to assist neighboring trees of the same species, even if some of this leaks into

◄ Pest control
When pine trees are attacked by pine sawfly larvae, they emit a chemical signal that attracts a species of parasitic wasp. These lay their eggs inside the larvae, which then get eaten from the inside out, killing the larvae but saving the tree.

the wider environment and helps other species to grow. Trees can also send and detect chemical signals through the air – for example, to warn of herbivore attacks. Acacias respond to browsing giraffes by releasing gas (see below). Trees also send chemical signals in response to communal threats from drought or disease. Neighboring trees, even of other species, respond with mechanisms to reduce water loss or trigger internal defenses.

PARASITOID WASP

▼ Chemical warfare
When a giraffe begins to browse an acacia's leaves, the tree responds by releasing ethylene gas, and this chemical warning triggers acacias downwind to flood their leaves with distasteful tannins. Giraffes have learned to browse upwind.

Coniferous Forests

Once the most prevalent plant group on Earth, conifers have been reduced to just over 600 species, but they still form a forest that encircles the northern hemisphere. They occur in both temperate and tropical forests and are more common in the far north.

Boreal forests

Forming a continuous band across northern Asia, Europe, and North America, boreal forests are conifer forests. Also known by their Russian name, taiga, they include pine, larch, spruce, and fir trees. In warmer areas, they grow alongside flowering trees such as willow, poplar, alder, and birch. These conifers are supremely adapted to cold weather and thin, nutrient-poor soils. In their northernmost extremities, boreal forests are somewhat sparse, with lichen coating the trunks and forest floor. Farther south, forests are denser, with ferns and flowering plants growing beneath the trees. The diversity of tree species is low compared to temperate or tropical forests, though there is some variation between continents. In North America, spruce and fir dominate; while Scots pine (Pinus sylvestris) is most significant in Europe; and larch reigns across Siberia.

BOREAL FOREST STRUCTURE

In the far north, the growing season is short, but evergreen conifers retain their leaves and can photosynthesize all year round. Boreal forests are dense, with few nonconiferous trees and a sparse ground cover.

Canopy

Understory

Soil layers

Shallow, widely spreading roots

Sparse ground layer

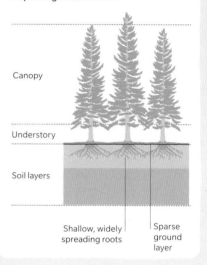

◄ Boreal wildlife

Several mammals can be found in taiga, including elk, moose, lynx, brown bears, wolves, and predatory weasels like this fisher (Pekania pennanti). They roam large territories to survive the harsh environment.

▼ Siberian taiga

Dense taiga forests, like this one in Siberia, comprise mostly conifers. The conical habit of conifers helps them shed snow in winter, preventing branch damage.

◄ Temperate rainforest

In areas with high rainfall, temperate forests are dominated by huge conifers with rich populations of ferns, mosses, and lichens among the trees, as in the Hoh Rainforest in Washington.

Cones start off light green and mature to bronze

▲ Wollemi pine

Discovered in 1994, this rare conifer occurs only in Wollemi National Park, Australia. Originally known only from fossils, *Wollemia nobilis* is critically endangered.

Temperate coniferous forests

Richer in diversity than boreal forests, temperate coniferous forests occur farther south, often in coastal areas with high rainfall, such as the Pacific Northwest of North America and northern Japan. They also occur inland at high elevation, in mountain ranges such as the Rockies (US), Alps (Europe), and Himalayas (Asia). These forests can host large conifers, such as kauri (*Agathis australis*) in New Zealand, redwoods in North America, or Patagonian cypress (*Fitzroya cupressoides*) in South America. The ground layer is richer than in a boreal forest, and nonconiferous trees are present. Some temperate conifer forests, such as the pine forests of the southeast US, depend on fire for regeneration. Here, grasses are common in the ground layer. In the wetter Pacific Northwest, fire is uncommon and ferns replace grasses.

Tropical coniferous forests

The rarest of the three conifer-dominated forest types, tropical coniferous forests are mainly found in Mexico, Central America, and the islands of the Caribbean, although pockets also exist in Sumatra, the Philippines, and the Himalayas. These forests contain a diverse array of coniferous and nonconiferous trees but a sparse layer of ground plants. In Mexico, conifer forests provide a valuable refuge for migratory birds and monarch butterflies.

► Butterfly refuge

Sacred fir (*Abies religiosa*) forests in central Mexico provide shelter to monarch butterflies (*Danaus plexippus*) that have migrated from Canada and the US for the winter. A single tree can house as many as 100,000 butterflies.

TEMPERATE DECIDUOUS FOREST STRUCTURE

The forest canopy is dominated by deciduous trees, while the understory includes saplings waiting for a gap to grow into, plus evergreen shrubs, such as holly and yew. The forest floor is the richest part of the forest.

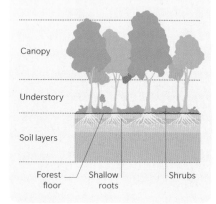

Canopy

Understory

Soil layers

Forest floor | Shallow roots | Shrubs

▶ Spring
For the plants of the forest floor, spring is the time to bloom. Bluebells (*Hyacinthoides non-scripta*) must set seed before the beech canopy above fully regrows its leaves.

Temperate Broadleaved Forests

Defined by the dominance of broadleaved trees and few or no conifers, these forests occur across temperate climatic zones. In colder regions, deciduous trees dominate, shedding their leaves in fall to survive. In warmer areas, evergreens reign.

Temperate deciduous forests

Compared to coniferous forests, the deciduous woods of eastern North America, western Europe, and eastern Asia are richer in species. In some, one tree species predominates, as in European beech woods, but in others, oaks, maples, birches, hornbeam, ash, and hickory are just some of the trees in the canopy. The woodland floor is very rich, with an abundant array of spring ephemeral wildflowers, which appear before the trees spread their leaves. Depending on location, temperate deciduous forests can include some conifers and evergreens. In the southern hemisphere, southern beeches (*Nothofagus*) dominate many forests in New Zealand, Chile, and Argentina, though conifers and evergreens may be part of the mix.

▲ Fall
The rich array of leaf colors in a North American woodland in fall is justly famous. Once shed, the leaves produce a thick mass of humus, promoting the growth of wildflowers and other plants.

Temperate evergreen forests

In warmer parts of the temperate climatic zone, evergreen species dominate the forest. Australia's eucalypt woods are one example, as are the rhododendron forests of the Himalayas. In Tasmania, there is only one deciduous tree, the tanglefoot (*Nothofagus gunnii*), with evergreen conifers and broadleaved trees, such as eucalypts, acacias, and tea trees, making up the bulk of the native forests. The Valdivian forests of southern Chile have a rich array of evergreens, including several members of the myrtle family, with a dense understory of bamboos and ferns. The mountains of central Mexico are famed for the richness of their pine-oak forests. Pines dominate at higher elevations and oaks at lower elevations, but the mixed forest contains many unique plant and animal species. The islands of the eastern Atlantic, including Madeira, the Azores, and the Canaries, hold some of the last fragments of laurisilva (see p.104), an evergreen broadleaf forest often dominated by members of the laurel family.

Long tail used for balance and steering during glides

▲ Greater glider
One of several marsupials restricted to eastern eucalypt forests, greater gliders feed on eucalyptus leaves and buds. Three greater glider species live in these forests.

Centurion, an Australian mountain ash (*Eucalyptus regnans*), is the world's tallest hardwood tree at 330 ft (100 m)

▲ Asian mixed forest
In the Himalayas, forest composition often varies with elevation. At middle elevations, oaks, rhododendrons, and magnolias form evergreen forest, while birches, maples, and alders are the main components of deciduous forest. Conifers dominate the higher reaches.

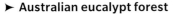

▶ Australian eucalypt forest
Along the eastern coasts of New South Wales and Queensland lies a forest dominated by eucalyptus. Most of the trees have thick evergreen foliage, and woods such as this are typical of upland areas in the Great Dividing Range.

Seasonal Tropical Forests

Not all tropical forest is rainforest. In many tropical regions, rainfall is seasonal and trees must survive a lengthy dry season. The absence of rain for part of the year has prompted the evolution of numerous survival techniques in trees, including water storage and defense mechanisms.

African dry forests

Across much of the African continent, a prickly forest of deciduous trees, comprising acacias and other species, forms a patchwork blanket over the landscape. This sparse woodland harbors a diverse array of birds and large mammals, including giraffes and antelopes and the predators, such as lions, that feed on them. Elephants also live in the woodland and use their great strength and size to push down even the thorniest of acacias to better feed on their tender shoots. The actions of elephants tend to encourage the growth of grass; the characteristic savannas of Africa are made up of patches of woodland and grassland, with the actions of animals and fire causing continuous switches between the two. On the island of Madagascar, dry seasonal forest occurs along the west coast, while in the drier south, spiny forest dominates with numerous succulents and prickly trees.

▼ Acacia trees

In a seasonally dry climate, trees must protect the water in their leaves. Acacias use thorns to ward off herbivores, although it does not always work and their typical umbrella shape results from browsing animals. Weaver birds take advantage of this shape to suspend their nests.

DRY FOREST STRUCTURE

Trees in seasonally dry climates must find ways to access water. Some have deep root systems to reach subterranean aquifers. (Acacias also have some roots spread near the surface.) In contrast, Africa's baobabs have widespread but shallow, stumpy roots that quickly absorb rain across wide areas; rain is then stored in the swollen trunk.

Baobab stores water in spongy trunk

Acacia

Soil layers

Deep roots | Shallow roots | Short roots

◄ Monsoon forest
The monsoon brings moisture-laden clouds from the Indian Ocean across India and Southeast Asia, replenishing thirsty forests such as this in Laos. Less diverse than rainforests, seasonally dry forests nevertheless are home to a wide diversity of wildlife, especially large mammals such as tigers.

Monsoon forests

Tropical rainforest is the jungle of human imagination, but in India, the jungle of Rudyard Kipling's *The Jungle Book* is a seasonal forest with a distinct dry season. Across much of India and mainland Southeast Asia, winter is hot and dry, and trees lose their leaves for an extended period. These are difficult times for the wildlife of the forest, as food is sparse and predators struggle to hunt without the camouflage of foliage. Respite comes with the monsoon, which brings heavy rains in summer. Trees replace their leaves and also produce flowers and fruits, creating a glut of food for forest dwellers. Similar tropical dry forests occur in southern Mexico and the Caribbean; several parts of South America; and islands such as Sri Lanka, New Caledonia, and Indonesia's Lesser Sundas.

▼ Jacobin cuckoo
Native to Africa and Asia, the Jacobin cuckoo (*Clamator jacobinus*) is known in India as a herald of the monsoon. It arrives in northern India with the rains, ready to feed on caterpillars that appear in wetter weather.

Around 80 percent of India's annual precipitation falls during the summer monsoon

KAKADU NATIONAL PARK

In the far north of Australia's Northern Territory lies Kakadu National Park, which covers around 7,600 sq miles (19,700 sq km). Within its boundaries can be found a diverse tropical landscape of monsoon forest, mangroves, savannas, and floodplains, home to a rich and varied assembly of wildlife, including more than 280 species of bird, over 100 reptiles, and over 70 mammals.

NOURLANGIE ROCK

Black and white coloration gives alternative name of pied cuckoo

Tropical Rainforests

Any forest between the two Tropic latitudes is a tropical forest, but tropical rainforest is defined by its lack of a dry season, with average monthly rainfall of 2½ in (60 mm) or more. High temperatures ensure that these forests experience high humidity all year round.

More than **25 percent** of all **medicines** used today are derived from **rainforest plants**

Lowland tropical rainforests

Some of the most diverse forests on this planet develop in the warm, humid tropics. Tropical rainforests are home to a rich array of mainly evergreen trees and the many plants, animals, and fungi that rely upon them. Lowland rainforests occur at low elevations in the Amazon Basin of South America, the Congo Basin of Africa, and the Indonesian Archipelago of Asia. Fragments are also found in Central America, Madagascar, Australia, and some Pacific islands.

These forests are complex, with four characteristic layers: emergent, canopy, understory, and forest floor. Different animal and plant species inhabit these layers, connected by trees and vines. Tropical rainforests have a closed canopy, and tree seedlings only grow when larger trees fall, letting light flood in. Beyond the rainforest lie seasonal tropical forests, which do have a dry season, as in the monsoonal regions of the Indian subcontinent and parts of West Africa and the Caribbean.

▼ **Vines in rainforests**
Vines are an important component of tropical rainforests, as they connect the different forest layers. Rooted in the forest floor, they grow through the understory and canopy, often flowering in the emergent layer. They are also used by animals, such as orangutans, to move around the forest.

TROPICAL FOREST STRUCTURE

A typical tropical rainforest has four distinct layers, the uppermost being the emergent layer, where the tallest trees emerge. Below that is the canopy layer, rich in epiphytic plants. An understory of palms, vines, and shrubs stands above the forest floor, which is dark with sparse ground cover.

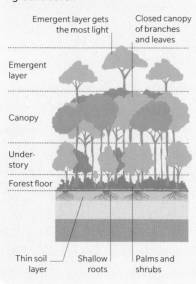

Emergent layer gets the most light

Closed canopy of branches and leaves

Emergent layer

Canopy

Under-story

Forest floor

Thin soil layer

Shallow roots

Palms and shrubs

Cloud forests

The nature of the rainforest changes as the elevation increases. With increasing altitudes, the trees become shorter and more heavily branched. The diversity of tree species also declines the higher one goes. Known as cloud, montane, or elfin forests, high-altitude rainforests typically receive most of their precipitation in the form of fog, which condenses on the foliage of trees and drips or flows down their trunks. The near-constant fog banks limit exposure to the sun and reduce the overall temperature, so many animals that live in such forests have adaptations such as thick fur coats that enable them to tolerate the cold, as with mountain gorillas in Africa and spectacled bears in South America.

While the range of tree species in cloud forests is less in comparison to the sheer variety present in lowland rainforests, by contrast, the diversity of epiphytes increases. Epiphytes are plants that grow attached to tree branches and do not come into contact with the soil. They are not parasites and do not steal resources from the host tree; their roots simply attach them to the bark. Epiphytic mosses are very common in cloud forests, and most tree trunks and branches are thickly coated, providing the perfect substrate for larger epiphytes such as orchids, bromeliads, cacti, and ferns. A rich diversity of animals relies on these hanging gardens.

▲ **Monteverde cloud forest**
The cloud forest within the Monteverde Reserve in Costa Rica is exceptionally rich, with 100 species of mammal; 120 species of reptile and amphibian; and 400 species of bird, including more than 30 hummingbird species.

Moist skin allows frog to absorb oxygen

► **Red-eyed tree frog**
Amphibians thrive in rainforests because they need high humidity to survive. Frogs, such as this red-eyed tree frog (*Agalychnis callidryas*), breathe through their skin, which must remain moist.

THE ORIGINS OF RAINFORESTS

Around 66 million years ago, an asteroid about 6 miles (10 km) wide struck Earth in what is now Mexico's Yucatán Peninsula, causing worldwide climate change and the extinction of 75 percent of life. Out of the ashes of this catastrophe developed today's rainforests, which are denser than their predecessors and composed primarily of flowering trees and plants. The exact cause of these changes is uncertain, but the extinction of the dinosaurs may be one reason. Without such large animals trampling and eating them, trees were able to grow larger and closer together. The extinction of most conifers and a large dose of nutrient-rich ash may also have helped seed our rainforests.

Using Trees

The predecessors of humans evolved in trees, and the first hominins (human ancestors) probably returned to trees for shelter and food. Discovering how to make fires and carve wood enriched life, and in time, humans began to cultivate trees for timber, food, and various other uses, both practical and for pleasure.

Wooden pin

c.8000–5000 BCE
In the tropics, early humans probably made simple shelters, although few survive. Sturdier structures were needed when they reached colder regions by the Neolithic period. The cool climate preserved some architectural remains, informing modern reconstructions (right).

NEOLITHIC LONGHOUSE

c.8000 BCE
Humans learned how to use whole trees for water transport early on. By around 8000 BCE, humans began paddling with wooden oars and carving out seating areas, as in this Pesse dugout canoe from Denmark.

c.3500 BCE
Timber is rigid yet easily carved, and wooden pins can hold pieces together. It was perfect for constructing the wheel, which first emerged in Mesopotamia, transforming agriculture and trade.

SUMERIAN CHARIOT WHEEL

c.1550 BCE
The Ebers papyrus, a digest of medical knowledge from ancient Egypt, mentions the use of willow bark as a painkiller. Much later, salicylic acid from willow bark was used in aspirin, although it is now synthesized.

EBERS PAPYRUS ANTICIPATES ASPIRIN

15th century
Strong, flexible, and durable, timber of oak or mahogany was ideal for building ocean-going ships, ushering in the European Age of Exploration.

PORTUGUESE CARAVEL

c.1200
Humans have long used wood to percussive effect. The *djembe*, an elaborate wooden drum, originated in West Africa around 800 years ago.

c.700
The Chinese developed *penzai*, a method of growing heavily pruned, miniature trees with pot-bound roots. The Japanese adapted this practice as bonsai.

MAPLE BONSAI

Pale spruce wood stained with dragon's blood sap

1666–1737
The resonance of choice timbers added to the unique sound of violins made by Antonio Stradivari and his family in Italy. Spruce was used for the front face, willow for the insides, and maple for the back and neck.

STRADIVARIUS VIOLIN

c.1715/16–1783
Lancelot "Capability" Brown, a landscape architect, designed gardens for more than 250 English country houses, featuring groups of mainly deciduous trees around lakes and rolling grassland.

BURGHLEY HOUSE, LANDSCAPED BY CAPABILITY BROWN

"Is not Italy so covered with trees that the whole land seems to be an orchard?"

MARCUS TERENTIUS VARRO, *On Agriculture*, 37 BCE

FIRST CAMPFIRES

c.1 MYA
Evidence from a cave in South Africa suggests that *Homo erectus* was making fires at least a million years ago. The first humans who moved into colder northern latitudes seem not to have started building warming fires until around 300,000–400,000 years ago.

c.10,000 BCE
Cave art in Kimberley, Australia, depicts people carrying wooden boomerangs and spears. The oldest known Australian boomerang dates back to 8000 BCE and was discovered in South Australia's Wyrie Swamp.

Wooden boomerang

c.9400 BCE
One of the earliest signs of horticulture comes from a cache of seedless figs, which cannot propagate without cultivation, found in a burned-out house near Jericho, Palestine. Carbon dating of the remains shows that the house burned down around 9400 BCE.

Willow twigs

RECONSTRUCTED EEL TRAP

c.10,000 BCE
Most wooden tools made by early humans decomposed long ago. However, eel traps made from water-resistant willow wood have been found, preserved in oxygen-depleted water or mud for 12,000 years.

AUSTRALIAN ABORIGINAL BOOMERANG

668–627 BCE
Early evidence of trees planted for pleasure comes from this bas relief of royal gardens in the ancient Assyrian city of Nineveh (now in Iraq), complete with irrigation canals.

ASSYRIAN ROYAL GARDEN AT NINEVEH

c.300 BCE
The ancient Greeks worked out how wooden wheels, made to rotate using running water, could be used to mechanize tasks such as grinding grain in watermills.

ANCIENT GREEK WATERMILL IN EGYPT

CHINESE PRINTING WOODBLOCK

c.600 CE
Under the Tang Dynasty, around 1,400 years ago, the Chinese invented the technique of using carefully carved wooden blocks to reverse-print characters and images onto cloth or paper, initially for religious texts.

OAK WINE BARREL

100 BCE
The Romans perfected methods for transplanting grape vines to form vineyards and for constructing leak-proof oak barrels to store, transport, age, and flavor wine.

1715–1774
The strength of oak, teak, and mahogany inspired the slender, curved forms of French furniture from the Louis XV period, which was often inlaid with "exotic" woods.

LOUIS XV CHAIR, FRANCE

1845
German inventor Friedrich Gottlob Keller filed the patent for a wood-cut machine to extract fibers from pulped softwood, typically from conifers. These fibers were then used to make paper.

2019
The Mjøstårnet Building in Brumunddal, Norway, is known as a "plyscraper"— a high-rise made almost entirely of wood. Wood construction helps reduce harmful carbon emissions.

Wood stores carbon dioxide

MJØSTÅRNET TIMBER BUILDING

Trees and the Environment

Wooded forests cover around 30 percent of the Earth's surface, growing wherever there is sufficient heat and moisture. Locally, they are important for biodiversity. As as a whole, they are a major source of the oxygen in the planet's atmosphere and important for the transfer of heat and moisture around the world.

Deforestation in Brazil
In this forest clearance in August 2020 in Mato Grosso state, southwest Brazil, every living thing has been removed and the stored carbon has been released as CO_2. The exposed soil will be used to support crops for a while until erosion leads to nutrient loss.

The carbon cycle

Living things take in carbon in various forms from the environment and give it back through various biological processes. For example, plants take in carbon dioxide (CO_2) from the air via photosynthesis and replace it during respiration. Together with the physical processes that move carbon through the air, land, and oceans, this creates the carbon cycle. The cycle is naturally balanced, but human activities—such as cutting down trees, which store carbon, and burning wood, thereby releasing it—are upsetting this balance. Overall, more CO_2 is being added to the air than is being removed.

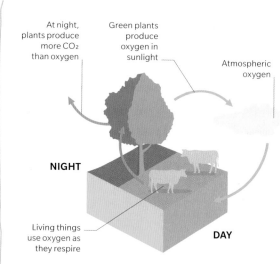

At night, plants produce more CO_2 than oxygen

Green plants produce oxygen in sunlight

Atmospheric oxygen

NIGHT

DAY

Living things use oxygen as they respire

▲ Moving oxygen
Animals consume oxygen and emit CO_2 when they respire. Plants do the same, but when sunlight is available, they also photosynthesize, converting CO_2 into sugars and oxygen. This creates a daily cycle of oxygen and CO_2.

The oxygen cycle

Forests, along with grasslands and the oceans, are major contributors to the release of oxygen into the air. Some of this oxygen is immediately turned back into CO_2 by the respiration of the trees in the forests. However, the rest of it is released and spread around the world by winds—without this movement, there would be insufficient oxygen for life in large cities, and forests would contain poisonous quantities of it.

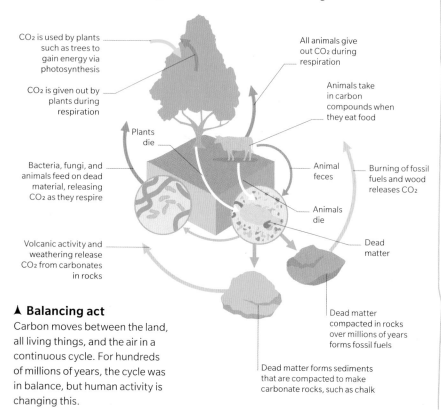

CO_2 is used by plants such as trees to gain energy via photosynthesis

CO_2 is given out by plants during respiration

Plants die

Bacteria, fungi, and animals feed on dead material, releasing CO_2 as they respire

Volcanic activity and weathering release CO_2 from carbonates in rocks

All animals give out CO_2 during respiration

Animals take in carbon compounds when they eat food

Animal feces

Burning of fossil fuels and wood releases CO_2

Animals die

Dead matter

Dead matter compacted in rocks over millions of years forms fossil fuels

Dead matter forms sediments that are compacted to make carbonate rocks, such as chalk

▲ Balancing act
Carbon moves between the land, all living things, and the air in a continuous cycle. For hundreds of millions of years, the cycle was in balance, but human activity is changing this.

An area of Amazon rainforest about the size of a soccer field is cleared every minute

Reforestation

Reforestation projects, such as the UN Trillion Trees replanting campaign, can address some of the issues of deforestation, such as capturing CO_2, or controlling flooding and erosion. The planting of canopy species can make a fairly quick improvement, but this is only the first step. Without comparable levels of biodiversity nearby, it is likely to take many decades to develop an ecosystem with the same richness as the areas that have been destroyed. As a result, replanting projects work best when they connect surviving pockets of forest.

Harming forests

When trees are cut down, many other living things lose their homes, and the lack of cover makes the area drier and often more susceptible to damage during heavy rainfall. Simply cutting down the trees—unless on an extensive scale—may cause relatively little harm. More serious problems occur when cutting is combined with other damaging conditions. In the above photograph, the devastation is permanent because the trees and understory have been destroyed. Light, sandy soil is exposed between stacks of brush; sandy soils do not retain nutrients, so when the nutrients in the brush are released (by burning or decomposition), without tree roots and other debris to hold them the rain will wash them away. Grazing can similarly change forest into grassland, while pollution can lead to a reduction in biodiversity.

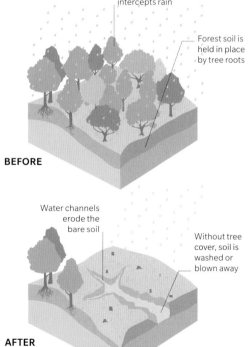

Tree canopy intercepts rain

Forest soil is held in place by tree roots

BEFORE

Water channels erode the bare soil

Without tree cover, soil is washed or blown away

AFTER

▲ **Irreversible damage**
Converting tropical rainforest to farmland is an unsustainable change. The forest soil is thin, and nutrients are cycled through it quickly by the trees. After a few years of farming, the land becomes infertile. Even if abandoned, the land may not return to forest for centuries, due to irreversible soil erosion.

▲ **Planting new forests**
A young girl prepares to plant a sapling. Replanting trees is beneficial not only to the plant and animal life in the immediate area, but also to humans everywhere.

CHAPTER 2

Nonflowering Trees

These trees are part of the group known as gymnosperms, which includes cycads, ginkgoes, and conifers (the largest group). They reproduce via seeds that are exposed—not protected within a fruit.

Queen Sago

Cycas circinalis

Cycads are notable as especially ancient trees. However, they are far from primitive and have had 300 million years to evolve into the specialist plants that can be seen today.

Cycads survive as a small group of around 360 species. In the distant past, they made up a major part of the world's vegetation, but today, they have been largely replaced by flowering plants (angiosperms). The cycads belong with ginkgo (see pp.46–49) and conifers in a loose grouping called gymnosperms, meaning "naked seeds" because their seeds are not encased in a fruit.

Cycads are sometimes called sago palms because they look very palmlike, with a spreading crown of long, feathery, evergreen leaves at the top of the trunk. However, in a sign of their primitive origins, these leaves uncurl, like those of a tree fern. The cones on male plants produce microspores, similar to pollen, which are carried by beetles and small bees, or in the wind, to ovules on the clustered floral leaves at the stem tip of female plants (see opposite page). The fertilization process is a relict of prehistoric times: the microspores swim through the nectar drops in hollows at the tip of the ovule to fertilize it.

Floating seeds

In queen sago, the fibrous seeds that develop on these floral leaves can float, allowing sea currents to disperse them to new sites. As a result, the species grows in dense stands along coastal areas of western India. Its seeds are poisonous to stop animals from eating them. The seeds are edible, but repeated soakings in water are necessary to remove the toxins. They can be dried and ground into a flour, similar to sago flour (which comes from the pith of true palm trees). This is used to make oatmeal, steamed cakes, and tortillas.

Other species

JAPANESE SAGO
Cycas revoluta

Species native to Japan, China, and Taiwan; can be distinguished by the shape of their oblong male cones.

CYCAS PLATYPHYLLA
Cycas platyphylla

Blue-leaved species from Queensland, Australia; egg-shaped male cone (strobilus) is 8 in (20 cm) long. No common name.

▼ Tree cycad
The treelike form of cycads means they are often mistaken for palm trees. However, the two are botanically very different.

◄ Female cluster
At the stem tip, female cycads produce a cluster of specialized leaves with round ovules on their surface.

GROUP: CYCADS

FAMILY: CYCADACEAE

HEIGHT: UP TO 16 FT (5 M)

SPREAD: UP TO 20 FT (6 M)

Male cone Solitary, conical; on separate plant from female; up to 20 in (50 cm) long

Stem Unbranched; thick, woody; covered in a dense stubble of diamond-shaped leaf bases

Crown of leaves, each 5–10 ft (1.5–3 m) long, with around 100 pairs of leaflets

Mature stems are stout and columnar, with a prickly covering of dead leaf bases

GROUP: GINKGOES

FAMILY: GINKGOACEAE

HEIGHT: 50–115 FT (15–35 M)

SPREAD: UP TO 30 FT (9 M)

Leaves Deciduous; fan-shaped; matte green, yellow in fall; alternate; up to 2¾ in (7 cm) long

Fruits Oily and smelly yellow-green husks; orange-yellow flesh partly encloses edible seed

Bark Grayish brown; corky ridges and fissures deepen with age

Groups of leaves typically grow in a whorl from a woody spur—a short side stem

Older leaves often split into two lobes by a deep notch, hence the scientific name *biloba* (two lobes)

Ginkgo

Ginkgo biloba

Fossils show that relatives of ginkgo were growing widely around the world 200 million years ago. Today, the sole surviving species is so unlike any other plant that it has a taxonomic group to itself.

This unique tree is a beautiful, deciduous species native to China. Stories about it abound—from English naturalist Charles Darwin describing it as a "living fossil," to claims that it was found as a fossil long before the first living specimens were discovered. Others suggest that fossil ginkgoes predate the dinosaurs. The truth is more complex.

The first published Western record of ginkgo was by Engelbert Kaempfer, a German naturalist and explorer who worked for the Dutch East India Company. In 1691, he came across a ginkgo growing in a temple garden in Nagasaki, Japan, now known to have been introduced from China. On his return from Japan, Kaempfer published a description of the species in his 1712 Latin book *Amoenitatum Exoticarum* ("attraction of the exotic"). His proposed name, "ginkgo," is unknown in contemporary Japanese or Chinese. It is thought that he borrowed the name from his assistant, a native of Nagasaki who spoke a local dialect.

► **Precious perch**
Because the hardy ginkgo repels insects, it is not of much dietary interest to birds. However, this large shade plant does provide a welcome perch for birds, such as this warbling white-eye (*Zosterops japonicus*).

Foliage is bright green as leaves emerge, turning darker green, then a spectacular yellow-orange in fall

" Among living plants, there is perhaps no more striking example of a genus that recalls the past than the Maidenhair Tree [Ginkgo] of China and Japan. "

A. C. SEWARD & J. GOWAN,
Annals of Botany Vol XIV, 1900

◄ **Distinctive leaves**
The fan-shaped leaves are unlike any others found today. They resemble the maidenhair fern, earning the species the name Maidenhair Tree.

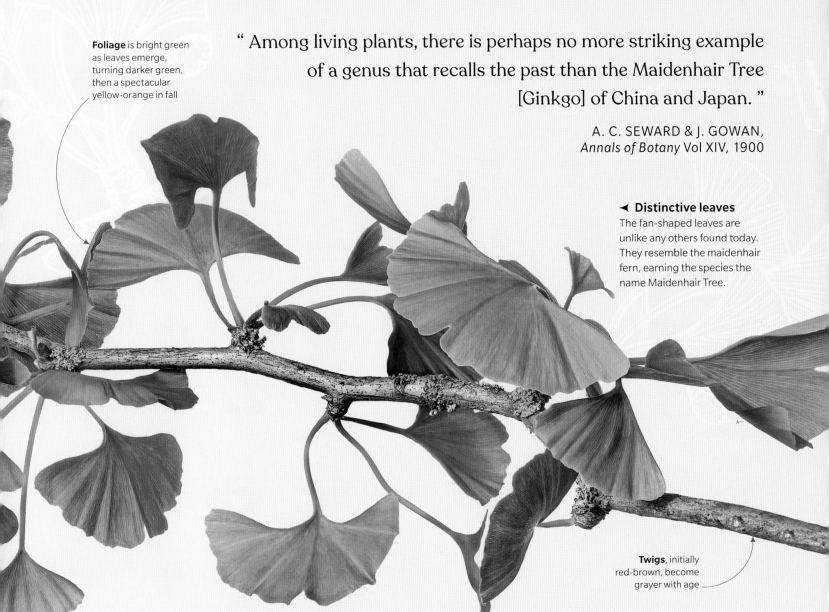

Twigs, initially red-brown, become grayer with age

Leathery, flat leaves are unlike the needle leaves of related conifers

Ovules develop in pairs at the end of stalks

Ginkgo is often called the **tree of hope** since six of them **survived** the **atomic blast** in Hiroshima, Japan, in 1945

▲ Female trees

Ginkgo is dioecious—the male and female structures grow on separate trees. While the males develop structures like catkins females develop exposed ovules.

In 1771, Sweden's Carl Linnaeus, the father of modern taxonomy, adopted it in the first published scientific name for the species, *Ginkgo biloba*.

Kaempfer collected seeds from the temple tree, some of which were planted in the Utrecht Botanic Gardens in the Netherlands. The garden still hosts some of the oldest ginkgoes growing outside Asia. From there, the species spread to Europe's stately gardens and arboreta—gardens cultivating plants for educational purposes—and was taken to North America in 1784.

Ginkgo is an elegant tree, with a narrow, columnar form at first, spreading into a more expansive crown as it ages. It is tolerant of air pollution and is widely planted along urban streets and in parks for its shade and beautiful golden fall colors.

Fossil connections

It was some time after Kaempfer that paleontologists made the link between ginkgo and the fan-shaped leaves being found in fossils from 251 to 50 million years ago. Some of the oldest, from 200 million years ago, when dinosaurs roamed the Earth, had multilobed leaves. Fossil leaves from 120 million years ago look more like modern *Ginkgo biloba*,

Edible kernel inside fleshy husk is considered a delicacy

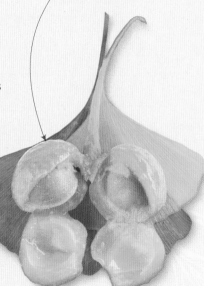

▶ Stinking fruit

Botanically, ginkgo fruit is regarded as a fleshy cone, only partially enclosing the seed. The yellow flesh stinks of rancid butter, so female trees are not planted in civic spaces.

and fossils with fruits from 65 million years ago are almost identical to the modern plants. It seems there was once a range of species in the genus *Ginkgo*, but these were not strictly "living fossils" because they continued to evolve and adapt, until today, when just one species survives. The modern ginkgo is so unlike other plants that it is placed by itself in a division of the living world called the Ginkgophyta. In contrast, the division Angiospermae includes all 350,000 species of flowering plants.

Ginkgo is relatively similar to conifers. As in conifers, pollen is carried to female flowers by the wind. The pollen grains grow into sperms, and fertilization requires the sperm cells to swim to the female ovule. Ginkgo is one of the few seed-producing plants to have motile sperm. The female flowers develop into a whitish, edible seed partly enclosed within a fleshy covering.

Wild survivors

For two centuries, ginkgoes were seen only in temple gardens. In the early 20th century, ginkgoes were found in the Dalou Mountains of Guizhou Province, China. Some of these were older than the earliest human colonists there, so it was concluded that the trees were native. Even so, far more survive in cultivation than in the wild.

Ginkgo has featured in Chinese medicine for more than 2,000 years. It is now used in the West to treat ailments that benefit from increased blood flow, from chilblains (inflammation of blood vessels), to tinnitus (ringing in the ears), and even memory loss.

FOSSILIZED RELATIVES

This fossil from Sealby Ness in Yorkshire, England, is estimated to be around 180–160 million years old. The leaves resemble those of modern ginkgo but have several divided lobes, so were named as a different species, *Ginkgo huttonii*. This was one of many closely related species that flourished at that time around Europe, Australia, North America, South America, and South Africa, all but one of which are now extinct. Because only leaves are easily identifiable from fossils, it is not known whether these ancient plants differed from modern ginkgoes in other features.

Leaves fell on ancient river delta mud and were fossilized

Leaf with four lobes, themselves slightly notched

FOSSILIZED GINKGO LEAVES

▲ Ancient tree

Starting in the 6th century CE, the Japanese planted ginkgoes from China in their temple gardens, believing this was the tree under which Buddha attained enlightenment. Some huge, 1,000-year-old trees still grow there.

GROUP: CONIFERS

FAMILY: ARAUCARIACEAE

HEIGHT: 100–165 FT (30–50 M)

SPREAD: UP TO 40 FT (12 M)

Leaves Evergreen; triangular with pointed tips; overlapping at base; up to 2 in (5 cm) long

Male cones Hang from branches solitarily or in groups; yellowish brown; 2¾–6 in (7–15 cm) long

Bark Thick and fire-resistant; gray-brown, resinous, deeply fissured; forms large, hexagonal plates

Female cones such as these will develop over two years into globular fruiting cones up to 8 in (20 cm) in diameter

Monkey Puzzle

Araucaria araucana

This distinctive coniferous tree looks notably different from typical conifers, partly as a result of the harsh conditions of its native environment.

Monkey puzzle, the national tree of Chile, is the best known member of an ancient family of trees called the Araucariaceae. These were widespread during the Jurassic and Cretaceous periods, 200 to 66 million years ago, but are now restricted to parts of South America and the Asia-Pacific region. It is a pyramidal tree, with whorls of horizontal branches, and a trunk up to 5 ft (1.5 m) in girth. The species grows wild on both sides of the Andes mountains in limited areas of south-central Chile and southwest Argentina, between altitudes of 3,000 and 6,000 ft (900 and 1,800 m).

At these altitudes, it is often windy with regular avalanches and landslides, volcanic eruptions, and wildfires, but the tree is highly adapted to cope with these conditions. The clasping form of its leaves may stop snow from building up and breaking branches, while its thick bark protects the living inner wood and buds from frequent fires. Trees are slow-growing but can live for at least 830 years.

It is relatively easily cultivated from seed and is highly prized as an ornamental tree in Europe and North America. The 19th-century English gardener who coined the name "monkey puzzle" was a clever marketeer for the species, giving it an intriguing name supposedly as a challenge for climbing monkeys; in fact, no monkeys live within its native range.

◄ Seed-rich cones

Female cones grow at branch tips, usually on separate trees to male cones. They mature into fruiting cones holding up to 200 seeds (piñones), which resemble large pine nuts.

People of the trees

Monkey puzzle (*pehuén* in Spanish) is of great religious and economic significance to native tribes in the southern Andes. One tribe relies so heavily on the tree that it is named the Pehuénche. They get wood for fuel and building materials from the trees, collect resin for medicines, and gather seeds. The latter are eaten raw, roasted, or boiled at harvest time (February to May) and throughout the winter months. Any surplus seeds are used to feed livestock or sold. In general, the heavy seeds are unlikely to disperse far from the tree, although animals including grass mice and parakeets help spread them. Although logging of monkey puzzle trees is banned, the area of native forest is declining sharply, partly due to the problem of uncontrolled forest fires.

► Monkey puzzle forest

Monkey puzzle grows in pure stands in mountainous regions, as here, or in mixed forests with various species of southern beech (*Nothofagus* species).

Glossy, dark green leaves are arranged in a spiral

> " [The monkey puzzle's] ecology
> is disturbance-driven ... "

MARTIN GARDINER, *Threatened Conifers of The World,* 2019

Other species

BUNYA-BUNYA
Araucaria bidwillii

Pyramidal or dome-shaped tree found in the rainforests of Queensland, Australia. Of great importance to native peoples within its range, who considered it sacred.

NORFOLK ISLAND PINE
Araucaria heterophylla

Popular ornamental tree in parks and gardens from Australia to California; native only to Norfolk Island, around 870 miles (1,400 km) east of Australia.

NEW CALEDONIA PINE
Araucaria columnaris

Tall and columnar, as its scientific name suggests; can grow to around 200 ft (60 m). Tends to tilt slightly depending on which hemisphere it grows in.

Female cones are around 2½ in (6 cm) long; when ripe, scales fall away to release seeds inside

Leaves are flattened, thick, and leathery, looking very unlike typical conifer needles

Bark of young twigs is smooth and reddish, marked with slightly raised scars

GROUP:	CONIFERS
FAMILY:	ARAUCARIACEAE
HEIGHT:	100–165 FT (30–50 M)
SPREAD:	UP TO 115 FT (35 M)

Leaves Evergreen; flat and thick, longer and thinner when young; in pairs or threes; up to 1½ in (4 cm) long

Bark Grayish and smooth; thick scales flake off, leaving a mottled appearance

▲ Illustration of mature twig
Few people get close views of the branches in the crown of a Kauri, high above the ground. Trees produce female cones from the age of around 40 years.

" ... living cathedrals ... evoking a bygone era when dinosaurs still roamed the Earth."

LES MOLLOY ON KAURI FORESTS,
Wild New Zealand, 1994

Kauri

Agathis australis

These imposing and venerated conifers can be found on New Zealand's North Island growing in some of the most ancient forests in the world.

When early settlers migrated from eastern Polynesia to Aotearoa (New Zealand) in the late 13th century, they found the islands dominated by rich forests. Their religion told them that all natural things, animate and inanimate, shared a universal life essence called *mauri,* so they became known as Māori. In the northern half of the North Island, they were especially impressed by the massive Kauri trees growing there, and they revered these giant trees like gods. Two of the largest that survive today are called Tāne Mahuta ("Lord of the Forest," right) and Te Matua Ngahere ("Father of the Forest").

The largest **Kauri tree** contains around **2,745 sq ft** (255 sq m) of timber, enough to **build a house**

► Sacred giant
Dwarfed by the huge tree above, a man looks up at Tāne Mahuta, the largest surviving Kauri at 148¼ ft (45.2 m).

Other species

QUEENSLAND KAURI
Agathis robusta

Sometimes called Kauri Pine; grows wild in two rainforest areas in Queensland, Australia, reaching a height of 128 ft (39 m).

AMBOYNE PINE
Agathis dammara

Massive tree from around Indonesia. The main source of copal, a white resin from the inner bark used to make varnishes.

WOLLEMI PINE
Wollemia nobilis

Known only as a prehistoric fossil until a single stand of living trees was found in 1994 in Australia. A truly extraordinary "living fossil."

▼ Māori canoes
The Māori constructed massive war canoes up to 82 ft (25 m) long from relatively buoyant Kauri trunks, hollowed out using fire and stone tools.

Fossils show that Kauri trees date back to the Jurassic period, 200–145 million years ago. They survived by being the tallest trees in their environment, emerging above the surrounding forest canopy. The lowest branches do not appear until 50–100 ft (15–30 m) above the base of the columnar trunks. The trunks also sheds flakes of bark, which stops other plants from climbing up them, and these flakes build up to a huge mound at the tree base, which helps exclude other competing plants.

The Māori valued Kauri gum for medicines, to start fires, as pigments for their tattoos, or to chew, and the relatively light timber was perfect for their canoes. Felling and fire reduced the forest around them, and, by the time the first Europeans arrived, forest in New Zealand had been reduced from about 78 percent of the land area to just 53 percent. The rate of forest destruction accelerated dramatically after the British colony was established there in 1841. The colonists found that the elasticity and length of the Kauri trunks made it perfect for constructing ships' spars. Timber merchants and shipbuilders set up steam-driven sawmills along rivers in the regions where the Kauri trees grew. Because most giant Kauris were felled, it is not known just how massive the largest trees might once have been.

Modern challenges

Today, less than quarter of New Zealand is forested. Kauri forest has been reduced to a scattering of remnant patches, estimated to cover no more than 18,400 acres (7,455 hectares), with the largest trees surviving only in particularly dense and inaccessible bush. The trees are fully protected from logging but today face a new challenge. Kauri dieback disease, caused by the fungus *Phytophthora agathidicida*, was first observed in the 1970s. It attacks the Kauri roots, then damages the tissues that transport nutrients to the crown. The leaves wither, the canopy thins, and branches die, until eventually the tree succumbs—and there is no known cure. Many forests are now closed to visitors to restrict the spread of the disease.

▲ Flaking bark
The Kauri trunk continuously sheds flakes of bark. This stops other plants from attaching their roots to it so they can scramble up the trunk.

Kauri is the largest tree in the family Araucariaceae and the third largest conifer

GROUP: CONIFERS

FAMILY: CUPRESSACEAE

HEIGHT: UP TO 60 FT (18 M)

SPREAD: UP TO 10 FT (3 M)

Leaves Evergreen; scalelike: pressed against stems in opposite pairs; $1/16$–$3/16$ in (2–5 mm) long

Male cones Borne at branch tips; yellow to brown; $1/8$–$3/16$ in (3–5 mm) long; release pollen

Female cones Spherical; fewer than male; 1–$1\frac{1}{2}$ in (2.5–4 cm) wide; open once mature or after a fire

Other species

LEYLAND CYPRESS

Cupressus × leylandii

Vigorous conifer resulting from a cross between *C. macrocarpa* and *C. nootkatensis*. Often used as a hedging plant.

MEXICAN CYPRESS

Cupressus lusitanica

Native to Mexico and Central America; fast-growing and sensitive to cold. Used ornamentally and for timber.

MONTEREY CYPRESS

Cupressus macrocarpa

Planted around the world as a windbreak; natural range is restricted to two sites on the coast of California.

◀ **Cypresses in art**

Dutch painter Vincent Van Gogh described the Italian cypress as "beautiful as regards lines and proportions, like an Egyptian obelisk." His *Cypresses* (1889) is one of about 15 paintings in the cypress series.

In Jewish tradition, **Noah** used **cypress** wood to build **the ark**

Italian Cypress

Cupressus sempervirens

A common sight across the Mediterranean Basin, this columnar evergreen has been planted as an ornamental tree since the rise of the Greek civilization.

Although wild Italian cypresses occur from Greece to Turkey and south to Libya, their native distribution is difficult to determine, as they are widely planted around the Mediterranean. The familiar narrow, pencil-like (or fastigiate) form does occur in seemingly wild trees, but natural populations are variable and can have broader, conical outlines as well.

Italian cypress is well adapted to life in hot, dry habitats. Its tiny leaves resist desiccation, and its foliage is less flammable than that of many other Mediterranean conifers. For this reason, it is often found planted along roads and fire breaks. The tree's mature cones protect its seeds from the man-made fires that are sometimes used to induce them to open.

Italian cypress owes both its English name and its Latin genus (*Cupressus*) to the mythical tale of Cyparissus and his love affair with a god. Depending on the author, that god is either Apollo (Greek god of music, arts, light, and medicine) or Sylvanus (Roman god of the countryside). Both versions tell the story of Cyparissus and a deer, which he loves immensely. When the deer is accidentally killed, an inconsolable Cyparissus weeps and asks to "mourn forever" (Ovid, in *Metamorphoses, Book X*), so the god turns him into a cypress tree. Cypresses have long been linked to mourning, and their wood is used to construct coffins. The tree "weeps" droplets of resinous sap when injured and does not recover when pruned excessively.

▲ **Cyparissus transformed**

This engraving by 16th-century Dutch artist Cornelis Cort depicts the mythical figure Cyparissus turning into a cypress tree after suffering the loss of his tame deer.

GROUP: CONIFERS

FAMILY: CUPRESSACEAE

HEIGHT: 65–160 FT (20–50 M)

SPREAD: UP TO 50 FT (15 M)

Male cone Ovoid, yellow; develops in late spring on the previous year's shoots

Bark Purple, gray and smooth in young trees; purplish brown and furrowed with age

▼ Cones and leaves
Incense cedar's side branches are typically slightly downward-pointing at the trunk, usually becoming level or upturned at the tips.

Mature cones are oblong, ripening from yellow-green to reddish brown; six scales open to release the seeds

Foliage is in flat sprays with whorls of four scalelike leaves, which have a small, bony, acute tip

Incense Cedar

Calocedrus decurrens

The bright green foliage of this stately conifer makes it easy to spot from a distance. It is well known for its aromatic wood, which is widely used in pencils.

Incense cedar is a distinctive feature of the wooded landscapes in the northwest of the US. It is found from western Oregon south to California and into western Nevada; at its farthest reaches, it also extends south into the Mexican state of Baja California.

The "cedar" part of its common name is slightly misleading, as the species is not related to the true cedars of the genus *Cedrus*; the "incense" part of the name refers to its wood, which is pleasantly scented. The wood is also soft and can be easily worked in any direction with minimal splintering, a property that makes it useful in the manufacture of pencils.

Hardy survivor

Incense cedar is a useful evergreen tree in horticulture, as it is tolerant of diseases such as *Phytophthora* root rot and honey fungus. It is adaptable to variable soil conditions, can tolerate hot summers, and is reasonably resistant to drought and fire. It is somewhat similar to another genus in the cypress family that grows around the same region, *Thuja*, as the two have comparable cones; however, those of incense cedar generally hang down under their own weight, whereas in *Thuja*, they are upright.

◄ Pure incense cedar

Incense cedars rarely grow in pure stands. However, such stands do exist, such as this one in the Red Buttes Wilderness in the northwestern US.

Other species

WESTERN RED CEDAR
Thuja plicata

Large, coniferous evergreen that grows widely in the Pacific Northwest in the US; not a true cedar of the genus *Cedrus*.

Common Juniper

Juniperus communis

Usually bushy and low-growing, this evergreen species is probably the most widespread conifer in the world. It is a tough survivor from the Arctic to mountaintops, growing in various forms that help it survive its environment.

The 50 or so species of juniper are typical conifers in their evergreen, needlelike leaves and conelike male flowers, which release wind-dispersed pollen. However, the female flowers—which grow on separate trees—develop into cones that look like berries, with swollen, fleshy scales that fuse together, each with a seed on its inner surface. The cones usually take two years to ripen but do not open to release the seeds as in other conifers. Instead, they rely on fruit-eating birds such as fieldfares, waxwings, thrushes, and woodland grouse, which swallow the rather bitter "berries"; digest the flesh; and spread the seeds in their droppings, dispersing the plants throughout suitable habitats.

The upper surfaces of juniper's needle leaves are bright green, with a broad, bluish-green band of stomata (gas-exchange pores) running lengthwise along the center of the leaf. The lower surface is distinctly keeled and gray-green in color, and some bushes look gray because all their leaves are turned to show their undersides.

A widespread tree

The different species of juniper are found from subarctic habitats in the far north; to hot, dry hillsides around the Mediterranean; to wet mountain forests in tropical Africa. They are

▶ Food in frost
Many birds and mammals, such as the mule deer shown here, eat the berrylike cones and leaves of juniper. This evergreen tree is an important source of food for such animals, especially in winters.

recorded at altitudes up to 16,700 ft (5,100 m) on Mount Everest in the Himalayas. Common juniper is somewhat less widespread but is found throughout most of Europe (although only in mountains in the south), in North African mountains, and in Asia south to the Himalayas. It is the only juniper found in both Eurasia and North America, as far south as New Mexico and Georgia.

High and low

In lowland habitats across Europe, common juniper can grow as a tree to a height of 50 ft (15 m). In fact, the tallest specimen recorded in 2018 was a tree in Ryd, Sweden, which was measured at 56½ ft (17.2 m) tall. The trees can form almost single-species juniper woods on dry chalk or limestone soils. However, more

Needles green with paler band on upper surface

Herbalists regarded juniper as a powerful herb against poisons and pestilence and an aid to childbirth

► Juniper up close
This sprig of common juniper shows its main characteristics: the prickly needle leaves and the "berries," which botanically are regarded as fleshy cones

Mature cones, after two years, are glossy black with a bluish bloom, around ¼ in (5–9 mm) in diameter

GROUP: CONIFERS

FAMILY: CUPRESSACEAE

HEIGHT: RARELY TO 50 FT (15 M)

SPREAD: UP TO 13 FT (4 M)

Male cone Small, cylindrical, solitary, yellowish; usually on separate plants from females

Bark Reddish brown, fibrous, frayed in peeling, vertical strips; smooth on younger branches

Young cones are berrylike and green, each with 2–3 seeds

62

Gin house
In London in the early 18th century, gin became cheaper to drink than ale. This prompted many rowdy "gin houses," as shown in this 1822 painting.

Other species

CHINESE JUNIPER
Juniperus chinensis

Variable from low bushes to trees; features short, scalelike mature leaves. Native over much of China and commonly planted in parks, gardens, and churchyards.

WESTERN JUNIPER
Juniperus occidentalis

Found to 10,500 ft (3,200 m) in the Sierra Nevada mountains of western US. Picturesque old trees of this species sometimes emerge from cracks in solid granite cliffs.

ROCKY MOUNTAIN JUNIPER
Juniperus scopulorum

Found in the Rocky Mountains from British Columbia south to New Mexico; typically grows as a shrub, but sometimes forms twisted, weathered old trees.

> " Juniper enters the recipes of many traditional meat dishes in the countries of Europe. "

G. M. ROUGEMONT, *A Field Guide to the Crops of Britain and Europe*, 1989

typically, this form (subspecies *communis*) grows in boreal forests throughout Scandinavia and in Scotland alongside Scots pine, Norway spruce, and other conifers. Grazing and weather often prune the plants in these areas to a much lower, shrubby form, rarely exceeding a third of their potential height.

In the tundra at the far north of its range and in the high mountains of southern Europe and Turkey, the Himalayas, and western North America, common juniper grows as a spreading, matlike shrub rarely exceeding 20 in (50 cm) in height. This subspecies, *nana*, is much better adapted to coping with gales and bitter winds. In mountains around the Mediterranean, an intermediate third subspecies, *hemisphaerica*, is also recognized. All three subspecies are slow-growing, so tall specimens should be valued as veteran trees—some can reach ages of up to 600 years old.

Selected uses

Juniper wood is durable, with a delicate fragrance, but is generally suited only for small carved objects. However, the berries are a valued crop, crushed and eaten in pâtés; in stews; and as marinades for game, especially venison. Juniper is used to preserve cold meats and, in Germany, is a common flavoring in sauerkraut.

However, juniper is probably best known as the flavoring for gin (and its German equivalent, *steinhäger*), although the base spirit is produced by the repeated distillation of wheat. The Dutch physician Franz de le Böe is reputed to have been the first person to produce a distilled spirit flavored with juniper in the 17th century. An early variety was used by Dutch colonists in the West Indies as an antidote against fevers. During the reign of Queen Elizabeth I of England (1558–1603), English soldiers serving in the Netherlands were offered a dram of this liquor to give them "Dutch courage," and it might have been these troops who first brought gin back to England, where it soon became the drink of choice for the privileged classes and later for people of all backgrounds. Today, local brands of gin are traditionally flavored with various "botanicals"—ingredients from the surrounding countryside—but juniper must still provide the dominant flavor before the drink can be properly classified as gin.

Folk beliefs

In folklore, juniper was said to be a powerful deterrent against witches and devils. Early herbalists valued its fleshy cones as a strong counterpoison, which was believed even to resist the plague. The cones were also said to be powerful against venomous beasts and as a treatment for "wind in any part of the body." When eaten, they are powerful diuretics, which the botanical guide *Flora of Great Britain & Ireland* notes "makes the urine smell of violets."

Fleshy scales coalesce around the seeds inside

▲ Fruit and seeds
Unlike the woody cones of other conifer trees and shrubs, the juniper cone is made up of swollen, fleshy scales, each carrying a single seed.

▼ Veteran of the hills
Bent by the prevailing wind and the years, this stately old juniper in Upper Teesdale in northern England is probably the last survivor of a forest that once stood on this hillside.

GROUP: CONIFERS

FAMILY: CUPRESSACEAE

HEIGHT: 130–360 FT (40–110 M)

SPREAD: UP TO 75 FT (23 M)

Leaves Evergreen needles, with two white lines below; arranged in spirals; up to ⅝–1 in (15–25 mm)

Cone Gray-green to brown; up to 1¼ in (3.5 cm) long, opening when mature to release seeds

Bark Reddish brown, thick, fibrous; furrowed when mature; young stems are green to brown

▼ Small leaves
Coast redwood leaves' small surface area helps reduce water loss through pores; white, waxy deposits on the undersides further decrease evaporation.

Seed cones release small seeds onto the forest floor. Germination rates are low, but seed production is high

◄ Trees in the mist
Fog is common along the north Californian coast, and it allows coast redwoods to grow to great heights by cooling air temperatures and reducing leaf water loss.

Needles are evergreen but eventually fall. Their litter burns quickly, preventing high-intensity fires that might kill the tree

Male cones develop at branch tips, releasing copious quantities of pollen

Coast Redwood

Sequoia sempervirens

The tallest of all living things, the towering coast redwoods are an awe-inspiring sight. However, their vast size also led to their overexploitation until the mid-20th century.

Along the coast of northern California and southwestern Oregon grows the tallest tree species in existence, made possible by the cold California current. Flowing from the north Pacific along the west coast, it brings cool waters south, moderating air temperatures along the coast. Prevailing winds create an upwelling of cold water, further cooling and generating bands of fog that roll inland. Without this current, air temperatures would be higher, rainfall and fog would be much less reliable, and coast redwoods would not have thrived.

At just over 375 ft (115 m), a tree known as Hyperion is the tallest recorded coast redwood. Great height brings complications, the biggest of which is transportation of water. Redwood leaves are constantly losing water through pores, and this creates suction, effectively pulling water up through the trunk from the roots. As trees get taller, gravity increasingly threatens to break this flow, but fog provides solutions. When air humidity is high, water loss through leaves is reduced. Fog water

▲ National parks
Harvesting timber of coast redwoods was destroying forests and wildlife, but most redwood forests are now protected by the US National Parks Service.

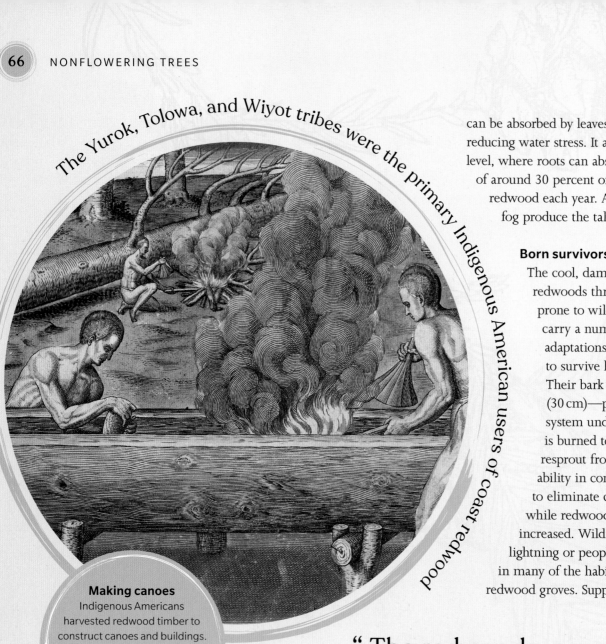

The Yurok, Tolowa, and Wiyot tribes were the primary Indigenous American users of coast redwood

Making canoes
Indigenous Americans harvested redwood timber to construct canoes and buildings. The wood splits easily lengthwise, making flat boards. Methods of canoe making included burning and scraping by hand.

can be absorbed by leaves and through bark, reducing water stress. It also drips down to soil level, where roots can absorb it; this is the source of around 30 percent of water used by a redwood each year. Areas with the most fog produce the tallest redwoods.

Born survivors

The cool, damp forests where coast redwoods thrive might not seem prone to wildfires, but redwoods carry a number of physical adaptations that hint at an ability to survive low-intensity fires. Their bark is thick—up to 12 in (30 cm)—protecting the vascular system underneath. If the tree is burned to ground level, it can resprout from the base, a rare ability in conifers. Fire also tends to eliminate competing tree species, while redwood germination is increased. Wildfires can be ignited by lightning or people and are common in many of the habitats that surround redwood groves. Suppressing fire may even

> " The redwoods, once seen, leave a mark ... that stays with you always. "
>
> JOHN STEINBECK,
> *Travels with Charley: In Search of America*, 1962

Other species

DAWN REDWOOD
Metasequoia glyptostroboides

Living specimens were only discovered in 1941, giving this tree "living fossil" status. Native to China. Fast-growing, with a fluted trunk and fibrous bark.

HEAD IN THE CLOUDS

Many of the tallest trees ever recorded are conifers, which lack the outward spread of most deciduous trees and so can generally grow taller. However, the heights of different coniferous species vary considerably, from the more than 330 ft (100 m) coast redwoods to their much smaller relatives, including pines, larches, and spruces.

CONIFER HEIGHTS

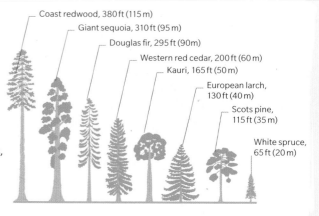

Coast redwood, 380 ft (115 m)
Giant sequoia, 310 ft (95 m)
Douglas fir, 295 ft (90 m)
Western red cedar, 200 ft (60 m)
Kauri, 165 ft (50 m)
European larch, 130 ft (40 m)
Scots pine, 115 ft (35 m)
White spruce, 65 ft (20 m)

be disadvantageous to the long-term survival of redwood forests and the many species that rely upon them, including endangered spotted owls, marbled murrelets, and Humboldt martens.

Redwoods as resources

Coast redwood forests were inhabited by at least 15 groups of indigenous peoples, many of whom utilized redwood timber. The wood from old-growth redwoods was often free of knots, making it easy to split, plus the timber is resistant to fire and decay. Naturally fallen trees or driftwood was utilized, and some native peoples used fire to bring down standing trees. The timber was split into boards using wedges made of elk antlers and used in the construction of buildings and canoes.

Many groups relied on harvesting acorns for food and burned vegetation to encourage oak growth, also benefiting redwoods.

In the early 19th century, logging of coast redwoods began in earnest and, as mechanization developed, loggers reached the most remote areas. The San Francisco earthquake of 1906 created great demand for lumber and also demonstrated the value of redwood timber, as buildings constructed with it were often spared fires. However, in 1918, the devastation of the forests led to the foundation of the Save the Redwoods League. In 1968, Redwood National Park was established, and today, around 82 percent of ancient coast redwood forest is protected.

Coast redwoods are among the **oldest living organisms**

▼ **Felling giants**
Before industrialization, much of the early coast redwood logging was done by hand using basic tools such as giant saws, despite the huge diameters of some of the trunks.

Sunlit canopy
The morning sun bathes the dense, undulating canopy of this eastern North American forest in a soft light. As the mist lifts, the intense green of needle-leaved conifers, such as pine and fir, appears in stark contrast to the beautiful yellow to red fall foliage of broadleaf trees, such as aspen and maple.

GROUP: CONIFERS

FAMILY: CUPRESSACEAE

HEIGHT: UP TO 310 FT (95 M)

SPREAD: 82–115 FT (25–35 M)

Male cones Yellow, solitary, and stalkless at end of short shoot; about ¼ in (6 mm) long

Female cone Green, oval; 2–3¼ in (5–8 cm) long; clustered on branches, ripening in second year

Bark Red-brown, fibrous, soft, spongy; up to 2 ft (60 cm) thick; highly fire-resistant

Tiny scalelike leaves, spirally arranged around shoots, give the blue-green foliage a rough feel

◄ **Redwood relatives**

Although closely related to coast redwood (see pp.64–67), giant sequoia differs from it in that it has scalelike leaves clustered around its shoots and cones that persist for several years.

Cones ripen to brown in their second year but can remain on a tree for 20 years before releasing seeds

Giant Sequoia

Sequoiadendron giganteum

While coast redwood is known for its height, giant sequoia is famous for its sheer size. It is world's the largest living tree, and it can survive for more than 3,000 years.

▲ **The mammoth tree**
"The Stump and Trunk of the Mammoth Tree" (lithograph, 1862) shows how a giant sequoia felled in Calaveras County, California, in 1857 became a tourist attraction, with 32 people dancing on its hewn trunk.

The biggest and tallest giant sequoias have long since been felled for their valuable timber. Today, only a few trees survive in around 75 isolated groves among conifer forests on the western slopes of the Sierra Nevada mountains in central California, at altitudes of 2,950–8,800 ft (900–2,700 m). The largest surviving tree in the Sequoia National Park, called "General Sherman," currently stands 217 ft (82.6 m) tall. Its trunk has a girth of 27 ft (8.25 m) and a volume of about 54,000 cubic feet (1,530 cubic meters). Battered by its 2,100 years of life, this giant sequoia has a broken top ending in a long, jagged spike. The tallest known living specimen—measured in 1998 at the Redwood Mountain Grove, also in California—was 311 ft (94.9 m) tall.

► General Grant

The second largest tree, "General Grant," can be found at Kings Canyon National Park in California. It has a thicker trunk than that of "General Sherman"—with a diameter of 29 ft (8.85 m)—but it is more than 3 ft (1 m) shorter.

This species was not recognized scientifically until 1853, when British plant collector William Lobb returned to England with samples from the tree. Two weeks after his return, botanist John Lindley rushed out a scientific paper naming the species *Wellingtonia gigantea* in honor of the British war hero Arthur Wellesley, the first Duke of Wellington. Its scientific name was amended in 1854 under the rules of the botanical code, as another, unrelated plant had the same genus name. However, the tree is still known as *Wellingtonia* in the UK.

Born of fire

Wild giant sequoias survive in soils that are irrigated by runoff from surrounding mountains or summer thunderstorms. These thunderstorms also start fires, which are a natural part of the species' ecology, as shown by its fireproof bark. Cones remain on the tree for up to 20 years, only occasionally opening to disperse a few seeds. However, rising heat from fires makes the cones open fully, dispersing the seeds onto soft, clear soil enriched by nutrients from burning.

In recent years, conservation efforts have suppressed natural fires, allowing brush to build up beneath the trees. As a result, fires now burn hotter and longer. This makes climate change the main threat to the survival of the species.

"General Sherman" has enough wood for **175 miles** (282 km) of standard planks—enough to build 35 five-room houses

Bristlecone Pine

Pinus longaeva

Twisted, battered, and eroded by the harsh climate of the Sierra Nevada Mountains in California and Nevada, bristlecone pines are known to be some of the oldest living organisms on Earth, with life spans of up to several thousand years.

GROUP: CONIFERS

FAMILY: PINACEAE

HEIGHT: UP TO 60 FT (18 M)

SPREAD: UP TO 40 FT (12 M)

Seed cone Unstalked, with thick, woody scales; seeds shed in third summer; 2¾–3½ in (7–9 cm) long

Bark Red-brown, thin, and twisted, with fissured, irregular, thick, scaly ridges

Bristlecone pines grow in the White Mountains of California and neighboring ranges in Utah and Nevada. Two very closely related species grow in other mountains in the region: the foxtail pine (*Pinus balfouriana*) and the Rocky Mountain bristlecone pine (*Pinus aristata*). The species featured here is sometimes called the Great Basin bristlecone pine to make this distinction clearer.

This species is found at elevations between 5,600 and 11,200 ft (1,700 and 3,400 m). At these altitudes, temperatures range from 158°F (70°C) in summer to −15°F (−26°C) in winter, and strong winds occur year round. Because this habitat lies in the rain shadow of the main Rocky Mountain range to the west, it receives very little precipitation, averaging just 12 in (30 cm) per year, which mostly falls as snow. It is too hot and dry for growth through most of the summer and too cold in winter. The trees

▼ Fallen ancient tree
This large felled bristlecone in the mountains of California displays twisted knots in its outer wood. A bristlecone of this size would have been very old.

can only actively grow for a very short period, when the snow melts in early spring and before temperatures get too high. This allows a growing season of only around six weeks. For the rest of the year, the tree effectively shuts down. As a result, a 5,062-year-old tree (see p.74) may only have been growing for the equivalent of 590 years.

The trees grow tallest, to around 60 ft (18 m), at the highest altitudes, where most snow gathers in winter to support their spring growth. Trees lower down the mountain, where the drought is more severe, rarely reach a third of that height. The trees grow so slowly that scientists need a microscope to distinguish and count the bands between their annual growth rings. The same factors that cause the tree's slow growth also explains its longevity. Few wood-rotting fungi can survive the drought and subzero temperatures, so dead branches can cling onto the last remnants of a living tree without rotting.

Dead or alive

In many of the oldest bristlecones, the trunk is dead around most of their girth. Only a narrow strip of living tissue survives on the protected side of the trunk, away from prevailing winds. The dead wood on the windward side gets

FEMALE CONES

Long, pink, protective **scales** will turn purple-brown with age

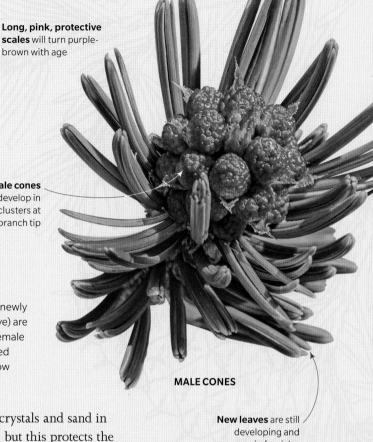

Male cones develop in clusters at branch tip

MALE CONES

New leaves are still developing and grow in fascicles (bundles) of five

▲ ► Female and male cones

At the stem tip of this newly emerging shoot (above) are a pair of very young female cones. The egg-shaped male cones (right) grow in early summer.

pummeled by ice crystals and sand in the frequent gales, but this protects the last living tissue in the "strip-bark." This characteristic results in typically twisted and battered trees that are only partially alive but are often extraordinarily old.

The first person to confirm their longevity was Dr. Ernest Schulman from the University of Arizona. During surveys in 1954 and 1955, he used a tree borer (a hollow metal tube with a sharpened tip) to dig into the trunks of

> " These trees were already ancient when Columbus landed in the New World. "
>
> SIR DAVID ATTENBOROUGH,
> *The Private Life of Plants*, 1995

Other species

SCOTS PINE
Pinus sylvestris

Handsome species found in boreal forests across northern Eurasia, with a subspecies forming the Old Caledonian Forests of Scotland.

PONDEROSA PINE
Pinus ponderosa

Ranges from British Columbia south to Mexico; iconic US tree with separate varieties on either side of the Rocky Mountains.

MONTEZUMA PINE
Pinus montezumae

Tall species with large branches; confined entirely to subtropical highland forests in Mexico and Guatemala.

living trees and extract a narrow column of wood through the breadth of the trunk. Back in the laboratory, he counted the growth rings and found that several trees were over 4,000 years old, overturning the previous belief that giant sequoias (see pp.70–71) were the oldest trees.

The death of Prometheus

However, even these records were soon eclipsed as the result of an unfortunate incident in 1964. Donald Currey was a geography graduate student studying tree rings as a clue to past climates. In 1964, he visited a particularly large, statuesque tree, which had been named Prometheus, in the mountains of Nevada. Exactly what happened next varies between sources. Some versions of the story say his tree borer broke in the trunk, others that the borer was too short to bring out a

Branches
are long and slender

◄ **Hardy survivor**
Growing in the White Mountains of Inyo County, California, this ancient bristlecone pine has a typically gnarled and knotted appearance. Its windward side is possibly protected by a layer of dead wood.

DENDROCHRONOLOGY

The wood of a tree is formed by a layer called the cambium. In spring and early summer, the cambium produces a band of large, light-colored cells with thin walls. In late summer, growth slows and the cambium makes a darker ring of small, thick-walled cells. Each concentric dark ring marks a year's growth, so counting them can provide an estimate of the tree's age.

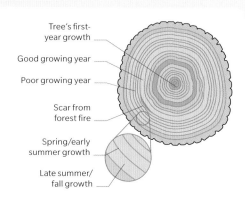

Tree's first-year growth

Good growing year

Poor growing year

Scar from forest fire

Spring/early summer growth

Late summer/fall growth

COUNTING TREE RINGS (TEMPERATE REGIONS)

---

complete core. Whichever it was, he decided, in desperation, to ask the Forest Service for permission to fell the tree. Unusually by modern standards, they agreed, and Prometheus was felled. Later, Currey counted its annual rings and found it was 4,862 years old, making it the oldest tree then known. Currey went on to a distinguished career as a professor of geography, but, throughout his life, his friends nicknamed him "Killer Currey" for cutting short the potential lifespan of Prometheus.

In 2010, even this record was exceeded when a tree at a secret location in the White Mountains was found to be 5,062 years old. (The locations of such ancient trees are typically kept secret to prevent damage from curious visitors or even vandals.) This makes it the oldest nonclonal organism currently alive, although some trees that spread by suckers, such as quaking aspen (*Populus tremuloides*, see pp.130–133), form clonal clumps that could be even older. At the time of writing, the tree is reported still to be growing strong.

► **Dramatic habit**
This striking bristlecone pine in Utah has grown into an unusually curved habit, possibly in response to the harsh, exposed conditions of the landscape.

The **oldest bristlecone pines** were growing when **the first pharaohs** were **building the pyramids** in Egypt

Cedar of Lebanon

Cedrus libani

The magnificent cedar of Lebanon is now desperately rare in the country after which it is named and is more common as a specimen tree in grand parks and gardens.

There are ongoing debates about whether there are four species of cedar around the Mediterranean and western Himalayas or only one species with several subspecies. The trees are all typically pyramidal in shape when young but become flat-topped with age. They occur in five discrete geographical areas, and trees in each area share distinctive characteristics, but it is not clear whether these merit species status. Matters are complicated further, as several cultivated varieties are grown in gardens with different shapes and forms and various colors of leaves.

The true cedar of Lebanon is found from the mountains of southern Turkey, where it grows at altitudes up to 6,500 ft (2,000 m), into Lebanon, western Syria, Israel, and Jordan, although it is no longer common. It grows only in sites where

> The oldest examples of cedar of Lebanon trees are thought to be **more than 1,000 years old**

▶ **Tree of life**
"Pilgrimage to the Cedars in Lebanon" was painted in 1907 by Hungarian artist Tivadar Csontváry Kosztka. Cedars were important in Hungarian mythology as symbols of fertility, the tree of life, and the tree of knowledge.

Male cones (strobili) are cylindrical, stiff, and up to 2⅓ in (6 cm) long

GROUP: CONIFERS

FAMILY: PINACEAE

HEIGHT: UP TO 125 FT (38 M)

SPREAD: UP TO 50 FT (15 M)

Leaves Evergreen; needlelike; long, densely clustered or singly at shoot tips; up to 1¼ in (3 cm)

Female cone Upright, brown, barrel-shaped with rounded tip; 3½–6 in (9–15 cm) long

Bark Dark gray and smooth initially, becoming darker and fissured with age

Dense clusters of dark green needle leaves give the stems a brushlike appearance

▶ **Strobili**
Male cedar of Lebanon cones are known botanically as strobili. When ripe, their outer scales open to release clouds of pale yellow pollen.

"Handsome conifers ... once covered the snow-clad mountain tops ... from southern Lebanon to southern Turkey."

JACQUES BLONDEL AND JAMES ARONSON,
Biology and Wildlife of the Mediterranean Region, 1999

◄ **Distinctive shape**
When mature, cedars have elegant ranks of horizontally spreading branches that make them unmistakable landmarks in native forests, parks, and gardens.

A **cedar of Lebanon trunk** on Mount Lebanon was recorded with **a diameter** at chest height of **$11^{1}/_{3}$ ft** (3.45 m)

fog gathers in the afternoon, allowing the trees to scavenge moisture from the air. However, it is surprisingly hardy when planted in parks and gardens around Europe and North America, where its elegant, horizontal spreading branches make it a choice ornamental.

As iconic trees, cedars feature in the cultural traditions of many countries. They are frequently mentioned in the Old Testament of the Bible. The First Temple of Solomon was built of cedar. Hiram, the King of Tyre, promised Solomon he would "...do all you want in providing the cedar and juniper logs. My men will haul them down from Lebanon to the Mediterranean Sea, and I will float them as rafts by sea to the place you specify" (1 Kings 5–6).

Downfall of the cedars

It might seem that Solomon's use marked the start of the downfall of cedar in its native range. Even before the start of Christian era, it was used for ship building, general construction, and decorative purposes. Felling increased in the last century—in part because of demands from two world wars—for construction work, railways, and fuel. Today, in Lebanon, just 14 fragments of the native cedar forest survive. Grazing, logging, urbanization, winter sports, and insect pests also

Solomon's temple
This print depicts the Biblical story of cedars being cut down for the construction of the First Temple in Jerusalem. Among its lavish decorations were walls carved from cedar, overlaid with gold.

contributed to the decline of the native cedar forests.

If the definition of the species is extended, it has a much wider range. *Cedrus stenocoma* is native to southwest Anatolia. *Cedrus atlantica* is found in the Atlas mountains of Algeria and Morocco and comes in two forms with shining green leaves or with leaves that are bluish gray or even whitish. *Cedrus deodara* grows wild in the mountains of the western Himalayas from Afghanistan to northwestern India. Finally, *Cedrus brevifolia*, with short, thick, and blunt leaves, is endemic to the Troodos mountains in western Cyprus.

Other species

ATLAS CEDAR
Cedrus atlantica

Grows in the Atlas mountains (Algeria and Morocco). Considered a local variant by some botanists (as with all three listed here).

DEODAR CEDAR
Cedrus deodara

Conical in shape with a narrow, spirelike tip. Grows 3,900–10,800 ft (1,200–3,300 m) up in the Western Himalayan mountains.

CYPRUS CEDAR
Cedrus brevifolia

Found only in the mountains of western Cyprus. Typically grows to around 65 ft (20 m) in height; needles are shorter than those of other cedars.

HOLY CEDARS

As shown in this 19th-century print, cedar trees are part of the cultural identity of the state of Lebanon. Only 14 "wild" cedar groves still survive there, and these would not still be standing unless they were regarded as sacred or marked important burial spots. One of the largest stands, at Bsharre, has been protected since 1999 as a World Heritage Site in the holy valley of Qadisha as the "Forest of the Cedars of God" (*Horsh Arz el-Rab*).

PRINT SHOWING THE CEDARS OF GOD

Japanese Larch

Larix kaempferi

This fast-growing, deciduous conifer is native to a relatively small area in Japan and grows into a tall tree that is attractive in new foliage in early spring, and later bursts into a blaze of distinctive fall color.

▲ Fall foliage

With its native range largely in mountains, Japanese larch grows well on bare ground and rocky slopes, which is helped by the trees coning at a young age.

GROUP: CONIFERS

FAMILY: PINACEAE

HEIGHT: UP TO 115 FT (35 M)

SPREAD: UP TO 50 FT (15 M)

Leaves Deciduous; spiny; set in whorls on the current year's long shoots; up to around 1½ in (4 cm) long

Female cone Produced on short shoots with some leaves at the base; ripen in the first fall

Bark Smooth red-brown or purplish brown when young; becomes fissured and scaly in old trees

Japanese larch, as its name indicates, is a member of the larch family, deciduous conifers of the genus *Larix* that are found across vast areas of the world's boreal forests. Like its relatives, it thrives in warm summers but can tolerate short growing seasons. Larches' deciduous foliage allows them to survive cold winters, which results in them being the most northerly of all trees, growing beyond 71 degrees north. The larches found in boreal forests extend across northern North America, Russia, and Asia. Farther south, larches occur in mountain areas in Europe, North America, and Asia, as far south as 27 degrees north. Japanese larch is one of the southern, mountain-dwelling species and is native to a small number of sites in central Honshu, the largest of the Japanese islands.

Speedy growth

Japanese larch is characterized by its cones, which mature to have reflexed scales, meaning they bend outward, and by its one-year shoots,

► Cones on short shoots

The male and female cones are carried on short reproductive shoots that are 3 years old or older. These shoots arise at the base of some of the vegetative shoots, which bear the leaves.

Male cones are formed on leafless short shoots, after which the shoot dies

Japanese larches typically take **around 50 years** to grow to **their full height**

Mature cones are upright with reflexed scales, ripening in the fall

Female cones have ovule-bearing scales and bract scales, which expand to cover the seeds after pollination

Leaves are gray-green or bluish, with pale bluish-green stomata on the lower surface

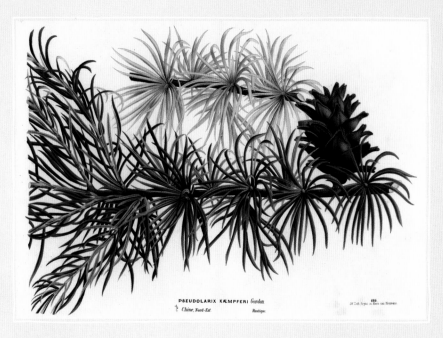

translates as "plant killer"—are algaelike plant pathogens that, in suitable environments, are destructive killers; infected Japanese larches are effective at spreading *Phytophthora*. This vulnerability has restricted the tree's potential use in forestry. In contrast, other species such as European and Dunkeld larches (see below) are far less susceptible.

Timber tree

Japanese larch yields a light and naturally durable timber with a reddish-brown coloration. It can be used for construction, cladding, furniture, and decking on fishing boats. In the past, it was used for fencing and other purposes that made use of its natural resistance to decay; however, it has subsequently been overtaken by modern timber preservation treatments, which offer better and longer-term protection from the elements. Japanese larch has been extensively planted for timber in the UK and Europe, as well as in Japan. Its high silica content means that it can blunt cutting edges when being worked.

▲ Kaempfer's larches
Japanese larch is named after naturalist Engelbert Kaempfer (see pp.46–48). This 19th-century lithograph shows the deceptively similar golden larch, also (formerly) named after Kaempfer as *Pseudolarix kaempferi*. It can be distinguished from Japanese larch by its larger cones.

which are reddish purple and usually bloom in the first year, becoming grayer in later years. The ability of Japanese larch to grow on heavier soils and clay soils and at a faster rate than European larch attracted the attention of British foresters, who produced a hybrid with European larch. This was found to grow even faster due to heterosis, or hybrid vigor, which occurs when two close species or lines are crossed. In the wetter western parts of Britain, Japanese larch has been found to be susceptible to *Phytophthora ramorum*, often better known as Sudden Larch Death. *Phytophthora*—which

◀ Japanese larch bonsai
Japanese larches are a popular choice for bonsai trees, as they can grow on nutrient-poor soils, and have attractive flaking bark and good fall color.

Other species

DUNKELD LARCH
Larix × eurolepis

Hybrid of Japanese and European larches; fast-growing and used in forestry. Intermediate in cone between its parent species.

EUROPEAN LARCH
Larix decidua

Medium-size larch native to central Europe; used for its timber. Has a slim habit when young, widening with age.

TAMARACK
Larix laricina

Grows across northern North America; characterized by its small cones, each with around 20 rounded scales.

White Fir

Abies concolor

This tough yet elegant evergreen species is native to the mountains of North America and can withstand a range of conditions, from heat to cold.

A tall conifer, white fir can form extensive forests in parts of its range. In regions to the south of its range, it becomes an associated species, such as in giant sequoia stands (see pp.70–71). It is characterized by its leaves having stomata on both sides, although those on the upper side are in a broad wavy band compared to those on the underside, where the stomata are in two well-defined bands.

Fire damage

The thin bark full of resin blisters makes young trees susceptible to forest fire damage. This is beneficial where the species occurs with giant sequoia, as the sequoia's thick bark resists fire damage, so fire prevents white fir from overwhelming the redwood. With time, the white fir's bark becomes corky and somewhat tolerant of forest fires. However, the fresh foliage will burn easily, and the species relies on its fecundity to restock areas affected by forest fires.

White fir may not produce cones or seeds for the first 40 years or so of its life. When they do appear, its cones are mainly carried at the top of the trees. They ripen in one growing season and then break apart to release the seeds, leaving the narrow central stalk, or rachis, standing upright on the shoots. The cones vary in color from light blue to olive green while they are young and still growing, but ripen to brown when mature. The male cones are carried on the underside of branches in the lower crown; they open in the spring and are around ³⁄₈–³⁄₄ in (1–2 cm) in length.

Blue-green leaves are needlelike and flattened in shape

Leaf tips are bluntly pointed

▲ Leaves
The leaves of white fir give off a pleasant lemonlike scent when crushed. They have a distinctive blue-green color, as seen here.

GROUP: CONIFERS

FAMILY: PINACEAE

HEIGHT: 100–165 FT (30–50 M)

SPREAD: 16 FT (5 M)

Leaf Lax on the shoot, curved upward; gray-green to bluish green; in whorls; up to 2¼ in (6 cm) long

Cone Cylindrical or ellipsoidal; olive-green, yellow-green, or pale blue

Bark Smooth with resin blisters in young trees, becoming furrowed and corky

---

WHITE FIR LOGGING

White fir trees have long been harvested for lumber in large volumes in the US. White fir is a versatile softwood and can be used for construction, framing, decking, flooring, paper pulp, and more. It is also one of the popular tree species cultivated commercially as a Christmas tree.

LOGGING TRAIN, OREGON, c.1890

◄ **Stems shed snow**
Norway spruce has a conical shape because its branches are arranged in whorls, the lowermost whorl being the oldest and longest. This shape helps trees drop excess snow, preventing damage.

Fresh green "tips"
grow on spruce stems each spring and are widely harvested for food in Scandinavia

► **Needle arrangement**
In all spruces, needles are attached to the stem via a peglike structure called a pulvinus. When the needles are shed, the pulvini remain, so spruce twigs are easily identifiable.

Norway Spruce

Picea abies

This tall, slender conifer makes up much of the dark spruce forests of Europe that have inspired so many folk tales. It also makes a familiar Christmas decoration in northern Europe and beyond.

GROUP: CONIFERS

FAMILY: PINACEAE

HEIGHT: UP TO 165 FT (50 M)

SPREAD: UP TO 50 FT (15 M)

Cone Hangs from branch tip; has pointed brown scales; opens when dry, releasing winged seeds

Bark Pale brown to gray; scaly; young stems brown with prominent pegs where needles attach

New growth develops from buds formed the previous year; scales protect buds from winter

Sharp-pointed needles grow on most spruces, distinguishing them from firs, which have rounded needles

▲ Spiral spruce
The needles of Norway spruce are placed in a spiral, as this is the most efficient arrangement, allowing the tree to capture maximum light and produce the most food via photosynthesis.

Forests have long exerted a sense of awe and can have great emotional resonance among the people who live near them. Maybe this is because, historically, forests were dangerous places to travel through, filled with outlaws and wild animals, and this sense of foreboding has inspired numerous stories and legends. In many of the tales collected by the brothers Grimm, the dark forest signifies danger or is a place of magic, and other tales of adventure often involve an epic journey into the woods, from the *Epic of Gilgamesh* to J. R. R. Tolkien's fantasy novels.

Evergreen forests can be especially daunting because their dense canopy makes navigation difficult—very little light reaches the forest floor, and the sky and horizon are obscured. In northern Europe, Norway spruce is a major component of these dense, imposing forests.

This coniferous species can form pure stands, in which at least 80 percent of the forest is made up of the same species. The saplings are shade tolerant and grow slowly under the canopy of other tree species, eventually overtaking them. Norway spruce is found in an almost continuous swathe from Norway to western Russia, where it begins to intergrade with the closely related Siberian spruce (*Picea obovata*). Farther south, it has a more interrupted distribution, occurring mainly in the mountains of central Europe, including the Alps and Carpathians, and into the Balkans. A useful timber tree, it is widely cultivated and can also be found in western Europe and North America, where it has become naturalized.

Uses and customs

Norway spruce is well established as a source of timber and pulp for making paper. It has been grown since the 16th century but was only

QUEEN VICTORIA'S CHRISTMAS TREE

A ROYAL TRADITION

The first royal Christmas tree in the UK was erected by Queen Charlotte, wife of King George III, but the tradition was popularized by their granddaughter, Queen Victoria, and her husband Prince Albert. Pictures of them and their young family enjoying this tradition were printed by the press, and the public was quick to adopt this new Christmas tradition. Queen Charlotte's tree was a yew, but Prince Albert preferred spruce imported from his home in Germany.

Spruce beer, which can be alcoholic or not, is flavored with spruce buds and leaves and is rich in **vitamin C**

widely planted for forestry from the 20th century onward. Since then, its popularity has waned with the introduction of Sitka spruce (*Picea sitchensis*) from North America, which produces a greater yield per unit area. However, as the climate changes, becoming drier, Norway spruce may return to popularity among foresters because it is more tolerant of dry soils than Sitka spruce, and trials are underway to determine the best source of Norway spruce seed for future plantations.

Norway spruce was also famed for dominating the Christmas tree market. Its rapid growth and festive scent made this species the top choice in many European households, but it also has a disadvantage—needle drop. If not watered regularly, this spruce rapidly sheds its needles, leaving a bare skeleton of a tree. Its role as a Christmas tree has now been largely taken by the Turkish native Nordmann fir (*Abies nordmanniana*), which does not drop its needles even if the watering regime is inconsistent. Nordmann firs are slower growing and therefore more expensive to produce, causing the price of Christmas trees to rise. They also lack the resinous scent of a spruce, which to many is the traditional scent of the Christmas season.

◄ **Tonewood**
Hardwoods are used to make the bodies of stringed instruments, but softwoods such as spruce are preferred for the soundboards, as they transmit sound well.

Soundboard of lute is made from spruce

► **Mysterious forest**
Dark Spruce Forest (1899), painted by Norway's most renowned artist, Edvard Munch, captures the mystery and dread of a Norway spruce forest, evocative of tales of myth and legend.

> " ... a line of spruce in the distance would appear an inkblot, a punctuation to the endless grey sentence of the morning. "

KATE WALPERT, *The Sunken Cathedral*, 2015

Other species

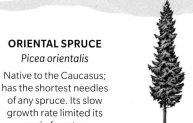

ORIENTAL SPRUCE
Picea orientalis
Native to the Caucasus; has the shortest needles of any spruce. Its slow growth rate limited its use in forestry.

SERBIAN SPRUCE
Picea omorika
Restricted to Drina River valley on the Serbia–Bosnia border. Narrow and elegant; cultivated as an ornamental.

SITKA SPRUCE
Picea sitchensis
Largest of all spruces; this fast-growing species from the Pacific coast of North America can reach over 295 ft (90 m).

Douglas Fir

Pseudotsuga menziesii

Native to western North America, this towering, evergreen conifer is one of the world's largest. Despite its common name, is not a true fir at all, but instead is a member of a small genus whose botanical name means "false hemlock."

GROUP: CONIFERS
FAMILY: PINACEAE
HEIGHT: 295–330 FT (90–100 M)
SPREAD: UP TO 65 FT (20 M)

Leaves Evergreen; dark green, needlelike; held radially on the shoots; up to 1¼ in (3 cm) long

Bark Initially smooth and gray; thickens to a corky, deeply ridged texture, turning red-brown

◄ Douglas fir stand

Stands of Douglas fir occur in the temperate Great Bear Rainforest of British Columbia, Canada. The bears that give the forest its name rip off its thick bark to gorge on the sap beneath.

LEWIS AND CLARK CABIN

WORLD'S LARGEST LOG CABIN

The world's largest log cabin was built in Portland in 1905, part of an exhibition celebrating the centennial of the Lewis and Clark Expedition. A central colonnade comprised over 50 unpeeled Douglas fir tree trunks. The building fell into decline and, always vulnerable to fire, was razed to the ground by a massive blaze in 1964.

Other species

EASTERN HEMLOCK
Tsuga canadensis

Long-lived, broadly conical conifer with purple-gray bark and short needles; has a number of dwarf forms that are popular garden plants.

WESTERN HEMLOCK
Tsuga heterophylla

Tall, elegant conifer with soft, pendulous foliage; tips of trees arch gently downward. Native to North America; widely planted as hedging.

Found from British Columbia to central California, including coastal regions, Douglas fir tolerates a range of conditions, from mild maritime to the more severe weather of the Sierra Nevadas, where it can grow up to an altitude of 5,900 ft (1,800 m) above sea level. In forests, the lower branches are generally shed, with the majority of the foliage held in the upper portion, while in a more open site, it is more likely to branch from nearer the base of the trunk. Trees can survive to a great age, with some specimens reaching over 1,000 years old. Douglas firs are monoecious, with male and female cones appearing on the same tree—the males in clusters on the undersides of shoots, the females at the stem tips—changing in color from yellow to pink to light brown.

First described by Europeans in the 18th century, this species had long been used by Indigenous people to make fish hooks and snowshoes, also providing firewood and branches for bedding. Mature forests are a habitat for the red tree vole, which nests in its branches and feeds on its needles, preferring them to those of other conifers. When crushed, the needles have a sweet, resinous smell. Douglas fir is now commonly grown throughout Europe and parts of South America.

This conifer is one of the world's most important timber trees, owing to its strength and durability, and is widely planted throughout temperate regions, doing best in areas of high rainfall. Not only is the wood excellent for making frames and trusses for house building, but it makes an ideal flooring material, readily taking paints and stains. It has a further use as a Christmas tree, the whitish stripes on the undersides of the needles giving it a frosted appearance that adds to its appeal.

Douglas fir can be planted as a garden tree, and it thrives in cool temperate climates, doing less well in hot, humid conditions or in areas with excessively dry summers. Garden forms seldom reach the heights achieved by trees in their natural range.

Cylindrical female cones hang downward; the three-parted bracts distinguish this species from all other conifers

► Food source

Smaller birds are able to cling onto ripe cones in order to feed on the seeds beneath the scales. The seeds are also eaten by small mammals, including the Douglas squirrel.

" A sun-loving tree ... excellent stands of this species followed resettlement forest fires. "

LEO ANTHONY ISAAC,
Reproductive Habits of Douglas-fir, 1943

Changing seasons
An early snow blankets the boreal forest surrounding Fairbanks, Alaska, in soft, white powder. While the tall, stately spruces in this predominantly coniferous forest add a splash of green to the wintery landscape, broadleaf trees such as aspen, birch, and poplar display their fall colors in bursts of yellow and orange.

GROUP: CONIFERS

FAMILY: TAXACEAE

HEIGHT: 50–70 FT (15–20 M)

SPREAD: UP TO 70 FT (20 M)

Leaves Evergreen; pointed, slim, two white lines below; grow in two rows on either side; up to 1½ in (38 mm)

Male cone Male and female cones grow on separate trees; males are yellow, spherical

Bark Reddish brown, flaking; trunk is often strongly fluted; young stems are green to brown

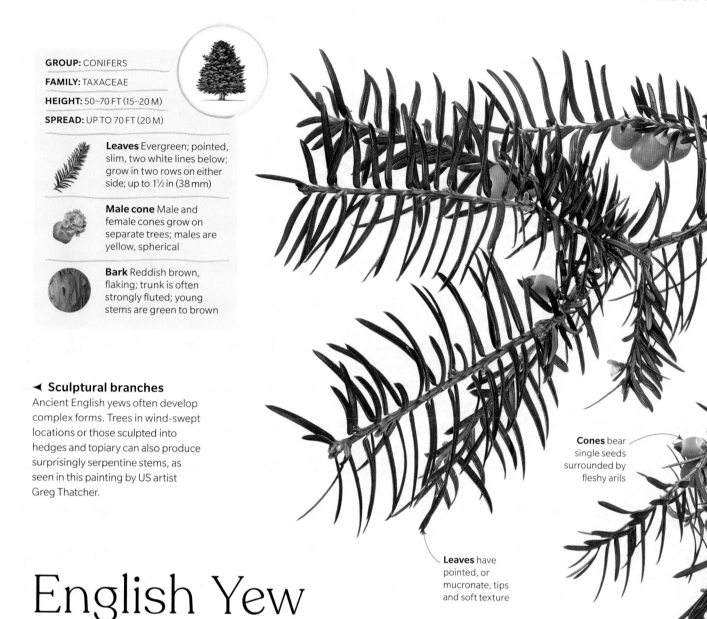

Cones bear single seeds surrounded by fleshy arils

Leaves have pointed, or mucronate, tips and soft texture

◄ **Sculptural branches**
Ancient English yews often develop complex forms. Trees in wind-swept locations or those sculpted into hedges and topiary can also produce surprisingly serpentine stems, as seen in this painting by US artist Greg Thatcher.

English Yew

Taxus baccata

With mournful foliage and traditional associations with graveyards, yews can seem gothic and forbidding. However, these long-lived trees have a rich history and unusual characteristics.

Trees feature in the folklore of societies on every continent, and in Europe, the yew has fueled storytellers' imaginations for millennia. Although colloquially known as English yew, this evergreen tree resides from the British Isles east to Iran and south via Italy to North Africa; its precise natural distribution is difficult to deduce due to humans aiding its spread. It often occurs singly or in small groups within the understory, and forests dominated by yew also occur. However, it is within the grounds of churches and other religious buildings in Europe that yew has found its role in legend.

English yews possess several characteristics that have inspired awe and reverence. Almost all parts of the tree are poisonous, containing taxine alkaloids that, if ingested in sufficient quantity, can cause cardiac arrest. Poisonings typically

▲ **Leaves and cones**
The dark, evergreen needles of yew provide a perfect backdrop for the bright red arils (seed coverings) that surround the yew seeds.

occur through consumption of the leaves, although toxin levels are highest in the seeds and symptoms can occur after breathing in pollen or sawdust from yew timber. Yews, as with many evergreens, are also venerated due to their ability to retain leaves throughout the dark and cold of winter—holly, ivy, and mistletoe are similarly revered. They also have an astonishing capacity to regenerate, with felled trees resprouting from the base, and stems can root when in contact with the soil, allowing new trees to develop. Finally, yews are well known for their longevity, with trees potentially reaching ages of over 2,000 years—although accurately dating ancient yews is fraught with difficulty. Trunks often become hollow with age, so tree rings cannot be counted. Many elderly groves are the result of trailing limbs rooting to create a large clonal organism that dates back millennia, even though the individual trunks might be only a few hundred years old.

> " Of vast circumference
> and gloom profound
> This solitary Tree!—a
> living thing/Produced too
> slowly ever to decay. "
>
> WILLIAM WORDSWORTH,
> "Yew-Trees," 1815

Weapons of war

The wood of English yew has long been valued. It is a softwood, like that of other conifers such as pine, making it flexible and easy to work with. However, it is one of the hardest of the softwoods, and this combination of strength and flexibility made yew ideal for the construction of longbows. The medieval English longbow was used for game hunting and in warfare and is celebrated for its role in helping English forces dominate the French during the Hundred Years' War in battles

STRAIGHT GRAIN

Popular with artisans, yew timber tends to be rich in knots, and older trees are typically hollow. As a result, it is used for the construction of small items, for carvings, and as veneer. Yew wood is durable and is resistant to decay and insect attacks.

DIFFERENT YEW TIMBERS

The English army at Crécy included around 6,000–7,000 longbowmen

Other species

KOREAN PLUM YEW
Cephalotaxus harringtonia
Native to Japan, Korea, and northeast China. Evergreen shrub or small tree that produces plumlike cones, each with one large seed.

JAPANESE NUTMEG-YEW
Torreya nucifera
Grows in Japan and South Korea; has sharp-tipped evergreen needles and nutmeg-sized seeds with a green fleshy coating.

CALIFORNIA NUTMEG
Torreya californica
Restricted to California. Closely resembles its Asian relations—the only other American *Torreya* is *T. taxifolia*, found in Florida.

Battle of the bows

At the Battle of Crécy (1346), English soldiers (on the right) used longbows to defeat a French force of mercenaries armed with crossbows, then later to break up French cavalry charges. Such was the importance of archers that the yew wood used to make bows was highly valued.

such as Agincourt and Crécy. Such is its significance that yew was widely planted to provide stavewood for bows around this time, and the 1472 Statute of Westminster required all ships arriving in England to provide four bow staves per ton of cargo unloaded. Yew wood's qualities also made it popular for the construction of musical instruments, and the bowls of many medieval lutes were fashioned from this wood. Modern piano cases and acoustic guitar soundboards and sides may also be built from

yew. With its significance in folklore and as a source of bow wood, English yews are a common sight around older buildings, but they have also been widely planted as landscape trees and as manicured topiary and hedges, the latter dating back to Ancient Rome. Yew's slow growth rate means that such shaped trees need to be pruned infrequently, which saves on labor. They can resprout from old wood, and drooping branches of old trees can root and grow into new trunks. Elderly hedges can be readily rejuvenated by hard pruning, a process that would kill many other hedge types.

Birds and berries

Yews are conifers, but their cones are unlike those of pines, spruces, and cedars. They are hugely reduced, each bearing only a single seed, which is surrounded by a fleshy structure called an aril. The aril, which is the only part of a yew that is not toxic, is usually red and is therefore attractive to birds that typically feed on berries. Yews do not produce berries, as real berries are only produced by flowering plants, but their cones effectively behave like berries and allow the seeds to be distributed over long distances from the parent plant.

▼ Yews among the gravestones
Yews are common in European churchyards and in some cases predate the church buildings. As yews were considered sacred in pagan tradition, their sites were often chosen for church construction.

Totara

Podocarpus totara

Superficially similar to European yews, the podocarps—including totara—are found in warm temperate regions of the Americas, Africa, east Asia, and Australasia.

The totara is an evergreen conifer endemic to New Zealand, with a huge significance in Maori culture. A slow-growing species, trees can also be extremely long lived, although determining the precise age of large specimens is not possible, as ring patterns can be difficult to read. Initially spreading and bushy, trees develop massive trunks as they mature. Older trees can have aerial roots.

Its flowers are unisexual and males and females are usually borne on separate trees (dioecious). The fruit produced by a female—technically a cone—comprises two fused, fleshy scales, bright red when ripe, that form an oval. At the tip is a rounded receptacle containing one or two seeds. The name "podocarp" is from the Greek *podos*,

GROUP: CONIFERS

FAMILY: PODOCARPACEAE

HEIGHT: UP TO 100 FT (30 M)

SPREAD: UP TO 49 FT (15 M)

Leaves Evergreen; narrow, sharply pointed with raised midribs on the undersides

Bark Thick and dark brown to silver gray; peels in strips when mature

▼ Survivor

This totara tree on Banks Peninsula on the South Island of New Zealand is the remnant of a wooded area that was cleared.

meaning foot, and the tree's fruit is said to resemble a foot kicking a soccer ball. For its hardness but relatively light weight, totara timber was prized by the Maori for building their war canoes (*waka taua*)—a lengthy process that could take several years from selection of a suitable tree to the finished artifact. The largest canoes, accommodating up to 100 warriors, could be up to 79 ft (24 m) in length and comprised separate pieces bound together with ropes. Natural oils in the wood prevented rotting and ensured the vessel would be watertight. Traditionally, once a totara tree had been felled, a replacement seedling would be planted to appease Tane, the god of the forest, for removing one of his children.

▼ Carved canoe prow

This wooden Maori war canoe prow, thought to be carved from totara wood, is intricately carved on each side with cascading patterns of loops and spirals.

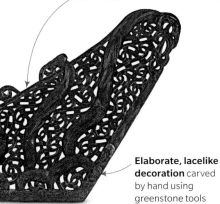

Patterns in Maori carving are often inspired by elements from nature, such as spiders' webs or fish scales

Elaborate, lacelike decoration carved by hand using greenstone tools

Other species

YEW PLUM PINE
Podocarpus macrophyllus

Native to southern and eastern China and southern Japan; the northernmost species of the genus *Podocarpus*.

CHILEAN PLUM YEW
Prumnopitys andina

Coniferous evergreen tree native to parts of Chile and Argentina. Formerly known as *Podocarpus andinus*.

CHAPTER 3

Flowering Trees

These trees are part of the highly diverse group known as angiosperms. This group includes magnoliids, monocots—often not considered "true" trees at all—and eudicots. Their seeds develop enclosed within a fruit.

► **Bountiful blooms**
Large magnolia flowers can be up to 10 in (25 cm) across and have a strong lemon fragrance. They open each morning and close at night for a few days—a process known as nyctinasty—before disintegrating.

Cream-colored flowers
are singly borne at the end of shoots

Branches, with their broad evergreen leaves, are prone to collect winter snow and snap

Leaves are dark glossy green above and covered in rust-colored hairs below, especially when young

GROUP: MAGNOLIIDS

FAMILY: MAGNOLIACEAE

HEIGHT: 60–80 FT (18–25 M)

SPREAD: UP TO 30 FT (10 M)

Leaf Evergreen, elliptic, alternate; 1²⁄₄–6 in (4–15 cm) long and ²⁄₄–1²⁄₄ in (1.5–3.5 cm) wide

Fruit Woody cone 2³⁄₄–4 in (7–10 cm) long; each carpel splits longitudinally to release one seed

Bark Gray, rough, splitting into plates; young twigs smooth, green to brown, covered in silky hairs

Southern Magnolia

Magnolia grandiflora

Southern magnolia's saucer-shaped white flowers set against its glossy, dark green foliage are a striking sight. Native to the US, this tree has an ancient lineage.

Magnolias represent an early form of flowering plant and feature several characteristics that are rare in more recently derived trees. Typical flowers feature sepals, which protect the bud, and petals that are ornamental, but in magnolias, the two are not differentiated. This shows that these two distinctive structures had yet to fully evolve when magnolias first appeared an estimated 130 million years ago. Each magnolia bloom comprises 6 to 12 petal-like structures called tepals. These robust and leathery tepals can withstand visits from the somewhat clumsy beetles that frequent magnolia flowers to feed on pollen. Beetles were pollinating flowers before the evolution of social insects such as bees, and many early angiosperms still rely on them to do so.

Stately bloom

Magnolia has strong associations with the southern United States. In 2020, the state of Mississippi voted to redesign its flag, removing the controversial Confederate battle insignia.

▲ Setting seed
Female structures (carpels) at the center of each flower become woody and conelike after flowering. Each carpel releases a red seed with a fleshy coat on a thread, as seen in this botanical illustration.

Other species

SAUCER MAGNOLIA
Magnolia × soulangeana
Deciduous magnolia first developed in France, the result of a cross between *M. denudata* and *M. liliiflora*. A low, spreading tree with tuliplike blooms in white and purple.

STAR MAGNOLIA
Magnolia stellata
Native to Japan. Deciduous shrub that produces abundant white flowers, each with many tepals. Well suited to small gardens and can be grown as a hedge.

> " *Fragrant o'er all the western groves The tall magnolia towers unshaded.* "

MARIA GOWEN BROOKS (*c.*1794–1845), American poet

The new flag features a magnolia blossom, the state flower. Often referred to as the Magnolia State, Mississippi claims *Magnolia grandiflora* as its state tree as well. This graceful tree is distributed across many southern states, from Virginia to Florida and Texas. Although a native of the coastal US, it has been cultivated across a much wider area.

Despite its many cultural associations with the southern US, the name "magnolia" is not of American origin. The genus was first named in 1703 by a French botanist, Charles Plumier, in honor of another, Pierre Magnol. Magnolia was first brought to Europe by English botanist Mark Catesby in the 18th century. It was not the first American magnolia to reach Europe—*Magnolia virginiana* was already established in gardens—but the grandeur of the new magnolia meant it quickly outshone its compatriot. It grows as a freestanding tree in warm, temperate regions and as a large, ornamental wall shrub in cooler areas.

► Magnolia money
President Andrew Jackson planted a magnolia tree along the White House south portico, and it was pictured on the $20 bill until recently.

◄ Male flowers
Flowers on male plants are similar in outward appearance to the female flowers. Both types appear in spring.

Pollen grains attract flying insects

Leaves are glossy and firm in texture, with slightly wavy margins

GROUP: MAGNOLIIDS

FAMILY: LAURACEAE

HEIGHT: 20–60 FT (6–18 M)

SPREAD: UP TO 30 FT (10 M)

Fruits Purple-black berries, up to ½ in (1.5 cm) long, contain a single seed

Bark Bark can crack and peel, probably as a response to cold

► Female flowers
Female flowers are greenish yellow and around ⅜ in (9 mm) across. As bay trees are dioecious, female and male flowers grow on separate trees.

Bay Tree

Laurus nobilis

Widely grown for its fragrant leaves, which can be used to impart flavor to a range of dishes, bay tree is planted as a familiar garden plant throughout temperate regions. However, it also has a distinguished history dating back to ancient times and has given rise to a rich seam of cultural symbolism.

This evergreen tree or shrub of variable size is densely packed—often all the way to ground level—with tough, dark green, aromatic leaves, although mature plants sometimes develop a clear trunk. It is native to the Mediterranean region but is now more widely planted as an essential component of herb gardens; in formal schemes, it is often clipped to a firm pyramid or cone or is trained as a standard (a trimmed, treelike plant). While the species is capable of growing to considerable size, most plants grown in gardens are usually kept much more compact by regular trimming. In mild regions, bay is also often used as hedging.

Bay is a member of a large family of plants, the laurels (Lauraceae). While the genus *Laurus* comprises only two species—the other is *Laurus azorica*—the family Lauraceae is vast and extremely diverse, with nearly 3,000 species, and includes many other trees and shrubs that are familiar to gardeners. Plants are either male or female (dioecious), although it is possible to tell the two apart only when they are in flower, and even then only by close inspection. Female trees, if the flowers are fertilized, produce single-seeded, purple-black, berrylike drupes in fall.

Fresh leaves are available year round for use in cooking, but they are also often dried for winter use. They are essential in a *bouquet garni*, a herb bundle used to flavor stews and pâtés, and a single leaf can impart a subtle fragrance to various puddings. The essential oil in the leaves is used in aromatherapy and cosmetics. A few cut stems thrown on an open fire in winter will flash and crackle as the oil ignites.

Laurel forests

The laurels as a family are found mainly in warmer regions, where, in areas of high humidity, they can form colonies known as laurisilva forests. These often include other evergreens that bear a superficial resemblance, such as magnolias and myrtles.

Laurel forests evolved millions of years ago. In the warm, humid climate prevalent across the globe before the ice ages, they covered much of

> " Deep in the palace, of long growth, there stood A laurel's trunk ... "
>
> VIRGIL
> *Aeneid, Book VII,* 19 BCE

► **Representing resurrection**
In Western art, the bay tree has often been used to symbolize Christ's resurrection, as seen here in Italian artist Girolamo dai Libri's *Madonna and Child with Saints* from around 1520.

◀ **Laurisilva forest**
Laurel forests—known by type as laurisilva forest—evolved in ancient times. Surviving remnants of these trees offer clues to ancient climates.

the available land mass. In the northern hemisphere, as Earth cooled and the air became drier, they largely died out, leaving only bay laurel in the Mediterranean; fragments of earlier forests cling on in the Canary Islands, Madeira, and certain neighboring mountainous regions.

Mythology and symbolism

Bay's association with the Greek god Apollo (according to Ovid in his *Metamorphoses*) derives from the myth of Daphne, a young nymph who was pursued by him against her will. For her own protection, her father, the river god Peneus of Thessaly, transformed her into a bay tree. In ancient Greece, where bay was a symbol of wisdom, peace, and protection, wreaths woven from the stems in the form of a headdress—in honor of Apollo—were traditionally awarded as prizes to victorious generals, athletes, poets, and musicians. The practice was continued in classical Rome. Near the entrance of a burial vault in Naples, believed to be the poet Virgil's tomb, a specimen was planted in his honor. The tree no longer survives; visitors to the site would cut branches as souvenirs, an overenthusiastic pruning regime that resulted in its death.

Crowning a hero with laurels—in various disciplines—was revived in Renaissance Italy, when a distinguished poet would earn the title Poet Laureate. One of the first to be honored in this way was Petrarch (1304–1374), whose sonnets rank among the most famous of all love poetry.

NATURAL PEST CONTROL

The bay sucker is a small, grayish-white psyllid (plant louse) that feeds on the foliage of bay trees during the summer months, causing damage to the leaf edges. To deter the bay sucker without using pesticides, it is possible to encourage the insect's natural enemies into the affected area—predators such as wasps, ladybugs, and some birds. This can be done by planting a range of plants to attract these animals.

LADYBUG SEARCHING FOR BAY SUCKERS

Cinnamon

Cinnamomum verum

This small evergreen tree is native to Sri Lanka. An earlier botanical name, *Cinnamomum zeylanicum*, references the island's historic name of Ceylon.

A member of the laurel family, the cinnamon has aromatic bark, timber, and leaves. The common name is also used to identify a color—a soft, warm, reddish brown, which also describes the inner bark from which the spice of the same name is derived. While other related species are also cropped for cinnamon, *Cinnamomum verum* is considered to have the finest flavor.

As the source of spice, cinnamon has long been an important economic plant. In ancient Egypt, oil from the bark, around 90 percent of which is the organic compound cinnamaldehyde, was used in embalming. More recently, it has been used in incense and to flavor toothpaste and medicines. Oil from the leaves is also used in cosmetics and perfumery.

A classic flavor

In culinary usage, cinnamon sticks are usually broken to release their flavor or are ground to a powder, which is then added to a range of dishes; many cooks consider the spice an essential addition to any apple-based dessert.

Conspicuously veined leaves taper to a point

▲ Cinnamon leaves
The leaves, the source of a delicately flavored oil, are arranged in pairs; to distill the oil, they are stripped from young shoots during the rainy season.

▼ Cinnamon sticks
Inner bark is peeled from the tree and rolled into "quills" or sticks, then dried in a shady area to preserve the oils.

Brittle, papery surface texture

GROUP: MAGNOLIIDS

FAMILY: LAURACEAE

HEIGHT: 30–50 FT (10–15 M)

SPREAD: 45–60 FT (14–18 M)

Leaf Evergreen; narrowly oval; leathery and glossy green; opposite; 2¾–7 in (7–18 cm) long

Bark Reddish brown; on mature trees, outer bark can turn grayish brown

Embalming
Cinnamon was used in embalming in Ancient Egypt. This scene from a papyrus shows a ceremony before the burial of the embalmed body.

1   2   3   4   5   6

Nutmeg

Myristica fragrans

This aromatic evergreen tree is famous for its principal economic crop, the spice of the same name, and it also produces another spice, mace. It is native to the Banda Islands of Indonesia, where trade in nutmeg was the source of conflict and oppression by colonizers for centuries.

GROUP:	MAGNOLIIDS
FAMILY:	MYRISTICACEAE
HEIGHT:	33–66 FT (10–20 M)
SPREAD:	33–66 FT (10–20 M)

Leaf Evergreen; shiny above, glaucous beneath, petiole grooved; alternate; 3⅛–6 in (8–15 cm) long

Bark Smooth, gray-brown or brown, containing a watery pink or red sap that can be used as a dye

Nutmeg has been a coveted spice for thousands of years, reaching India by the 6th century CE and spreading to Constantinople and then farther west. Initially, it was not known from where the spice originated, and when Arab traders deduced the origin in the 13th century, they decided that this information was commercially sensitive and kept it secret. This was maintained for a further three centuries until Portuguese and Dutch traders tracked the trees down to the Banda Islands, part of the Molucca Islands in modern-day Indonesia—also the original home of the sugar cane. The Portuguese and Dutch vied for control of the islands, which led to gross

Fruit is solitary and pendulous, ripening to a yellow color

In the 17th century, nutmeg was believed to have aphrodisiac properties

mistreatment of the islanders, and established the Dutch East Indies as a colony there by force, lasting until after World War II. However, it was an earlier war that hastened the spread of the nutmeg tree—during the Napoleonic Wars, Britain had briefly occupied the islands and took the opportunity to send trees to Sri Lanka, Malaysia, and Singapore, and from there to

Zanzibar off the coast of Tanzania and the West Indies, especially Grenada. Nutmeg was also cultivated in the Indian state of Kerala.

The tree is tropical in origin and is intolerant of more than the lightest frost. It is widely grown for its fruits; Indonesia, Guatemala, and India between them produce 85 percent of the annual nutmeg harvest of around 185,000 tons (167,800 tonnes). Seedling trees start fruiting at about 6 to 8 years old, but until then, it is not possible to know whether they are male or female trees—only female trees produce the nuts, and in nature they grow in around equal

Leaves are elliptic to oval with a glossy, dark green upper surface and untoothed margins

◀ **Parts of the tree**
This 19th-century French engraving—made from a botanical illustration—shows, from left to right, the nutmeg tree's flowers, drupe, habit, aril, and seeds.

▲ **Nutmeg seed**
This split and ripe nutmeg seed from Kerala, India, is ready for harvest, with the aril visible within the drupe. The seed is contained inside the aril.

Health handbook
This illustration from the *Tacuinum Sanitatis*, a medieval handbook of health, shows a nutmeg tree being used to make a health-giving beverage. Nutmeg was thought to have a range of health benefits and was used in traditional medicine to treat various ailments.

Nutmeg has traditionally been used to treat rheumatism and cholera

Rough exterior surface grates easily

▲ Grated nutmeg
A familiar sight in many kitchens, grated nutmeg can be used in cakes and puddings, as well as in savory dishes such as stews and curries.

numbers. Given the inherent variability in fruit production between seedling trees, grafted trees are sometimes used, with selected fruiting clones and sufficient male trees to ensure effective pollination. Peak nut production in trees is at around 20–25 years of age, with commercial production tailing off at about 60 years.

Spice of life
The fruit is a drupe that, when ripe, splits open to reveal the seed—the nutmeg—and the aril that partially covers it, which yields mace. The fleshy covering or pulp is sweet and is used to make jam, or desserts in Indonesian culture. It can also be made into a juice or pickles. Mace is the fruit's crimson-colored layer that lies beneath the pulp and largely covers the seed. It is removed from the seed, flattened, dried, and grated to form the spice. The seed is dried for 6 to 8 weeks in the sun: this causes the kernel to shrink away from the seed coat, which is cracked. The flesh of the nut is then extracted and ground to make the commercial nutmeg.

It can also be grated. The tastes of mace and nutmeg are similar, with nutmeg having a sweeter taste and mace being more subtle; the latter also has a bright orange color. They are used to flavor savory and sweet dishes in Indonesian, Indian, and European cuisine.

A versatile kernel

Apart from yielding the spice, the kernel can be used to make other products. It can be pressed to produce nutmeg butter, a reddish-brown, fatty product that has the same smell and taste as the spice. Pressing the kernels also gives an oil that can be reduced to myristic acid, which can be used as a replacement for cocoa butter. In addition, ground nutmeg can be steam-distilled

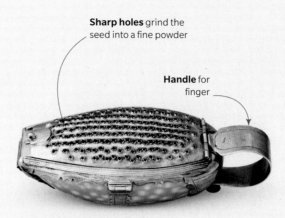

Sharp holes grind the seed into a fine powder

Handle for finger

▲ **Nutmeg grater**
This antique British nutmeg grater from around 1690 is set into a cowrie shell, which forms the receptacle into which the spice is grated.

Other species

MACASSAR NUTMEG
Myristica argentea

Native to Papua; has small, globose seeds sometimes used to adulterate true nutmeg.

MYRISTICA MALABARICA
Myristica malabarica

Grows on lowland, swampy sites in southwest India; its aril completely encloses the seed.

> " It is desirable always to obtain seed from thence, for the culture of the valuable Nutmeg. "

Hooker's Journal of Botany and Kew Garden Miscellany, on Banda, 1857

to produce a light yellow to colorless essential oil that contains several organic compounds. Uses for this oil range from perfumery to cooking, or as ingredients of toothpaste and some cough medicines. The oil has a similar taste to the powdered spice and can be used to soothe irritation or as a scent in soaps—unlike the ground spice, it leaves no gritty residue.

The dose makes the poison

In large enough doses, nutmeg is known to produce some psychological or neurological effects, although it is safe at the levels typically used in cooking or cosmetics. Its psychoactive effects potentially include psychosis, convulsions, delirium, nausea, or headaches. The effects of intoxication take several hours to develop and can persist for some days, sometimes leading to death. Large quantities can induce early labor. It can also interfere with the action of some drugs or painkillers. Pets may be attracted to the scent of nutmeg, which can be fatal if they eat too much of it.

▲ **Batavia in 1723**
This Dutch colonial port, in what is now Jakarta, Indonesia, was the hub of the Dutch East India Company's nutmeg trade in Asia. The native Bandanese people had been trading nutmeg for centuries.

Dragon's Blood Tree

Dracaena cinnabari

Statuesque and seemingly timeless, these magnificent evergreen trees are shaped like half-opened umbrellas. Famed for their dark red "dragon's blood" sap, as well as their unusual appearance, they are among the most striking of the many unique plants that grow wild in the harsh landscape of the Soqotra Islands, located off the Horn of Africa.

GROUP: MONOCOTS
FAMILY: ASPARAGACEAE
HEIGHT: UP TO 30 FT (9 M)
SPREAD: UP TO 40 FT (12 M)

Leaves Evergreen; stiff, sword-shaped; clustered at end of young branches; 1–2 ft (30–60 cm) long

Fruits Globose, fleshy berries; ripen green through black to orange-red; contain 2–3 seeds

Bark Initially gray and smooth, becoming fissured; often with wounds from resin extraction

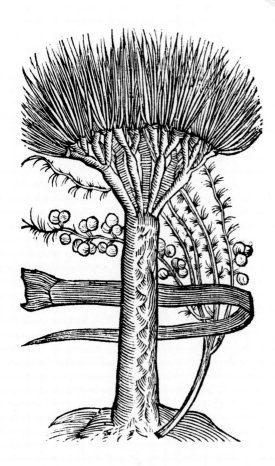

◄ Monumental grove
The limestone plateau of Firmihin on Soqotra Island is a stronghold for the dragon's blood tree. The trees there are mature, large, and a popular sight for visitors, but there is virtually no regeneration of young trees.

► Dragon and fruits
This engraving from 1640 depicts the plant and fruits of the related dragon tree (*Dracaena draco*) native to Madeira, the Canary Islands, and the Cape Verde Islands.

> " This strange and admirable tree groweth very great, resembling the pine tree. "

JOHN GERARD, describing dragon's blood tree, in *Generall Historie of Plantes*, 1633

The 60 to 100 species of *Dracaena* are so distinctive that their taxonomic relationship is obscure. Although they are usually placed in the asparagus family, some classification systems suggest they are related to the agaves or possibly belong to their own family, the Dracaenaceae. A few grow as trees, but most are low-growing shrubs. Some are kept as houseplants, possibly the most familiar of which is mother-in-law's tongue (*Dracaena trifasciata*).

Precious sap
Several trees produce a red sap when their bark is cut, but the dragon's blood tree has been the best-known source of this since Roman times. According to legend, the first tree grew from the congealed blood of a wounded dragon as it fought an elephant to the death. The dried sap was highly prized in the ancient world. Egyptians embalmed their dead with it, while Romans used it as a pigment in paint, as a dye to stain glass and enhance precious stones, for treating dysentery and burns, and as glue for loose teeth. Later, it was valued as stain for the wood of high-quality violins. Although it is now largely replaced by synthetic dyes, locals of the tree's native Soqotra—an archipelago in Yemen—still use it to cure stomach problems, dye wool, decorate pottery, and as lipstick.

The uniqueness of the dragon's blood tree derives primarily from its habitat of Soqotra Island (sometimes anglicized as Socotra). It is

Dark red resin is brittle and insoluble in water

▲ Dragon's blood
The red resin sold as Dragon's Blood came from dragon's blood tree in historic times. Today, it is more likely to come from rattan palms in Asia.

◀ Channeling water
Built to collect water rather than repel it, this tree is shaped like a half-opened umbrella—its spokelike branches meet at a single point partway down the trunk. The shape funnels water from the leaves, to the branches, and down to the trunk and roots.

the largest of four islands, situated 140 miles (225 km) east of the Horn of Africa in the Indian Ocean. Politically, it is part of Yemen to its north. The landmass split off from Africa around 18 million years ago. Since then, relatively immobile species have evolved there in isolation. More than a third of the islands' vascular plant species (containing food- and water-conducting tissues) are endemic (only found on Soqotra).

Mountain fog
Soqotra is a mountainous island, rising to 5,085 ft (1,550 m). The lowlands are arid, but the mountains receive rain from the winter monsoon and are regularly bathed in mist and fog. Dragon's

blood tree is adapted to these conditions, with foliage that scavenges water from the mist and funnels it to the spongy branches, which store it. The dense crown shades the ground beneath, helping fallen seeds sprout, which explains the tree's tendency to grow in patches.

However, the climate of Soqotra is changing. Circumstantial evidence suggests that cloud and mist cover in the mountains has diminished over the years and become more patchy and unreliable. As a result of this "drying out" and overgrazing, many surviving stands consist only of old trees without any saplings to take their place when they die.

Their **degree of branching** suggests that dragon's blood trees may live for up to **500 years**

Other species

DRAGON TREE
Dracaena draco

Found on La Palma in Spain's Canary Islands; in the Madeira region of Portugal, fine old trees grow in urban squares. It was introduced to the Azores region of Portugal.

CORN PLANT
Dracaena fragrans

Ornamental native to tropical Africa; bears variegated, palmlike leaves; can be grown as a houseplant or a hedge; bears fragrant white flowers when mature.

▶ Mojave landmark

Joshua trees are a conspicuous species in the Mojave Desert, with stout trunks and spreading branches that end in a dense cluster of evergreen leaves.

Joshua Tree

Yucca brevifolia

Picturesque or slightly grotesque, the characteristic shapes of Joshua trees dominate the landscape of dry mesas and slopes at high altitude in the Mojave Desert in the southwestern corner of the US.

Joshua trees are endemic to the desert region of the US, where California, Utah, Arizona, and Nevada converge, at altitudes of 2,000–6,000 ft (610–1,800 m). The climate there is very arid, and most of the precipitation needed for growth comes in the form of winter snowfall, so the trees' narrow, succulent leaves conserve water.

Dead leaves form a mantle around young trunks and branches

◀ Bountiful bloom

By early spring, Joshua trees produce rounded flowers in large clusters that are 12–20 in (30–50 cm) across.

Moth partnership

The trees typically bloom from March to May, soon after the snows, but do not flower every year. It is thought that some combination of temperature and moisture triggers flowering. To produce their seeds, the trees rely on yucca moths (*Tegeticula* species). The female moth visits one of their flowers and gathers a small ball of pollen. She then flies to another flowering Joshua tree and lays her eggs in the green ovary in one of its flowers. Afterward, she rubs the collected pollen onto the stigma of the flower, pollinating it. By the time her larvae hatch, the flower's seeds will have developed. The caterpillars eat some of the seeds, but enough survive to be dispersed and grow into new plants.

Other species

ALOE YUCCA

Yucca aloifolia

Found from North Carolina to Florida and Alabama, Mexico, Bermuda, and some Caribbean islands; white-flowered yucca that grows to 23 ft (7 m) tall.

Quiver Tree

Aloidendron dichotomum

Its thick trunk and spreading crown make this low-growing tree a conspicuous feature of rocky, semidesert areas in southern Namibia and Namaqualand, South Africa. Normally, quiver trees grow as lone landmarks, but in a few places, they can form forest stands of hundreds of trees.

GROUP: MONOCOTS

FAMILY: ASPHODELACEAE

HEIGHT: UP TO 30 FT (9 M)

SPREAD: UP TO 26 FT (8 M)

Fruit Dry, green capsule, turning woody; splits to release many winged seeds

Bark Initially pale, turning golden brown; splits into sharp-edged scales

▶ **Quiver forest**
Forests of quiver trees are rare and are famous where they do occur, as seen here at Keetmanshoop, southern Namibia.

Spiky leaves can grow to around 12 in (30 cm) in length

Branches form distinctive, flared habit

Quiver tree was previously classified as *Aloe dichotoma*. Aloes are typically low-growing succulent shrubs; in 2013, seven species of treelike aloes were separated off into a new genus, *Aloidendron*, based both on their growth form and differences in their molecular biology. Quiver tree is probably the best-known member of the new genus. The shape of this species closely resembles that of the dragon's blood tree (see pp.110–112)—they both have branches that radiate outward from a single point at the top of the trunk, resembling a half-opened umbrella. However, the two trees are not closely related; rather, their similarity is an example of "convergent evolution," whereby two unrelated species have evolved similar adaptations that help them cope with challenging conditions, in this case the dry desert.

Parched landscapes

Quiver trees grow in desert and semidesert rocky areas that receive minimal rainfall, falling mostly in winter. They grow among black rock formations that absorb heat during the summer, when temperatures regularly reach 100°F (38°C). They have a widely spreading root system, both to forage for scarce moisture and to anchor them among the rocks and thin, sandy soil.

The copious nectar from their flowers attracts insects, birds, and baboons, but bees are the species' main pollinators.

The tree is a favored site for nesting colonies of social weaver birds. The name "quiver tree" refers to the indigenous San people of the region, who used hollowed-out branches from the trees to make quivers for their hunting arrows.

▲ **Forked branches**
Quiver trees' stems branch into two as they grow, a characteristic that can be seen looking up the branches of this tree photographed in Namibia.

" ... a tree as unsightly as it was curious. It was a species of the aloe ... "

SIR JOHN BARROW, *An Account of Travels Into the Interior of Southern Africa*, 1801

◄ **Spikes of orange-yellow flowers**
In June and July, the trees burst into flower, producing multiply-branched spikes of yellow, urn-shaped flowers. These are about 1¼ in (3 cm) long, with conspicuous, protruding, orange stamens.

Brightly colored petals attract sugar birds

Young, green stalks support panicles

Other species

TREE ALOE
Aloidendron barberae

Medium-sized tree with a thickset trunk; grows in coastal ravines in Mozambique and the east coast of South Africa.

GROUP: MONOCOTS

FAMILY: ARECACEAE

HEIGHT: 115 FT (35 M)

SPREAD: 40 FT (12 M)

Leaf Evergreen; divided into numerous leathery, dark green leaflets; up to 20 ft (6 m) long

Flower Pale yellow, with three petals, three sepals, and six stamens (male) or three-celled ovary (female)

Fruit Egg-shaped; green turning brown; up to 1 ft (30 cm) long; weighing up to 4½ lb (2 kg)

Coconut Palm

Cocos nucifera

Coconut palms line the coast of many tropical regions. They are famous for their massive, hard-shelled fruits, which can survive for months floating at sea—this may help explain why they are so widely dispersed.

Highly decorated silver gilt contrasts with the polished coconut to create a lavish drinking vessel

Coconut palms probably originated in the Indo-Pacific region, and Polynesians migrating into the Pacific around 4,500 years ago spread the palms more widely. Later, Malay and Arab traders brought improved coconut types to India, Sri Lanka, and East Africa.

During the 16th century, European explorers introduced the species into West Africa, the Atlantic coast of America, the Caribbean, and later to the tropical coast of northern Australia. Europeans established large coconut plantations in many countries, so today it is impossible to know coconut palms' true native range.

Layers of goodness

Coconut palm trees can bear up to 30 large round or oval nuts, each encased in a soft, green-gray, fibrous husk. Inside the nut's shell

► Coconut tankard
In the early 17th century, polished coconut shells mounted with silver gilt ornamentation became fashionable with the wealthy.

is the edible, snow-white, fleshy layer (the endosperm), and within this is a cavity partly filled with a sugar-rich liquid (coconut milk). This food store is what allows floating coconuts to survive for months at sea. The tiny embryo of the new plant is embedded in the endosperm, and its developing shoot and root emerge through one of three soft "eyes" situated at one end of the shell.

Virtually every part of the tree is useful to humans. Fibers from the husk can be combed into coir, used in the production of ropes and matting, and in peat-free composts. Its trunk provides building materials, and its leaves provide materials for baskets and roofing thatch. The flesh is made into coconut flakes or dried as copra. Oil extracted from copra is used in soaps and cosmetics and in the production of margarine.

▲ Desert island palm
The coconut palm grows in sandy, well-drained soils along seashores and in coastal forests in most tropical regions of the world. It needs an annual rainfall of 47–90 in (120–230 cm) to survive.

► Seafaring fruit
The fruits can float freely in coastal currents for many weeks and still germinate wherever they are washed ashore. This allows them to colonize remote islands and coral atolls.

" The coconut tree likes to hear the people talk. "

PROVERB, quoted in *Coconut Planter's Manual*, 1907

Standing firm
In Malaysia's Danum Valley tropical rainforest, this Shorea tree (of the genus *Shorea*) stands its ground against the weather. Rooted in shallow soil, this tall evergreen develops enlargements at the base of its trunk in the form of fluting. Called buttress roots, these help stabilize the tree against rains and winds.

◄ Magi mosaic
This 6th century CE mosaic depicts the adoration of the magi against a background of palm trees. In certain Islamic retellings of the birth of Jesus, the birth is said to have taken place under a date palm tree.

GROUP: MONOCOTS

FAMILY: ARECACEAE

HEIGHT: UP TO 75 FT (23 M)

SPREAD: UP TO 15 FT (4.5 M)

Leaf Evergreen; thorns at base of leaf stalk; pinnate with leaflets on opposite sides; about 20 ft (6 m) long

Fruit Roughly cylindrical, yellow to reddish brown; up to 2¾ in (7 cm) long

► Date palm orchard
Date palms are grown in avenues, with Egypt, Iran, and Saudi Arabia being the major producers. The fruits ripen at different rates and have to be harvested several times during the year.

Date Palm

Phoenix dactylifera

Famous worldwide for its sweet, sticky fruits, the date palm is widely cultivated across northern Africa, the Middle East, and South Asia.

Date palm trees usually have a single, straight, upright trunk, crowned with arching fronds—large leaves consisting of multiple leaflets—giving the tree its parasol-like appearance. However, this species can also develop multiple trunks, if the offshoots arising from the base of their stem are allowed to grow. As the trunk extends upward, the lower fronds are shed, leaving behind their woody bases and giving the date palm its characteristic trunk. Frequently grown next to the sea and naturalized in many tropical and subtropical regions, palm trees are robust—able to withstand coastal gales and periodic flooding. Young specimens, with fronds emerging from the base, are popular as houseplants.

In spring or summer, the trees carry cream flowers in clusters that hang down from the crown. These then turn into thick-textured date fruits, each of which contains a single, elongated seed. As the fruits ripen, their skin wrinkles. Yellow to reddish brown, they are eaten fresh, dried, or processed, with the Medjool variety of dates being prized for its caramel-like taste. Fresh fruits are sold intact, but when the dates are dried or processed, the seed is removed and can be used as cattle fodder by being ground up; soaked; or, occasionally, germinated.

Besides being grown for their fruits, date palms can be tapped for their sap (date honey), which can be drunk fresh, processed as sugar, or

Other species

SENEGAL DATE PALM
Phoenix reclinata

Elegant palm that produces several trunks that arch away from the center; fruits are rather dry.

WILD DATE PALM
Phoenix sylvestris

Native to India and Pakistan; has clusters of yellow to orange fruits that turn dark red to purple when mature.

fermented to produce an alcoholic drink—known to the ancient Egyptians as the "drink of life." However, tapping impedes fruit production, and is not routinely practiced. Virtually all parts of the tree can be put to use: its timber is used for building materials and fencing, while the leaves can be used as thatching. Fibers can be wound into rope or used as packaging material, while the woody leaf bases can be burned as fuel.

Temples to churches

Date palm has been cultivated in northern Africa and the Middle East for at least 5,000 years. Revered as a fertility symbol in ancient Egypt, it was widely planted in temple gardens. The ancient Egyptian builder Ineni grew date palms alongside fruiting plants such as figs and carobs, and tomb paintings show palms planted to shade ornamental pools filled with fish and water fowl, considered a food source in the afterlife.

The species shares its genus name, *Phoenix*, with the mythical bird, which it was believed to house, as mentioned in Shakespeare's play *The Tempest*—"Now I'll believe that unicorns exist, and that there's a tree in Arabia where the phoenix lives." Date palm is important in Abrahamic religions and is mentioned in the Torah, Bible, and Qur'an. In Judaism, it is one of the four plant species used during the Sukkot holiday—a festival that commemorates the years when the Jews wandered through the desert on the way to the Promised Land. According to Islamic teachings, the Virgin Mary gave birth to Jesus under a palm tree. In Christianity, the tree

Grayish-green leaflets are narrow and regularly spaced

▶ **Date palm leaves**
The leaves, called fronds, comprise a stout, arching midrib that bears leaflets on two opposite sides. The leaflets are shorter toward the leaf tip, producing a rounded outline.

◀ **Harvesting the crop**
Attached by harnesses, fruit pickers climb up the palm tree's trunk, using the old leaf bases as footholds. Adept pickers often climb the trees barefoot. Ripe dates offer little resistance but have to be picked with care to avoid bruising them.

> " Its fronds heave and swish—It thinks, maybe my leaves are feathers. "

RABINDRANATH TAGORE, "Palm Tree," in *Sishu Bholanath*, 1922

Leaflets vary in length along the midrib, the longest being up to 12 in (30 cm)

is associated with victory—implying the victory of the spirit over the flesh. This may have been an appropriation of a classical tradition that used the palm as a symbol of peace and victory following the capture of Jerusalem by the Romans in 70 CE. Dates were already available in Roman markets before this, and the Roman general Julius Caesar is believed to have been fond of the fruit.

Medieval pilgrims returning from the Holy Land to western Europe would carry date palm leaves as a token. The leaves were also used to decorate Christian churches on Palm Sunday. Victors in many fields are still awarded a metaphorical "palm," and the Palme d'Or is a coveted accolade at the Cannes Film Festival.

Palm leaves have also been widely used as a decorative motif and are frequently found on surviving fragments of ancient Middle Eastern architecture. Columns and pillars in Egyptian temples were often topped with palm leaves. The stylized form of the palmette, in which a number of fronds spread outward in a fan, enjoyed a revival in Art Deco design and remains common even today.

Stone object decorated with palm trees and guilloche—a fine, repetitive pattern

► **Decorative date palms**
Found in the Persian Gulf, this 3rd millennium BCE stone object is adorned with engravings of palm trees, a popular motif in the region at the time. The object has a handle and could be a weight.

GROUP: EUDICOTS

FAMILY: SALICACEAE

HEIGHT: UP TO 80 FT (25 M)

SPREAD: UP TO 50 FT (15 M)

 Leaf Deciduous; slim, pointed; pair of small stipules at base; up to 5½ in (14 cm) long

Male catkin Greenish-yellow catkins with numerous small flowers, which release pollen

 Bark Gray-brown with numerous shallow fissures; young stems yellow-green, shiny

► Weeping foliage

Long, drooping branchlets bearing thin, lance-shaped leaves are responsible for this tree's distinctive "weeping" habit. Male and female flowers appear on separate trees and are arranged in spiky clusters, or catkins.

Shallowly serrated leaves drip raindrops from their tips and are associated with mourning in some cultures

Chinese Weeping Willow

Salix babylonica

Native to China but cultivated elsewhere, this tree has a striking habit and is instantly recognizable. Its likeness has been used in many artworks, whether to evoke the splendor of a Chinese imperial palace or the rustic beauty of the English countryside.

Male catkins consist of small flowers without petals, which bear yellow pollen

► Ghosts and grace
In Japan, weeping willows are widely planted, especially along bodies of water. They symbolize femininity and grace, but also ghouls and evil spirits.

" Willows don't break under the weight of snow. "

JAPANESE PROVERB (Translation)

Given that the weeping willow is a common sight in many parts of the world, it is perhaps surprising to discover that its origins are not clearly understood. This weeping plant is most likely a mutant form of a more typical upright willow native to northern China—probably *Salix matsudana*, which today is treated by many botanists as being the same species. At some point, a weeping form of this willow was discovered, and its cuttings were taken and distributed widely. Weeping willows were transported along the Silk Road through Central Asia to the Middle East, and from there to Europe and beyond.

The origins of this tree were further confused when Swedish botanist Carl Linnaeus coined its scientific name, *Salix babylonica*, implying an origin in Babylon (now Iraq). The tree he described was in the Netherlands, but he was guided by Psalm 137 in the *Book of Psalms*, which reads "By the rivers of Babylon, there we sat down, yea, we wept, when we remembered Zion. We hanged our harps upon the willows in the midst thereof." Even though the trees that line the Euphrates River in Iraq are poplars rather than willows, the Linnaean name remains.

Willows and water

Willows are a common sight at wetlands, marshes, and estuaries. Many willows have the remarkable ability to survive and thrive in

▲ Moving motifs
Weeping willow motifs are widely used in Chinese art. This paper fan by calligrapher Wu Xizai (dated 1852) features a cicada perching on an fall willow stem; each leaf is a single brushstroke.

water-saturated soil, and their spreading root systems help stabilize banks and shorelines. Such aquatic habitats are often subject to violent weather and rapid changes in water levels, which can result in trees being swept away. This is when willows demonstrate another key survival skill—their ability to root rapidly in new locations. Willow stems are rich in indolebutyric acid, a rooting hormone, and stems of all sizes can root within weeks. Extracts from willow stems are often used to encourage rooting in other plant cuttings, and their ease of propagation has made willows a popular choice for reforestation, windbreaks, and slope stabilization projects. Given their readiness to root, willow stems can be woven into a fence that will then root and grow leaves, known as a "fedge."

While willows readily reproduce by cuttings, they do produce flowers and seeds as well. In most willows, the plants are dioecious (with separate male and female plants). In Europe and Australia, most weeping willows are female, suggesting that a female clone was introduced and propagated by cuttings. In other parts of the world, male clones are more common. Traditionally, it was thought that only wind pollinated willow flowers. However, studies suggest that both insects and wind play a role, improving the chances of successful pollination.

Cultural connections

The weeping willow features in stories and folklore, is a recurring motif in arts and crafts, and is used in traditional medicine. In China, it

Nectar and pollen
Willow flowers produce nectar and pollen. They are a valuable food source for a variety of bees and other pollinating insects.

" The stiffest tree is most easily cracked, while the bamboo or willow survives by bending with the wind. "

BRUCE LEE (1940–1973), American-born martial artist and actor

Other species and varieties

CORKSCREW WILLOW
Salix babylonica 'Tortuosa'

Widely cultivated clone of Chinese weeping willow, grown for its upright form and twisted stems. Often harvested for floristry.

GOAT WILLOW
Salix caprea

A Eurasian species of deciduous shrub or small tree; one of the most common willows in Britain. Also known as pussy willow.

BAY WILLOW
Salix pentandra

Native to Europe and Asia. Deciduous shrub or small tree with leaves resembling those of the culinary herb bay.

is a symbol of immortality and rebirth, possibly alluding to its readiness to root from cuttings. In some parts of the country, willow boughs were carried during ceremonies to avert drought, or hats of woven willow worn to summon rain.

In 18th-century Britain, the import of Chinese arts and crafts led to a heightened appreciation of the aesthetic of the East. To cater to an increased demand for such products and motifs, British potteries created a chinoiserie willow pattern to use on their ceramics, a pattern that is still in production today.

In Chinese medicine, willow bark is used in the treatment of headaches, fever, and inflammatory conditions. Early European healers also employed willow bark for pain relief, as did some Indigenous American tribes. Willows contain the plant hormone salicylic acid, which was subsequently developed into the painkiller aspirin (acetylsalicylic acid).

NAPOLEON'S WILLOW

In 1815, French emperor Napoléon Bonaparte was exiled to the South Atlantic Island of Saint Helena, where he is said to have enjoyed sitting under a weeping willow and wished to be laid to rest there. This tree's cuttings were sent around the world, often under the name *Salix napoleonis*.

PAINTING OF NAPOLEON'S GRAVE, ST HELENA

▲ Weeping within the walls

Chinese weeping willows are also known as Beijing willows and are widely planted around the Chinese capital, including in and around the Forbidden City.

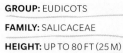

GROUP: EUDICOTS

FAMILY: SALICACEAE

HEIGHT: UP TO 80 FT (25 M)

SPREAD: UP TO 65 FT (20 M)

Leaves Deciduous; slender; dull green above, blue-green below; alternate; to 4 in (10 cm) long

Bark Dull gray; heavily fissured on mature specimens; source of salicin, a painkiller

◄ **Young female catkins**
Catkins arrive in early spring. Female catkins such as these grow up to 1½ in (4 cm) long, while male catkins are slightly larger, reaching 2 in (5 cm). Male and female catkins grow on different trees.

Bark on young branches is smooth, becoming textured with age

Female catkins lengthen after pollination

◄ **Mighty willow**
White willow is the largest of the willow species; it grows quickly but is prone to disease. Its crown sometimes grows into an asymmetrical leaning position, as seen here.

White Willow

Salix alba

Notable for its slender, shimmering leaves, the white willow has found both traditional and modern uses, as well as being a popular garden plant.

In common with all *Salix*, this deciduous species is usually found growing near water, located in Europe and parts of western and central Asia. A specimen seen in a seemingly dry landscape is a sure indicator of an underground water source. Increasingly, it is planted to consolidate wet ground to help manage risk in flood-prone areas, a process known as hydro-hedging.

Its common name relates to the coating of silky hairs on the leaves—although the leaves are varying shades of green, they appear to shine bright white in the breeze, especially in the first part of the year. The flowers, produced in conspicuous catkins, appear at the same time as, or just before, the new leaves.

The white willow has long been valued for its young, whippy stems, which are ideal for basketry (including baskets for hot air balloons) and fencing. Production of these is encouraged by cutting all the growth down to ground level (coppicing) or by allowing a trunk to develop over a period of years and then cutting back all the stems in the crown (pollarding). Some forms have bright red or yellow stems.

White willow was used in Europe to decorate Christian churches on Palm Sunday, if palm leaves were unavailable, and stems were woven into crosses. It is also associated with the moon in Celtic beliefs. The bark has been used medicinally as a painkiller.

Other species

CRACK WILLOW
Salix fragilis

One of the largest willows, with very brittle branches that can snap off in high winds.

VIOLET WILLOW
Salix daphnoides

Grows plum-colored shoots, covered in a white bloom when young; its fluffy male spring catkins are attractive.

▼ Fall leaf
Quaking aspens typically occur in cool climates and shed their leaves before the onset of winter. Snow buildup on leaves could cause branches to break.

GROUP: EUDICOTS

FAMILY: SALICACEAE

HEIGHT: UP TO 82 FT (25 M)

SPREAD: 33 FT (10 M)

Leaf Deciduous; almost circular; rounded teeth; alternate; up to 8 in (20 cm) in young trees

Female catkins Trees are dioecious; female flowers are green, lacking petals, in pendulous catkins

Bark White to pale green; chalky, smooth with prominent dark branch scars

Leaf stalk or petiole of aspens is flattened and catches the wind, causing the leaves to quake in the breeze

Mature aspen leaves are nearly round, but leaves on new shoots and suckers are triangular and twice as big or more

Quaking Aspen

Populus tremuloides

North America's most widely distributed tree, quaking aspen ranges from the heart of Alaska to the mountains of central Mexico. Some groves are thousands of years old.

Aspen bark contains the green pigment **chlorophyll**, used for **photosynthesis**, especially early in the season

Determining the age of a living tree can be difficult. With fallen trees, it is possible to examine the tree rings in the wood and count back through the tree's life. Every year during the growing season, the trunk expands to produce a new layer of conductive tissue, and this creates visible rings within the trunk. Living trees can sometimes be aged using rings, provided they have a wide enough trunk to allow a core sample to be removed. However, in quaking aspen, estimating age is especially difficult. Individual trunks can be felled and the rings counted, with ages ranging from 50 to 150 years—trees in western North America typically live longer than those in the north—but this is not the whole story.

Aspens are clonal organisms, and each tree can produce new stems from buds on the roots (see p.133). Over time, whole groves develop where each tree is connected to its neighbors and all are genetically identical. Older trunks die off but are replaced by new stems, the whole organism surviving for centuries. The Pando aspen grove in Utah covers an area of over 100 acres (40 hectares) with around 48,000 trees, all of which are part of the same single organism. Tree rings only tell us the age of individual stems, and there is no conclusive method for determining the true age of the colony, though current estimates suggest it is at least 14,000 years old.

► Fall foliage
As temperatures fall, green chlorophyll breaks down, revealing yellow carotenoid pigments, which give quaking aspens their fall colors. Some aspens also have red fall coloration.

Tree of sorrow

Jesus is crucified in this painting by 15th-century Italian painter Andrea Mantegna. In Christian tradition, aspen wood was thought to have been used to make the cross on which Jesus was crucified. Consequently, aspen leaves trembling in the wind are said to be the trees quaking in sorrow.

black bears, and the plant's rapid growth and ability to resprout ensure a reliable supply. Aspens host a range of insects—Weidemeyer's Admiral (*Limenitis weidemeyerii*) butterfly uses aspen and its relatives as food for its caterpillars. Beavers frequently harvest quaking aspen, feeding on the bark and smaller branches and using the larger stems in dam construction. Like aspens, beavers are keystone species, as they create habitats by damming, and many other plants and animals also rely upon them.

Population and survival

Since the 1990s, quaking aspen populations have been observed declining, especially in western North America. So far, no diseases or pests have been identified as the cause, and man-made factors such as fire suppression, excess cattle browsing, and climate change may be responsible. Other tree species may also play a role in this. Aspens are unable to grow in shade, and over time, evergreen conifer seedlings may establish themselves in aspen groves. These trees eventually shade out the aspens; conversely, wildfires could keep these seedlings in check. As habitats are degraded by human activities, browsing animals (and domestic livestock) feed more intensively on aspen, allowing little regeneration and further encouraging conifer encroachment. Models suggest that climate change will lead to more wildfires, which could benefit

Given their propensity to grow in large groves, it is no surprise that quaking aspens are an important component of the habitats they occupy. They are sometimes described as keystone species, an ecological term for an organism that, if removed from an ecosystem, would cause its collapse. Aspen leaves and stems are important food sources for browsing animals such as moose, hares, porcupines, grouse, and

Other species

BLACK POPLAR
Populus nigra

Native to Europe and parts of North Africa and western Asia; fast-growing, deciduous tree preferring damp habitats.

EUROPEAN ASPEN
Populus tremula

Similar to its North American sister species. Also has quaking leaves but with more coarsely toothed edges.

HYBRID COTTONWOOD
Populus × canadensis

The result of a cross between European black poplar and North American eastern cottonwood; used for windbreaks.

quaking aspens, as could the spread of certain damaging conifer-specific pests, such as mountain pine beetle. However, should non-native pests of aspen invade the forest, their clonal nature would make them vulnerable to eradication. As a result, the future for quaking aspens appears to be somewhat uncertain.

Quaking aspen and humans

Throughout its wide range, native peoples have made use of quaking aspen in many ways. The wood was used to make canoes, frames and other tools, and sometimes in cabins, though it was not favored for construction. Today, it is widely used to produce pulp for paper and for reconstituted building panels. The inner bark provides a sweet treat that can be eaten raw or cooked or processed into flour. The outer bark was used medicinally to treat a range of ailments from gout to fevers, while the white, powdery substance coating the bark was harvested for use

CLONAL COLONIES

Quaking aspen produces cotton-covered seeds that drift on the wind. This allows it to quickly colonize empty habitats—for example, after wildfires. However, the small seeds contain little nourishment and do not survive long. Clonal reproduction allows aspens to spread locally as new trees develop from buds on the roots of the parent. All these trees are genetically identical.

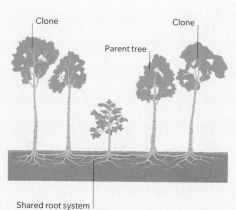

EXAMPLE OF A CLONAL COLONY

Clone · Clone · Parent tree · Shared root system

as a deodorant and antiperspirant. The roots, leaves, and buds were also put to various uses—quaking aspens were keystone to both human and natural communities.

The species also features in various mythological and folkloric beliefs. A person wearing a crown made from quaking aspen was thought to be able to visit the underworld and return, and aspen crowns have been found in European burial mounds. In Celtic mythology, the movement of the branches was said to be the tree communicating with the next world.

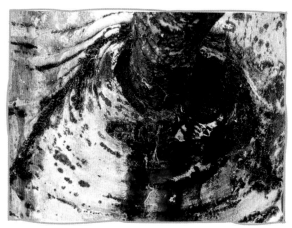

◄ Weeping wounds
Aspens release sap when the trunk is damaged to seal the wound and prevent insects and fungi from gaining access to the interior.

▼ Beaver food
Beavers select aspen over any other tree when feeding, but clonal aspen stems sprouting from roots produce a chemical that deters feeding, allowing them to mature.

" The quaking aspen, light and thin;
To the air quick passage gives. "

PATRICK HANNAY, Scottish poet, 1622

GROUP: EUDICOTS

FAMILY: BETULACEAE

HEIGHT: UP TO 98 FT (30 M)

SPREAD: UP TO 33 FT (10 M)

 Leaf Deciduous; oval, tapering to a point, with a toothed margin; alternate; up to 2 in (5 cm) long

 Catkins Male is cylindrical, drooping, ¾–2 in (2–5 cm) long; female is shorter, upright, then drooping

◄ Silver birch woodland
Pure woodland, like this in Germany, is surprisingly rare, found mainly on light, well-drained soils. The trees' characteristic silvery bark is dotted with knobby black plates and ridges.

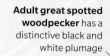

Adult great spotted woodpecker has a distinctive black and white plumage

Lichens commonly grow on the trunks of silver birch trees

Silver Birch

Betula pendula

One of 60 species of birch found in north temperate and arctic regions, silver birch is a graceful deciduous tree with silvery bark and slender, pendulous branches. Across Europe, it blends ecologically with two other species.

As an elegant specimen tree, silver birch is planted in parks, estates, and amenity areas; along suburban streets; and in domestic gardens around Europe and North America. It forms woodland on light soils in the slightly milder climates of southern and lowland Europe, western Siberia, Turkey, and Morocco, and it is recorded to the north of the Arctic Circle in Norway. It readily invades open heathland thanks to its wind-dispersed, winged seeds. However, it is typically a short-lived early colonist in these habitats and is eventually shaded out

as taller oaks or pines become established. The silvery-white bark in the upper crown of older trees is a distinctive feature, usually with big, black, knobby, diamond-shaped plates and ridges on the lower trunk. However, the bark can vary; to confirm the species as silver birch, it

► Woodpecker and birch
Young silver birches can have reddish-brown bark. In clean air areas, this soon gets colonized by lichens. Great spotted woodpeckers pry off the bark to find beetle larvae and dig their nest holes in older trees.

Other species

GRAY BIRCH
Betula populifolia

Native to eastern North America, from Nova Scotia south to North Carolina; birch with grayish-white bark that has been planted as an ornamental in Europe since 1750.

CHINESE RED BIRCH
Betula albosinensis

Birch from mountain woods in western China. Grows to 72 ft (22 m) tall; has coppery red bark that peels off in successive layers of papery, horizontal strips.

YELLOW BIRCH
Betula alleghaniensis

Characteristic tree of damp woodland in the Great Lakes region and northern Appalachians of eastern North America; bark peels off as thin, crisp flakes.

is essential to check the twigs, which are hairless, and the leaves, which have two rows of teeth, with longer, slightly irregular teeth interspersed with two to three shorter teeth (see right).

Birch trio

In many parts of Europe, including Britain, two other species of birch are more common but are often overlooked. In 1904, when the British naturalist Edward Step wrote his book *Wayside and Woodland Trees*, identifying birches was much easier because they were all regarded as a single, variable species, named *Betula alba*. He wrote: "[Birch] grows throughout the length and breadth of our [British] islands, and seems happy alike on a London common, in a suburban garden, or far up in the Scottish highlands. It penetrates farther north than any other tree, and its presence is a great boon to the natives of Lapland."

At the time, something very similar could have been written for Europe as a whole. Today, however, it is recognized that the tree he was

► Catkins and leaves
Silver birch foliage has a graceful form, with slender, pendulous, purple-brown twigs; shining green leaves that turn gloriously golden yellow in fall; and masses of nodding fruiting catkins in late summer.

writing about in Scotland was downy birch, *Betula pubescens*, which is the most common species in north and central Europe. The Laplanders' trees would now be named as scented birch, *Betula odorata*. This is found around northern Europe—including the hills of Scotland and Wales—and in the mountains of central Europe, although some authorities still regard it as subspecies *tortuosa* of downy birch. Diagnostically, both these species have downy twigs, and leaves with just

" Beneath yon birch with silver bark, and boughs so pendulous and fair ... "

SAMUEL TAYLOR COLERIDGE,
"The Ballad of the Dark Ladie," 1834

In **Celtic myth,** silver birch is a symbol of **purity and renewal**

SAMUEL TAYLOR COLERIDGE

Samuel Taylor Coleridge (1772–1834) was an English poet and philosopher. He had a great love of the English countryside, which inspired some of his poetry. In his 1802 poem "The Picture or the Lover's Resolution," he wrote "I find myself/Beneath a weeping birch (most beautiful/Of forest trees, the Lady of the Woods)." The "weeping" foliage confirms he had pendulous silver birch in mind.

a single row of equally sized teeth. They are shorter, bushier, less distinctive trees than silver birch, but most birch woodland in central and northern Europe is of downy birch, with scented birch growing mainly in the subarctic or higher hills. To make matters even more perplexing, all three species can inter-hybridize, creating a "confusion of birches."

Fruiting catkins are swollen and droop on short stalks; they later split open to disperse their seeds

Landscape trees

All these birches produce male and female catkins on the same tree, usually before, or as, the leaves open. The drooping male catkins are up to 2 in (5 cm) long, with numerous minute flowers. These release pollen, carried in the wind to the female catkins. These are shorter and initially erect, but they lengthen and droop as their fruits develop after pollination. They split to release nutlets that are less than $\frac{1}{10}$ in (just 2 mm) long, surrounded by a filmy wing that helps them spread in the wind.

All three species are important landscape trees with leaves that open lime green in springtime and turn golden yellow in fall. Silver birch's finely textured, heavy timber is used mainly for marquetry and veneers and in interior fittings and furniture. However, birch is undervalued as a timber crop and makes excellent flooring, among other products. Silver birch is the national tree of Finland, and its young branches are used by bathers to beat the skin gently in traditional Finnish saunas.

Leaves are edged with a double row of teeth; slightly curved, longer teeth are interspersed with 2–3 smaller teeth

◄ *Kalevala* **forest**

In this illustration to the epic Finnish poem *Kalevala,* the wise old hero, Väinämöinen, is sitting in typical boreal woodland with the distinctive trunks of Scots pine (left) and silver birch (right).

Paper Birch

Betula papyrifera

With its copper-colored to white peeling bark and its leaves that turn yellow or orange in fall, paper birch is a conspicuous feature in damp woodland in interior regions of northern North America. Its bark and timber were highly valued by Indigenous Americans.

▼ **Pure forest**
Paper birch forms pure stands in areas where the original forest has been felled or burned. It quickly regrows from cut stumps. Usually single-trunked, it develops multiple trunks if grazed.

GROUP: EUDICOTS

FAMILY: BETULACEAE

HEIGHT: UP TO 66 FT (20 M)

SPREAD: UP TO 20 FT (6 M)

Leaf Deciduous; oval, round base, pointed tip, toothed edge; alternately arranged; 3–5 in (8–12 cm) long

Male catkin Hangs from shoot tips in spring; green turning yellow; ¾–1½ in (2–4 cm) long

Bark Copper-brown, turning white in older trees; dotted with dark, horizontal pores

Canoe birch
Birch bark was used by Indigenous Americans as canoe waterproofing. Birch bark canoes are still made by Indigenous Americans, craftspeople, and enthusiasts.

" The species is an important successional tree, coming up readily after fires, logging, or the abandonment of cultivated land. "

Flora of North America, Vol.3, 1997

Paper (or canoe) birch is an important landscape tree in North America, growing from Labrador to southern Alaska and in northern US states. Its bright yellow fall leaves can contrast to its bark, which is shining, chalky white on older trees. It is particularly common in second-growth forests (recovering after felling or burning). It is wind-pollinated, with male and female catkins on the same tree. After pollination in early summer, the fruits develop in fall. Tiny, winged seeds released from the catkins blow readily in the wind, allowing the tree to colonize newly opened habitats.

The species is best identified by its bark, which peels off in papery sheets and gives the species its common name. It was an important tree to the indigenous people within its range, who used the bark as the outer waterproof lining for their canoes, for covering their shelters, or as writing material. They made baskets and cradles from its twigs and arrows, snowshoes, spears, and sleds from its wood. The sap and inner bark provided an emergency food supply, and its resin may have had medicinal uses. In many parts of its range, its sap is still tapped and used to make syrup and homemade beer and wine. Its bark can also be used as a fire starter even when damp.

Birch bark is a staple food for moose in winter. Although it has low nutritional value and is difficult to digest because of the amount of lignin (an organic polymer) it contains, it is an important food for the animals because of its sheer abundance and accessibility when snow covers the ground in winter.

Other species

RIVER BIRCH
Betula nigra

Bushy tree from wet woods and stream sides in eastern US; bark flakes off in curling, paper-thin strips.

CHERRY BIRCH
Betula lenta

Birch from woods in eastern US; glossy, reddish-brown bark can be easily mistaken for cherry.

Decorated lid inlaid with porcupine quills and brass tacks

► **Birch box**
This beautiful, decorated Indigenous American box, 9 in (23 cm) in length, was made sometime between 1890 and 1910 and demonstrates the versatility of paper birch timber.

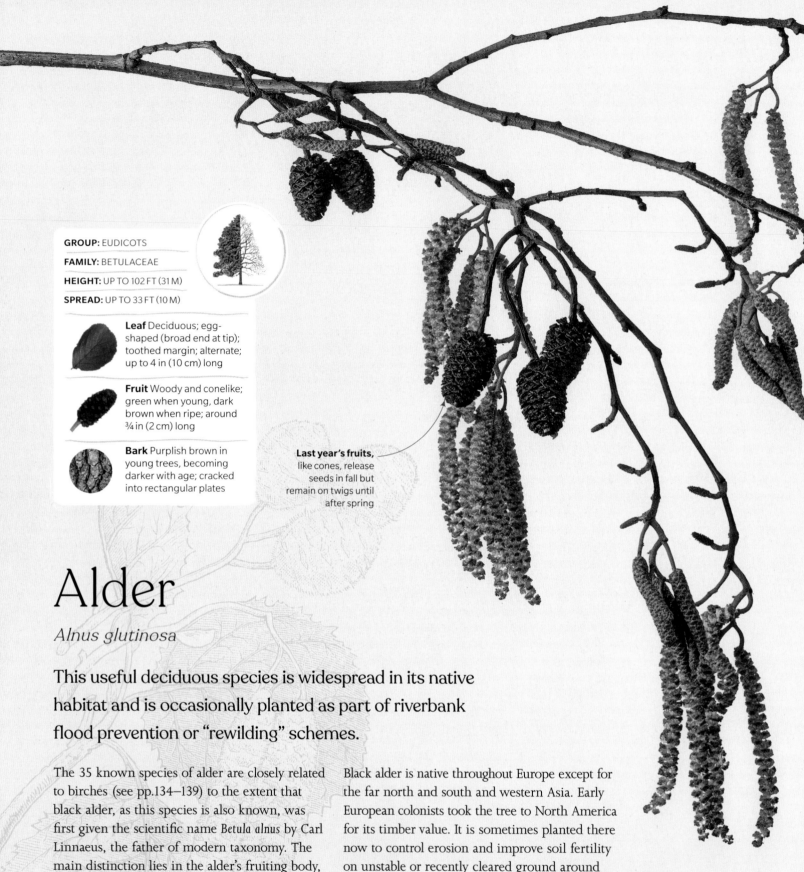

GROUP: EUDICOTS

FAMILY: BETULACEAE

HEIGHT: UP TO 102 FT (31 M)

SPREAD: UP TO 33 FT (10 M)

Leaf Deciduous; egg-shaped (broad end at tip); toothed margin; alternate; up to 4 in (10 cm) long

Fruit Woody and conelike; green when young, dark brown when ripe; around ¾ in (2 cm) long

Bark Purplish brown in young trees, becoming darker with age; cracked into rectangular plates

Last year's fruits, like cones, release seeds in fall but remain on twigs until after spring

Alder

Alnus glutinosa

This useful deciduous species is widespread in its native habitat and is occasionally planted as part of riverbank flood prevention or "rewilding" schemes.

The 35 known species of alder are closely related to birches (see pp.134–139) to the extent that black alder, as this species is also known, was first given the scientific name *Betula alnus* by Carl Linnaeus, the father of modern taxonomy. The main distinction lies in the alder's fruiting body, described as a "false cone" because it differs botanically from the cones of true conifers. The woody scales are made from fused floral leaves (bracts), and the fruit inside is technically a nut, which floats in water and is carried down streams to germinate on riverbanks.

Black alder is native throughout Europe except for the far north and south and western Asia. Early European colonists took the tree to North America for its timber value. It is sometimes planted there now to control erosion and improve soil fertility on unstable or recently cleared ground around sand dunes and mine spoils. Escaped plants grow wild around the Great Lakes area, and elsewhere it is planted as an ornamental tree.

Today, alder's main value is as a landscape tree in wet woodlands, often intermixed with willows. Because of this specialized habitat, these

▲ Spring catkins

Clusters of tiny flowers appear in catkins, usually in February and March. Wind carries pollen from male to female catkins on the same or nearby trees.

▶ Alder swamps

Black alder grows in damp ground beside lakes and streams. It is often the dominant species that colonizes swamps and marshes in woodlands around Europe, here growing with water violet.

Catkins appear before leaves open, which assists wind pollination

Female flowers grow in stubby, purplish-brown catkins at end of short stalks

Male flowers are numerous in dangling catkins up to 2¾ in (7 cm) long, shedding clouds of pollen in spring

DIVERSE WILDLIFE

Alder is a valuable tree for biodiversity. Mature trees host lichens; mosses; fungi; and more than 140 species of insects, including birch sawflies, whose larvae feed on its leaves. Birds such as siskins and lesser redpolls eat its seeds, and leaves falling into streams are food for aquatic insects.

Most of **Venice** is supported on alder's **water-resistant timber** in the canal pilings that **hold up the city**

BIRCH SAWFLY LARVAE ON ALDER

stimulating rapid regrowth of multiple stems, which can be harvested for poles or small timber. Pollarding is similar, but the trunk is cut at a higher level so that the land between the trees can be grazed by sheep or cattle without them eating the new shoots.

Alder wood is relatively hard and easily worked, so historically it was made into broom heads, tool handles, and the soles of clogs. Today, it is more likely to be used in plywood, veneers, or wood pulp. Because of its habitat, alder wood is resistant to water damage, so it is used in riverbank piling, water pipes, and boats.

Leather and gunpowder

The bark of alder is rich in tannins and was valued in the leather tanning industry, producing a rich orange color. In the past, the wood was also partly burned to form charcoal, the main ingredient of gunpowder. The powdered charcoal was mixed with sulfur, which lowered the temperature needed to ignite the gunpowder and increase its rate of combustion, and with potassium nitrate (saltpeter), which released oxygen to enhance the explosive power.

Today, many alder populations are being damaged by an algalike organism, *Phytophthora alni*, which eventually kills the tree. This is one of the most devastating diseases of natural ecosystems to have arisen in Europe in the last century.

▲ Van Gogh's clogs
The wood of alder was perfect for carving into the soles of clogs, once widely worn by factory workers. These clogs were painted by Vincent van Gogh.

are some of the most natural woodlands that survive in developed regions. The roots of alder contain hollow nodules; bacteria living in these "fix" nitrogen from the air to make nitrates, which help the alder grow in poor soils and enrich the surrounding soil in the process.

Cut-back trees

Although black alders can grow into tall trees, they are mostly lower-growing with multiple stems because they have been coppiced or pollarded in the past. In coppicing, the trunk is repeatedly cut down to nearly ground level,

Young shoots are grayish brown, covered with numerous sticky glands

Winter leaf buds are distinctly stalked, protected by tough, oblong, reddish-brown scales with gray spots

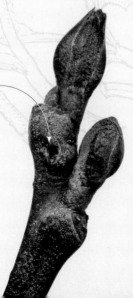

► Spring awakening
Shown here in sequence, the young leaves of alder trees emerge from their winter buds in late spring, well after the catkins appear—a key difference from birches.

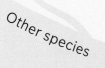

Other species

RED ALDER
Alnus rubra

Largest native alder of North America, found in western states from Alaska to California; fast-growing species that can reach 82 ft (25 m) in height.

GRAY ALDER
Alnus incana

Typical, gray-barked subspecies native to Europe, from Scandinavia south to the Alps and the Caucasus, with two more subspecies in North America.

ITALIAN ALDER
Alnus cordata

Unlike other alders, thrives in dry mountain soils; found in southern Italy, Corsica, and Albania. Hybridizes with black alder in Corsica.

" Once enjoyed, an alder swamp ... remains perennially and primevally enchanting. "

GEOFFREY GRIGSON, *The Englishman's Flora*, 1996

New leaves are often slightly notched at tip

Opening leaf is slightly sticky, hence specific name *glutinosa*

Bud scale around next developing leaf

Leaf stalk is yellowish-green and hairless

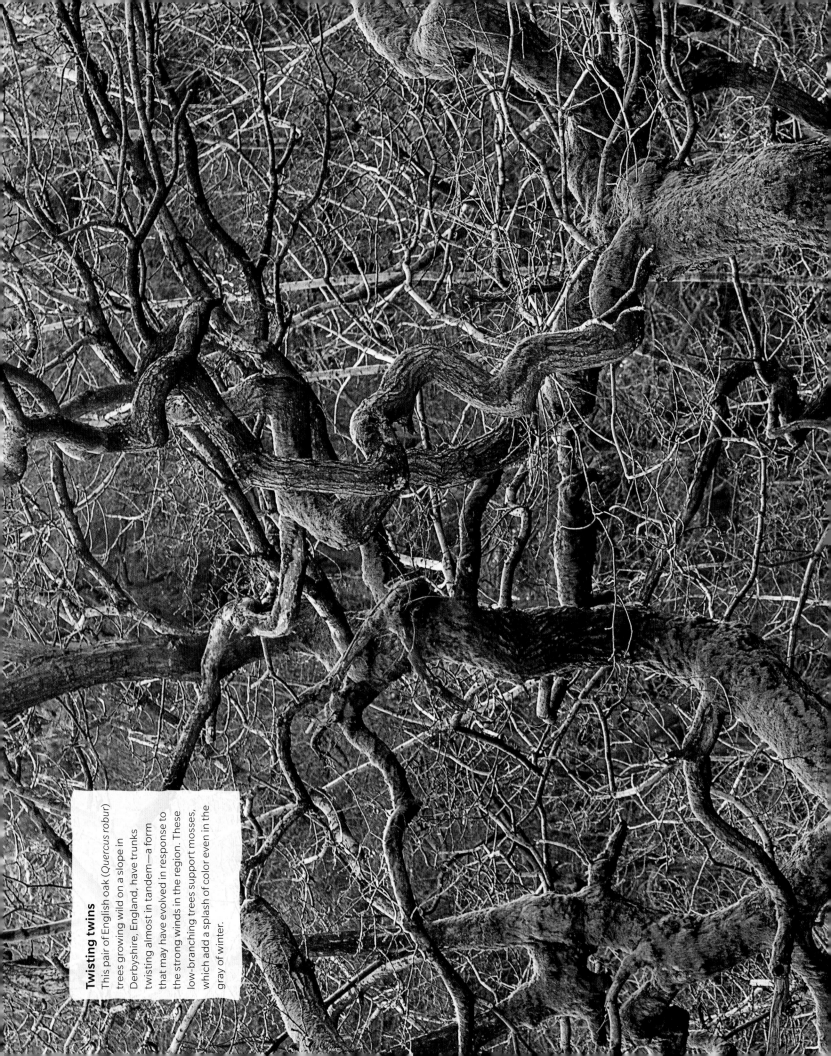

Twisting twins

This pair of English oak (*Quercus robur*) trees growing wild on a slope in Derbyshire, England, have trunks twisting almost in tandem—a form that may have evolved in response to the strong winds in the region. These low-branching trees support mosses, which add a splash of color even in the gray of winter.

Wild Apple

Malus sylvestris

Its beautiful pinkish-white blooms make this small, deciduous tree particularly noticeable when in flower. The small fruits it bears are a valuable food source for many mammals.

Also known as crab apple or sour apple, wild apple is a broadly spreading tree that is native to the Caucasus and northern Iran. While it is most often found growing in ancient woodlands or old hedges, its flowers and fruits grow best in open settings. The tree may have a single trunk when in a woodland setting, where it can grow up to 49 ft (15 m) tall. However, it is usually somewhat shrubby, with several stems sprouting from the base. Its low-domed crown is dense, with twisting branches that are laden with clusters of slightly fragrant blossoms in spring and marblelike fruit in fall.

New shoots of wild apple are slightly hairy at first, becoming smooth and hairless by summer. The leaves have a finely serrated margin, with

Of the **7,500 varieties of apples** cultivated in the world, 2,500 are grown in the US

Each flower cluster has 4–7 flowers and 2–4 leaves

▼ **Flowers in spring**
In spring, wild apple flowers appear along with smaller, young leaves. The showy white blossoms can also be tinged with pink.

Elliptical to obovate leaves have a short point at the apex and a rounded or wedge-shaped base

Flowers have five petals and 20 stamens

GROUP: EUDICOTS

FAMILY: ROSACEAE

HEIGHT: UP TO 30 FT (10 M)

SPREAD: UP TO 20 FT (6 M)

Leaf Deciduous; ovoid; dark shiny green above, whitish green below; alternate; 1¼–2¾ in (3–7 cm)

Bark Smooth and dark brown, becoming fissured and cracking into small squares in old trees

small round teeth; the side veins in the leaves are looped and do not extend to the leaf margin. The flowers are carried in small umbels—all arising from the same point—on last season's spur shoots when the leaves are half expanded. These are followed by globose or oblate (wider than long) "crabs," or fruits, which are ¾–1½ in (2–4 cm) across and set on a short stalk. When ripe, these become shiny green with some russet markings and a noticeable cluster of five sepals on the top. The creamy white flesh of the fruit is juicy but sour to the taste and rubbery in texture. A wild apple contains five cells, each with one to two light brown, oval seeds. In fall, ripened fruits may litter the ground beneath a tree, resembling greenish-yellow marbles with a cavity or

" An apple tree in full blossom is like a message, sent ... from heaven to earth, of purity and beauty. "

HENRY WARD BEECHER, American minister, c.19th century

Flowers briefly smother the leaves and provide rich pickings for bees

▼ **Wild apple tree**
In open settings, this tree forms a rounded crown, but in woodlands, it tends to grow taller, often on a single stem.

The Fall

In the Bible, Genesis tells the story of how Adam and Eve fall from grace when they eat the forbidden fruit—often said to be an apple—at the behest of the serpent.

played a significant part in the development of the tang or astringent flavor in some cider apple varieties.

In literature and folklore

Apples are mentioned in many works of literature—from poetry to prose. English playwright William Shakespeare mentions crab apples in plays such as *A Midsummer Night's Dream* and *King Lear*. Myths and folklores feature apples as well. In Norse mythology, apples were associated with youthfulness. Wild apple is a symbol of love and marriage in Celtic folklore, its seeds used to divine information in rituals. In the Old Testament's Book of Genesis chapter 2 verse 1, God tells Adam and Eve not to eat the forbidden fruit—often depicted as an apple—from the tree of the knowledge of good and evil. However, this association is superficial, and the only actual tree mentioned in the account is the fig tree.

indentation at both ends. Although eaten by many animals, raw wild apples are unfit for human consumption because of their acidic taste, but they can be used to make an edible jelly. The wood from this tree is extremely hard and dense, which makes it suitable for carving or turning small items such as chess pieces.

▼ Leaves and fruits

In fall, wild apples ripen to globose or oblate fruits that are juicy, with a sour taste and a rather rubbery texture.

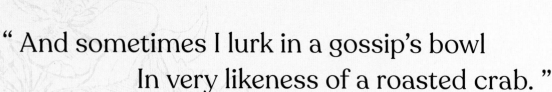

> " And sometimes I lurk in a gossip's bowl
> In very likeness of a roasted crab. "

WILLIAM SHAKESPEARE, *A Midsummer Night's Dream*, 1605

Famous relative

Wild apple is superficially very similar to the orchard apple (*Malus domestica*). However, it has smaller fruits than those of its cultivated counterpart. Another key difference between the two *Malus* relatives is that while wild apple is largely glabrous or hairless once the shoots and leaves are mature, the shoots, leaves, and flowers of orchard apple are persistently hairy.

Wild apple is not a direct ancestor of the orchard apple, despite their many similarities. However, the two species are capable of hybridizing, and wild apple probably has

▼ Muntjac deer

These small- to medium-sized Asiatic deer are one of the several small mammals to treat the fallen fruits of wild apple as a major fall food.

Five-lobed calyx (sepals) persists at the top of the fruit

Mature leaves are twice the size of those that appear with flowers

ORIGINS OF APPLES

A wild apple forest grows in Tian Shan, translated as "heavenly mountains"—a mountain range on the borders of China, Kazakhstan, and Kyrgyzstan. Here, the orchard apple's wild ancestor *Malus sieversii* is said to produce a variety of apples depending on how the trees are pollinated. The forest is believed to be the origin of modern apple varieties.

TIAN SHAN FOREST

Other species

APPLE TREE
Malus domestica

Small, deciduous tree with hairy shoots and leaves; bears fruits that are sweet when fully ripe and has larger flowers than those of wild apple.

JAPANESE CRAB APPLE
Malus floribunda

Small tree; bears massed flowers that are a rich rose color as buds, then pale pink, masking the branches in spring; followed by yellow fruits ¾ in (2 cm) across.

SWEET CRAB APPLE
Malus coronaria

Small tree from eastern North America; has clusters of 4–6 violet-scented white flowers in May or June followed by yellow-green, harshly acidic fruits ¾–1½ in (2–4 cm) across.

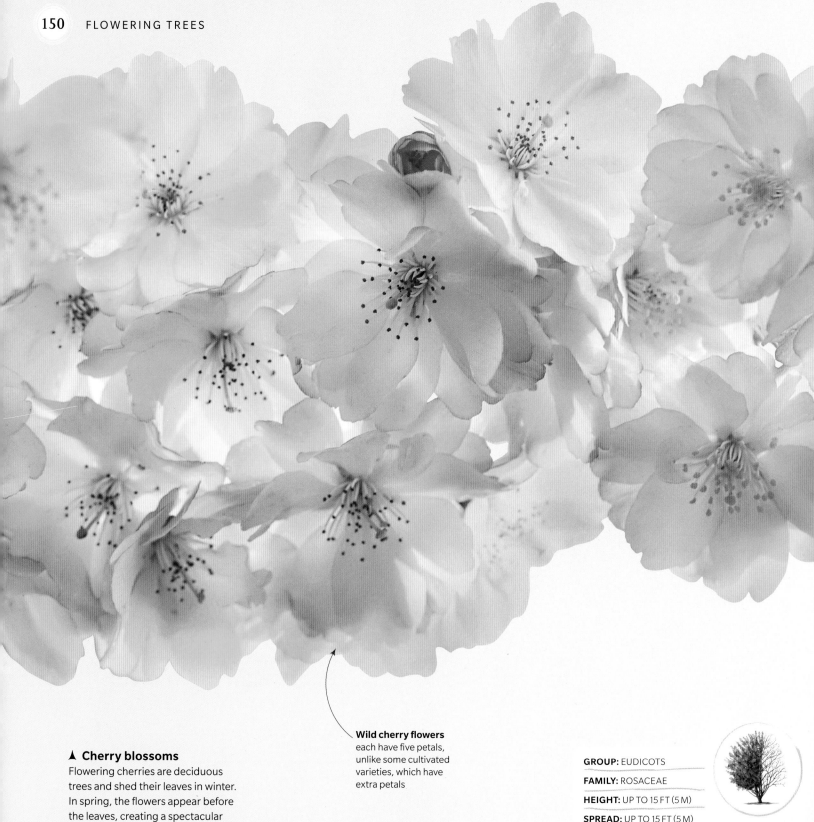

Wild cherry flowers each have five petals, unlike some cultivated varieties, which have extra petals

▲ **Cherry blossoms**
Flowering cherries are deciduous trees and shed their leaves in winter. In spring, the flowers appear before the leaves, creating a spectacular show of pure blossom.

GROUP: EUDICOTS

FAMILY: ROSACEAE

HEIGHT: UP TO 15 FT (5 M)

SPREAD: UP TO 15 FT (5 M)

Leaf Deciduous; margins toothed, colored yellow and red before falling; alternate; 2–5 in (5–13 cm)

Bark Smooth, gray-brown, horizontal lines of lenticels; young stems reddish green with cream lenticels

" In the cherry blossom's shade there's no such thing as a stranger. "

KOBAYASHI ISSA, poet, c.19th century

Leaves are often bronze when young

Cherry blossoms include a tuft of male pollen-bearing stamens surrounding a central female ovary and stigma

▲ **Birds and blooms**
Cherry blossom is a common motif in Japanese art. This woodcut print by Katsushika Hokusai features a weeping cherry in flower with a visiting bullfinch—these birds feed on fruit flowers.

Japanese Cherry

Prunus serrulata

It is not often that one tree's flowers can bring a nation to a standstill, but the springtime blooming of the Japanese cherry does just that.

Japanese flowering cherries, or sakura, are a cultural phenomenon. The arrival of the flowers in spring is the subject of much anticipation, and flower forecasts are presented alongside the weather. Viewing the blossom is a nationwide obsession that attracts people of all ages, from the older generation who sit on blankets below the boughs sipping sake in a centuries-old tradition called *hanami*, to teenagers with selfie sticks posing for the perfect picture for social media. Flowering cherries are often planted around schools, as peak blossom season coincides with

the start of term, allowing pupils to indulge in this botanical institution as they enter their classrooms. Increasingly, sakura is used to encourage international tourism and promote Japanese culture abroad. The mascot for the 2020 Tokyo Paralympics, Someity, is named after a type of cherry blossom.

Tradition and modernity
Hanami has its origins in the 8th century CE; wild plum blossom was initially the focus

Cherry flowers are **pickled** in salt and vinegar and used in **confectionery** and **blossom tea**

► A popular festival
Hanami, the tradition of viewing cherry blossoms, is centuries old. This gathering in Ueno Park, Tokyo, was photographed around 1890, and crowds still attend there.

of attention, but cherries soon eclipsed it. The tradition began among the elite of the imperial court but gradually spread and is now a firm fixture at every level of Japanese society. Cherry blossoms have many symbolic meanings in Japan. Their ephemeral nature, with peak bloom lasting only three days, encourages people to appreciate the fleeting nature of life. In contrast, the age-old tradition of *hanami* is respected as a much-valued part of Japanese culture. Cherry blossoms appear on the 100-yen coin, in Japanese tattoo art (*Irezumi*), and on the logo of the national rugby union team. During World War II, sakura was used by the government to promote Japanese nationalism, and cherry trees were planted in nations occupied by the Japanese Empire, including Korea and China.

Several species of sakura
The wild origins of sakura cherry trees are a source of much uncertainty. *Prunus serrulata* is native to Japan, Korea, and much of China. Although it does produce cherries, they are small and sour to taste. The flowers may be pink or white, and each has five petals. Sakura appear to derive from hybridization between several wild

cherries native to Japan, particularly Oshima cherry (*Prunus speciosa*), a white-flowered tree native to Oshima Island and the Izu Peninsula of Honshu, and pink-flowered Yamazakura (*Prunus jamasakura*) from central and southern Japan. Both species are treated as forms of *Prunus serrulata* by

► Ceramic sakura
This pottery teapot with cherry blossom motifs was made in early 17th-century Japan. It forms a component of a traditional tea ceremony.

Design echoes curtain used to surround picnic area during traditional *hanami*

Other species

YOSHINO CHERRY
Prunus × yedoensis
Widely planted sakura tree; white- or pale pink-flowered cherry of hybrid origin; its actual parentage is disputed.

FUJI CHERRY
Prunus incisa
Native to Japan; shrub or small tree with white or pale pink flowers and fiery fall leaf color; amenable to container culture.

TIBETAN CHERRY
Prunus serrula
Western Chinese species with white flowers; mainly notable for its glossy, copper-colored bark.

A cherry tree can remain in bloom for one or two weeks, but it keeps its "peak color" for only three days

Fleeting flowers

Given their very short season, sakura must be enjoyed quickly, as seen in this print. Their ephemeral nature is in part why the cherry blossom is regarded so highly. Today, weather forecasts and apps help people predict peak time for *hanami*.

Stylized blossoms depicted on advertisement

▲ **Floral favorite**
Printed in the early 1900s, this Japanese Government Railways travel poster features an iconic pagoda together with a spray of cherry blossoms.

some botanists, and recent studies using DNA suggest that other wild cherry species have also contributed to the development of modern sakura varieties.

In Japan, sakura are classified based on characteristics such as color, number of petals, and tree habit. Typical cherry blooms each have five petals, but those with double blooms have more than five petals per flower and are called *yae-zakura*. *Shidare-zakura* are cherries with weeping stems and include some of the oldest recorded varieties. One tree located in Fukushima Prefecture, the Miharu Takizakura, is said to be 1,000 years old. Most sakura are pink- or white-flowered, but yellow- and green-flowered forms have been developed. New varieties are still being bred; one breeder bombarded plants with radiation to stimulate mutation, developing the variety "Nishina Otome," which flowers all year round.

Japanese cherry trees were introduced to Europe in the latter part of the 19th century, after Japan opened its ports more widely to foreign trade. They soon became a fashionable addition to European city streets, gardens, and parks and inspired many artists of the time, including Vincent van Gogh and Claude Monet.

Blossom in the 20th century
Sakura have been used as a diplomatic calling card at the highest level, and gifts of cherry trees have long been used to cement alliances between Japan and other nations. Japan donated over 3,000 cherry trees to the US in 1912 as a gift to the American people. They were planted in Washington, DC, beginning with a ceremonial planting by US First Lady Helen Taft and Viscountess Chinda, the wife of the Japanese ambassador. These trees would form the foundation of the National Cherry Blossom

Festival in the city, which continues to this day. The 1912 trees replaced a previous batch delivered in 1910, which were found to be diseased and so were destroyed.

The English gardener and ornithologist Collingwood Ingram was a renowned authority on Japanese cherries, having traveled to Japan and grown many varieties at his home in Kent in the south of England. In 1926, he was asked to address the Cherry Society of Japan and while visiting, he viewed a painting of a white sakura that was thought to be extinct. He recognized the plant as one he had seen in England and was able to reintroduce it to Japan. Collingwood became fondly known as "Cherry" Ingram.

▼ Staggered blossoms

Yoshino Mountain, Nara Prefecture, is famed for its four cherry groves, which were planted at different elevations so that the blossoms appear in succession.

FLOWERING TIMES

The timing of each year's cherry blossom season is culturally important in Japan. Historical records have been kept in the city of Kyoto that date back 1,200 years and show that the flowering times did not vary significantly until the 1800s, when they began to occur earlier in the year. Increasing urbanization has caused a heat island effect that contributes to this development, while the rise of global warming has also added to this change in timing.

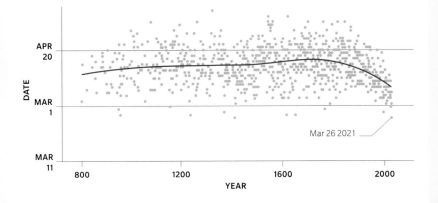

The **first almond trees** were brought to **California** by Spanish explorers in the **1700s**

◄ *Baburnama* **illustration**
For centuries, almonds have been important in commerce. In this 16th-century illustration from *Baburnama*, memoirs of Mughal ruler Babur, almonds are being weighed for transport in a village near Samarkand in present-day Uzbekistan.

Almond

Prunus dulcis

Hard outer coating protects the edible seeds

Almonds were one of the first nut trees to be cultivated around 5,000 years ago. Now 1.5 million tons (1.35 million tonnes) of almonds are grown commercially, mostly in the US and the European Union.

Probably native to Southeast Asia, the almond tree is a relatively small, deciduous species known for its beautiful blossom and edible seeds. It is widely planted and naturalized around the Mediterranean basin and western Asia. It thrives in regions that have warm climates with plentiful water supply but is easily damaged by cold weather. It is also grown in other regions with a warmer climate, including California—the largest producer of almonds in the world—South Africa, and Australia. In

2019–2020, more than 1.1 million tons/ 1 million tonnes of almonds were harvested in US, followed by the European Union (151,000/137,000), Australia (122,000/111,000), China (49,600/45,000), and Turkey (16,500/15,000).

The almond fruit is like a Russian nested doll. Its edible seed develops within a hard, pitted stone enclosed inside a green, fleshy outer layer called the hull. Unfit for human consumption, the hull is eaten by rodents and birds, such as crows and magpies. In this process, these animals scatter

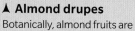

▲ **Almond drupes**
Botanically, almond fruits are classed as "drupes"—fleshy fruits with one or more seeds, each surrounded by a stony layer. The fruit splits open as it ripens.

Bowl-shaped delicate flowers have five petals. They are mostly white in color and have a pale pink center

GROUP: EUDICOTS

FAMILY: ROSACEAE

HEIGHT: 13–33 FT (4–10 M)

SPREAD: UP TO 20 FT (7.5 M)

Leaf Deciduous; lance-shaped; dark green on top, paler below; finely toothed; up to 4¾ in (12 cm) long

Seed Fleshy, green fruit encloses a woody, dry shell that contains the edible almond seed

Bark Dark gray or brown; smooth when young, becomes cracked and fissured as it matures

Each flower is about 1¼–2 in (3–5 cm) wide

Flowers are borne singly or in pairs in early spring before the leaves emerge

▶ Flowering almond

There are a large number of almond tree varieties, depending on the geographical area and the climatic conditions of each region. The flowering variety bears attractive pink flowers in March and April.

the stones from which seeds germinate. Almond's distinctive flowers are white or pink fading to white; they appear on the tree in early spring before the leaves open, sometimes as early as February, and are pollinated by insects.

Sweet and sour

There are three varieties of almonds. The edible form is the sweet almond (*P. dulcis* var. *dulcis*), whose seeds can be eaten raw or cooked. It contains around 40–60 percent unsaturated oil and 20 percent protein. The oil from its seeds is used in confectionery, baking, and making cosmetics. The second variety is the bitter almond (*P. dulcis* var. *amara*), which is probably the original wild type. It has a pungent taste because of the presence of a chemical called amygdalin that releases the deadly poison cyanide and can be toxic to humans. Bitter almond oil is used as food flavoring (in small quantities) and in cosmetics. The third (*P. dulcis* var. *persicoides*) is valued for its showy pink flowers.

▲ **Fine flavour**
This poster (1900) advertising French food shows a woman savoring cookies made using almonds sourced from the region of Provence.

> " Almond is a flavoring of the most original and refined sort; it is regretted that ... few dishes make use of it today. "
>
> G. M. DE ROUGEMONT, *A Field Guide to the Crops of Britain and Europe*, 1989

◀ **Almond orchards**
Many almond varieties need to be cross-pollinated with other varieties to produce fruits. The vast commercial orchards in California require 1.4 million hives of bees to pollinate the trees.

Other species

APRICOT
Prunus armeniaca

Deciduous tree native to Asia; bears fruit, which comprises edible pericarp (the fleshy outer layer of the fruit) and a stone within.

PLUM
Prunus domestica

Cultivated deciduous tree; hybrid between Cherry Plum and Sloe; grown for the sweet outer flesh of its fruits.

China peach
This painting on a porcelain vase from the Qianlong Period (1735–1795) features peaches, which are a symbol of longevity in Chinese culture.

GROUP: EUDICOTS

FAMILY: ROSACEAE

HEIGHT: UP TO 26 FT (8 M)

SPREAD: 20 FT (6 M)

Leaf Deciduous; dark, shining green; narrow and lance-shaped, with a finely toothed margin; alternate; 2–6 in (5–15 cm) long

Flower Rose-pink or sometimes white; opens before leaves; borne singly or in pairs; 1–1⅓ in (2.5–3.5 cm) across

Bark Grayish brown; develops narrow cracks and fissures as it ages

Peach

Prunus persica

Peach trees arose in the mountain areas of China and have been cultivated there for thousands of years. They were taken along the ancient Silk Road to Persia and grown by the Romans.

Peach trees are deciduous and low-growing, with spreading branches that are readily pruned, making harvesting easier, and typically live for only 10–20 years. Young plants often appear spontaneously around waste tips and habitation from discarded stones, but these rarely reach maturity, while double-flowered varieties are frequently grown for show in gardens.

This species was grown commercially for its edible fruit around warmer parts of Europe from the 13th century, but it is now cultivated in warm regions around the world. World production of peach fruits in 2018 was estimated at 27 million tons (24.5 million tonnes), almost two-thirds of which came from China. In the US, most of the national production comes from the state of Georgia, known as the "peach state."

The fresh fruit cannot be stored for more than a few weeks, so most of the cultivated peaches are canned, dried, or processed to make jellies, jams, juice, or wine. Peaches contains about 8 percent sugar, which is mostly sucrose.

Peach fruits have velvety, edible skin, while nectarines—a closely related species—have smooth, glossy skin. The difference results from the mutation of a single gene, making smooth-skinned nectarines appear on the branches of a tree that otherwise produces fuzzy peaches.

► Peach blossom
The flowers of the peach tree appear in spring. They can be small and rose pink in color or larger but paler pink or white. Most varieties are self-pollinating.

Young leaves
tightly folded in the leaf bud unfurl as growth begins

Flower buds
open before the leaves in spring at the end of shoots

GROUP:	EUDICOTS
FAMILY:	ROSACEAE
HEIGHT:	UP TO 50 FT (15 M)
SPREAD:	UP TO 40 FT (12 M)

Leaf Deciduous; ovate to elliptical, shortly pointed or rounded tip; alternate; up to 4¾ in (12 cm) long

Fruit Obovoid, with a dimpled base and a persistent calyx, spotted with small lenticels

Bark Brown or black; figuring into small plates of scales

> " Apple wood will scent your room,
> Pear wood smells like flowers in bloom. "

LADY CELIA CONGREVE, poet and World War I nurse,
"The firewood poem," 1930

Clusters of 7–9 flowers, 2–3¼ in (5–8 cm) across, are carried on spur shoots, which may be spiny

Pear

Pyrus communis

Pear is a large, long-lived tree mainly found in orchards. In addition to being cultivated for its fruit, pear boasts beautiful blossoms that blanket the tree in spring.

Believed to have originated in western Asia more than 2,000 years ago, pear is now cultivated the world over. Its foliage is a glossy mid to dark green on the upper surface and a paler subshiny green below. Initially hairy, the leaves become hairless by fall. The main vein is a strong feature up the middle of the leaf, but the side veins are small, if many. There is no fall coloration of note, with leaves turning black before falling off, but in some trees or seasons, the leaves turn an attractive yellow or red. Pear has a dense, hard wood that lends itself to carving and cabinetry, among other uses.

Flavorful fruits

Pear is grown for its fruits, which are sweet with a slightly floral flavor when ripe and come in a variety of shapes and sizes. In some forms, they can be almost round rather than the distinctive

obovoid "pear" shape—enlarging from the end of the stalk and broadest near the tip—that has come to be associated with them.

The common pear of Europe can be identified by the persistent calyx (sepals) at the apex of the fruit. Asiatic pears are derived from a different species. While they look similar to their

Pears would be left to ripen further after being picked to allow for them to grow softer and sweeter

◄ **Cider press**
This 17th-century illustration shows how apples and pears were turned into cider by crushing and pressing them and then treating the extracted juice with yeast found on the fruits' skin. Pear cider is called perry.

European counterparts, they usually have more "spots" or lenticels. Also, the calyx at the end of the fruit is absent, having fallen off to leave a circular depression. What both types of culinary pears have in common is that they are very juicy when ripe and have slightly gritty stone cells in their flesh. In the unripe fruit, the stone cells render the flesh inedible unless cooked; when the fruit ripens, which occurs abruptly, the flesh takes on a buttery texture and becomes pleasant to eat. These fruits are also crushed and fermented to make perry, or pear cider.

► Pear varieties
Hundreds of different varieties of pears have been named. The fruits produced can, therefore, come in a variety of shapes, colors, and sizes—from rounded with russet-yellow color to green and obovoid.

PYRUS communis.   POIRIER commun.

Flowers bear a 5-lobed calyx, 5 clawed petals, 18–20 stamens, and 3–5 separate styles

◄ Pear blossoms
There are more than 1,000 cultivars of pear. This branch of the French Doyenné du Comice cultivar bears nectar-rich flowers that attract prolific pollinators such as bees and moths.

Leaves are half expanded at flowering time. They are glossy green with a small-toothed margin

Other species

CALLERY PEAR
Pyrus calleryana
Often found planted as a street tree; similar foliage to the pear; fruit is ¾ in (2 cm) across; calyx disk falls off before ripening.

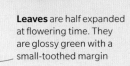

WILLOW-LEAVED PEAR
Pyrus salicifolia
Leaves covered in silvery gray hairs that fall away from the upperside in summer. Most often seen in weeping form.

Fleshy, oval to rounded, dark red fruits ripen in late summer to early fall

Hawthorn

Crataegus laevigata

A common deciduous hedgerow plant native to western and central Europe, hawthorn is an essential addition to any mixed wildlife hedge and has become popular choice in gardens where a small tree is required. Its fruits are eaten by both wildlife and humans.

Straight or zigzagging stems are set with sharp thorns

Hawthorn branches are often used as nesting sites by birds, such as this tree sparrow

GROUP: EUDICOTS

FAMILY: ROSACEAE

HEIGHT: UP TO 30 FT (10 M)

SPREAD: UP TO 26 FT (8 M)

Leaf Deciduous; shallowly lobed toward tips, glossy; alternate; up to 2 in (5 cm) long

Bark On mature specimens, grayish bark becomes fissured and forms platelets

◄ **Bird on hawthorn branches**

In winter, birds feed on the haws; small birds appreciate protection from the elements and predators that the dense tangle of stems provides.

This compact, spiny, shrubby tree is found throughout Europe, where it often grows as part of areas of ancient woodlands; it is also found as far south as North Africa. It hybridizes freely with the closely related species *Crataegus monogyna*, to the extent that the true species *Crataegus laevigata* has become rare. Hawthorn continues to play a valuable role in agriculture in the form of hedging to contain and shelter livestock, especially in windswept areas. In groups, it forms a virtually impenetrable barrier even when out of leaf over winter, and for this purpose regular trimming can help prevent trees from developing a clear trunk.

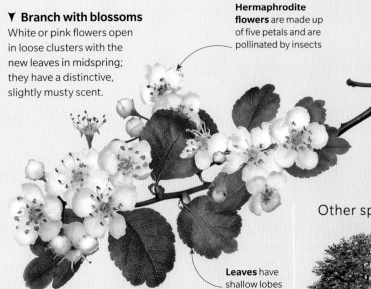

▼ Branch with blossoms
White or pink flowers open in loose clusters with the new leaves in midspring; they have a distinctive, slightly musty scent.

Hermaphrodite flowers are made up of five petals and are pollinated by insects

Leaves have shallow lobes

Other species

COMMON HAWTHORN
Crataegus monogyna

Found in similar range to *Crataegus laevigata*; can be distinguished by its much more deeply lobed leaves.

COCKSPUR HAWTHORN
Crataegus crus-galli

Native to North America; has ferociously sharp spines; in fall, leaves turn vivid orange to scarlet or purplish red.

> " I found the whole path throbbing with the fragrance of hawthorn-blossom. "

MARCEL PROUST, *Swann's Way,* 1913

Hedge laying is a traditional technique that has been practiced for hundreds of years. Individual plants are chopped almost through, just above ground level, so that the upper part of the trunk can be bent over at an acute angle. Side branches are then woven together into those of the neighboring tree as in basket making. Despite the damage inflicted, trees continue to grow, but a low top line is maintained.

Beliefs and traditions

Hawthorn has long been believed to have magical properties, both good and bad. It is traditionally associated with death and funerals, and as a result, flowering stems are avoided for use in interior decoration. According to legend, a vampire can be dispatched by driving a stake made of hawthorn wood through the heart. When hawthorn flowers are cut, they give off a foul smell that was traditionally said to be similar to that of the Black Death.

Possibly because it flowers around Easter time, hawthorn has become associated with Christian symbolism, including Jesus's crown of thorns (see box, right). One story tells how the biblical figure Joseph of Arimathea visited Britain, where he stuck his staff into the ground at Glastonbury in the southwest. This sprouted and grew as the "Glastonbury Thorn," a tree that flowered twice a year, in spring and again around Christmas.

The wood of hawthorn is very hard and is often used to make tool handles, while its berries (known as haws) have historically been used to make food and drink products such as jellies, wine, and preserves.

CROWN OF THORNS

Three of the biblical gospels refer to a crown of thorns that was placed on Jesus of Nazareth's head at the crucifixion. This was popularly believed to be hawthorn throughout western Christendom. An object said to be this crown was a venerated relic from the 5th century CE. Individual thorns appear in various later reliquaries.

JESUS AT THE CRUCIFIXION

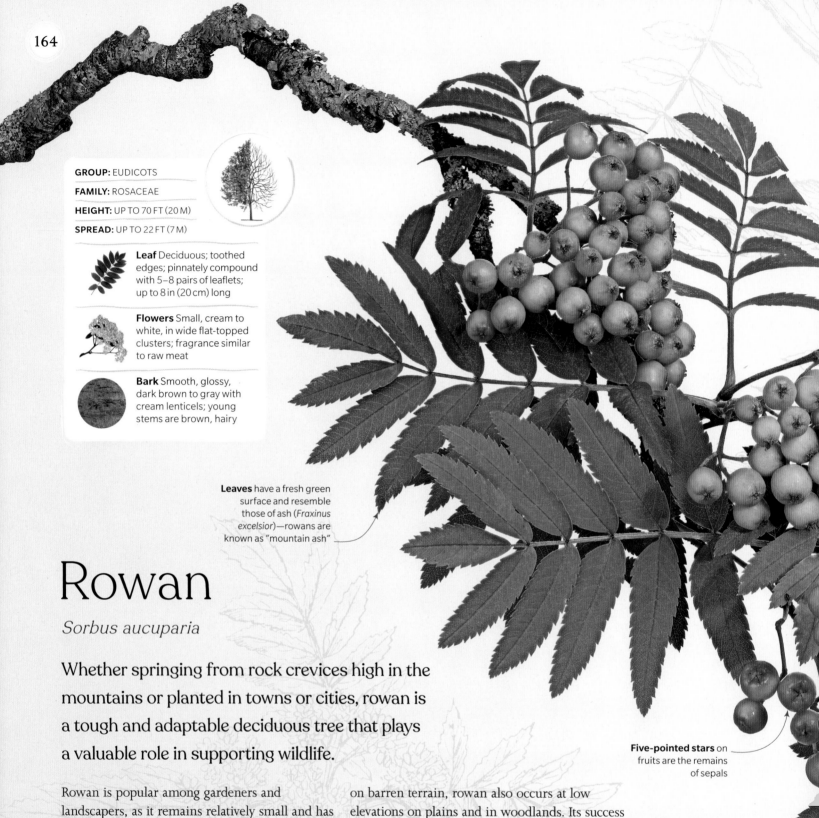

GROUP: EUDICOTS

FAMILY: ROSACEAE

HEIGHT: UP TO 70 FT (20 M)

SPREAD: UP TO 22 FT (7 M)

Leaf Deciduous; toothed edges; pinnately compound with 5–8 pairs of leaflets; up to 8 in (20 cm) long

Flowers Small, cream to white, in wide flat-topped clusters; fragrance similar to raw meat

Bark Smooth, glossy, dark brown to gray with cream lenticels; young stems are brown, hairy

Leaves have a fresh green surface and resemble those of ash (*Fraxinus excelsior*)—rowans are known as "mountain ash"

Rowan

Sorbus aucuparia

Whether springing from rock crevices high in the mountains or planted in towns or cities, rowan is a tough and adaptable deciduous tree that plays a valuable role in supporting wildlife.

Rowan is popular among gardeners and landscapers, as it remains relatively small and has pretty flowers, vivid fall leaf color, and fruits that provide a much-needed source of food for hungry birds in winter. However, it is in its mountain home that rowan (or mountain ash) stands out most. Native across a broad swathe of territory from Iceland and Britain across to the Russian far east, it is the only deciduous tree to be found among the stunted vegetation of mountainous regions. Although able to thrive on barren terrain, rowan also occurs at low elevations on plains and in woodlands. Its success at colonizing a wide variety of habitats is in part due to its fruits, which are eagerly consumed by a range of birds and mammals. These are especially important to birds such as thrushes and waxwings that migrate in winter once their breeding ranges succumb to winter weather. Once eaten, the birds transport rowan seeds some distance from the parent tree, allowing the plant to widen its distribution.

Five-pointed stars on fruits are the remains of sepals

▲ Bright berries
Growing up to around ¼ in (8 mm), rowan berries are a food source for birds and can be used in cooking as a flavoring for beverages and to make jelly.

Rowan fruits may not be all they seem. Typically, fruits and seeds are produced as a result of sexual reproduction between two plants of the same species, but rowans can crossbreed with other species in the genus *Sorbus*, such as whitebeam and service tree, to produce hybrid species with intermediate foliage. Hybrids are typically sterile, but rowans utilize a process called apomixis—asexual reproduction—that allows sterile plants to set seed. As a result, in the British Isles alone, there are over 45 species of *Sorbus*, most of them found nowhere else on Earth.

Colors vary from yellow through orange to red and often appear in late summer before those of other fruiting trees

Fruits are not berries, but pomes, and are more akin to apples and pears with a tough core at the center

Clusters of fruit can contain 80 or more pomes on a branch

► Mountain ash fairy
Rowan trees were often planted near homes or their branches used as adornment on walls in the belief they repelled witches or evil spirits. English illustrator Cicely Mary Barker's mountain ash fairy is a fanciful depiction of this attribute.

The Mountain Ash Fairy.

" Rowan-tree and red thread, put the witches to their speed! "

SCOTTISH PROVERB, THOMAS DAVIDSON, *Rowan Tree and Red Thread: A Scottish Witchcraft Miscellany of Tales, Legends and Ballads*, 1949

Other species

SERVICE TREE
Sorbus domestica

Leaves resemble those of rowan, but fruits are cherry-sized. Native to Europe and North Africa, but rarely common; widely planted.

WHITEBEAM
Sorbus aria

Unlike rowan, whitebeam leaves are not divided into leaflets and are starkly white beneath. Native to much of Europe and North Africa.

Sugar Maple

Acer saccharum

Native to eastern North America, where it is a main component of naturally occurring hardwood forests and the primary source of maple syrup, this deciduous tree gives New England its reputation for spectacular fall leaf color. Its leaf is also well known as the national symbol of Canada and is represented in stylized form on the Canadian flag.

GROUP: EUDICOTS

FAMILY: SAPINDACEAE

HEIGHT: 120 FT (35 M)

SPREAD: UP TO 50 FT (15 M)

Leaf Deciduous; palmate, papery in texture; opposite; 3–8 in (8–15cm) across

Fruit Seeds carried in pairs in two-winged samaras, falling in fall

Bark With small grooves; on mature specimens, furrowed and gray in color

Sugar maples are long-lived, with life spans of up to 300 years or more. They naturally form dense, rounded crowns, although in forest situations where crowding can occur, they will grow taller with narrower crowns. Their fall color can vary depending on the season, with leaves turning yellow, orange, or brilliant red, and it is possible for different colors to be present on a single tree at the same time.

Thriving in areas with cold winters, sugar maple needs a sharp drop in temperature to stimulate production of its sweet sap, so attempts to introduce the tree outside its natural range for commercial reasons have proved largely unsuccessful. Virtually all of the world's maple

▲ Seasonal color
North America's sugar maple forests are a popular tourist destination in fall, and city dwellers are happy to drive miles to witness the banks of trees exploding in rich color.

syrup originates in Canada and the US, where a single tree can yield up to 15 gallons (60 liters) of sap per year; Quebec is the main producer and exporter. Sap can also be extracted from the red maple (*Acer rubrum*), although this has a shorter season, so it is less popular with growers. While the Florida maple (*Acer saccharum* subsp. *floridanum*) can yield sap in warmer areas, it is seldom

Maple syrup production uses **40 times as much sap** as the finished **amount of syrup**

Leaves usually have five lobes, with some notching on the upper three

Thin-textured leaves turn crisp before they are shed

planted commercially. It is not known exactly when the tree's sap was first harvested, but archaeological evidence suggests that indigenous peoples were skilled in its extraction long before European settlers arrived. They taught the colonists how to tap the trees and, with its ready availability, the syrup rapidly became their principal sweetener. Sugar maple is also economically important for its timber, which is widely laid as flooring in bowling alleys and basketball courts. It is also used to make baseball bats and musical instruments, especially members of the string and drum families. Certain forms of the tree have a decorative, wavy grain and are popular with cabinet makers. It was commonly planted as a street tree in the 19th century, but it was found to be intolerant of urban pollution. It has since been largely

▲ **Fall leaves**
Sugar maple leaf coloration in fall can be patchy, with yellow, orange, and red appearing simultaneously on the same tree; leaves may not all color at the same time.

Other species

NORWAY MAPLE
Acer platanoides

Fast-growing species native to southwest Asia and Europe; now naturalized in parts of the US.

OREGON MAPLE
Acer macrophyllum

The most massive of the maples native to North America; also has the largest leaves—up to 12 in (30 cm) across.

RED MAPLE
Acer rubrum

Striking maple with showy red flowers in early spring and leaves that turn brilliant red in fall.

replaced in this role by Norway maple (*Acer platanoides*)—an invasive species that should be planted judiciously.

A billion-dollar industry

Sugar maple syrup begins life as sap. Through photosynthesis, trees produce starch during the growing season, which is stored in their trunks and roots over winter. In spring, as water is transported from the root system to the stems and leaves, this starch is converted into sugar that rises in the sap. Sap is collected in early spring (when snow may still be on the ground) while trees are still dormant but the temperature is just above freezing. Traditionally, a tap was drilled into the trunk and the sap was allowed to drip into a large bucket attached to the tree. Today, a network of pipes attached to a stand of trees pumps the sap through to a large tank, where it is boiled down to drive off excess water and concentrate the syrup. Further processing removes any impurities before the syrup is pasteurized to preserve flavor and color. Bottled maple syrup typically has a shelf life of up to four years.

Comfort food

Maple syrup has a distinctive, complex flavor, with hints of caramel. As a naturally occurring product, it can vary in color from pale golden to a rich dark brown depending on when the sap was collected. Early in the season, the trees' sap is pale, becoming darker as the temperature rises in spring. The darker the color of the sap, the stronger the flavor of the resulting syrup. With a fluid pouring consistency and much less viscous than honey, maple syrup is perennially popular as a sweet garnish to pancakes, waffles, oatmeal, and other dishes.

▲ **Maple Sugar Magic**
Sugar maples are used to make maple sugar, a traditional sweetener in parts of North America. This trading card from around 1880 advertises a popular brand.

Acid rain is a major cause of decline in sugar maple populations

Maple sugar orchard
A painting from 1941 by American folk artist "Grandma Moses" (Anna Mary Robertson Moses) shows a simple New England dwelling with children playing in the snow among a stand of sugar maples, where a few grown-ups are tapping the trees.

GROUP: EUDICOTS

FAMILY: SAPINDACEAE

HEIGHT: 25–50 FT (8–15 M)

SPREAD: UP TO 30 FT (10 M)

Leaf Deciduous; slender; divided into five to seven (sometimes nine) lobes; up to around 4¾ in (12 cm)

Fruits Winged pairs of samaras; seeds are carried in pairs

Bark Gray-brown in color; heavily textured bark featured on several varieties

▶ Leaves and flowers

Japanese maples are valued less for their flowers—which are attractive up close but not particularly showy—than their leaves, which can produce a vivid display both on emergence and before they are shed.

Leaves are fine textured and divided into lobes that are pointed at their tips like outstretched fingers

Spring flowers are small and produced in loose clusters

Japanese Maple

Acer palmatum

These dainty, deciduous trees are much loved by gardeners and can grow into dramatic explosions of shape and color.

Japanese maples are found not only in Japan— where they grow in cool, shady woodland and form an understory to taller growing trees— but also in similar habitats in China, Korea, Mongolia, and even parts of eastern Russia. They favor cool places, thriving in leafy soil, protected by their larger neighbors from the worst effects of frost, drying winds, and heat from the sun.

A notable feature of this species—whose common name is also sometimes applied to another species, *Acer japonicum*—is its variability. Unlike many other trees, its genes are unstable

enough to produce plants with different leaf sizes, shapes, and colors. This has resulted in the vast number of garden forms available today, many with evocative names. All have the same elegant form—a broad, airy canopy of leaves supported by one or more trunks that age gracefully, their gnarled branches tracing ever more intriguing shapes. This attribute is possibly one of the reasons bonsai enthusiasts are so fond of this species. Even without the extensive training that

◀ Artistic influence

This woodblock print depicting Japanese maple leaves is dated 1760–1764 and illustrates *The Tale of Genji*, an 11th-century text.

▶ Fall vista

The blaze of color presented by the foliage of some Japanese maple trees in fall—red, orange, or yellow—is unrivaled.

Bark usually roughens as trees mature

bonsai demands, Japanese maples can make impressive container plants. Their leaves have the five or more lobes characteristic of maples, but these can be slender and pointed and are sometimes themselves finely divided, producing a delicate, feathery appearance. Besides the typical green, they can be bright orange-yellow, yellow-green, or deep reddish purple. In some forms, they are margined with creamy white; in others, the new leaves are a brilliant shrimp pink as they emerge in spring and are easily mistaken for flowers. Whatever the interest of their spring foliage, this is usually outshone by the glorious fall display, when leaves turn bright red, orange, or yellow before being shed as the tree enters its winter resting period.

Other species

GOLDEN FULL MOON MAPLE

Acer shirasawanum 'Aureum'

Deciduous tree or large shrub; yellow-leaved with crimson flowers. Native to Japan; named after botanist Homi Shirasawa.

AMUR MAPLE

Acer japonicum

Also known as Japanese maple. Native to Japan and southern Korea; cultivated ornamentally in Europe and the US. Grows to a height of around 33 ft (10 m).

Dramatic branching
Japanese maple 'Ornatum' (*Acer palmatum* 'Ornatum') has an attractive rounded habit that makes it a welcome addition to many a garden. As the tree matures, its branches start to curl. This beautiful branching is especially apparent in winter, when this hardy tree sheds its leaves and weathers the cold with striking grace.

Horse Chestnut

Aesculus hippocastanum

Horse chestnuts make majestic trees for parks and large gardens, with attractive flowers in large "candles" in spring or early summer, followed by glistening fruits in fall.

Horse chestnut is a large, deciduous tree native to the Balkan peninsula that has been widely planted in Europe and in the US. It found great popularity as a decorative tree in parks and gardens from the 17th century. (In small gardens, it is tolerant of being pollarded, but a wiser choice for gardeners is to use one of its smaller growing relatives.)

It is also found in on the streets of many towns and cities. In recent history, it was a view of an urban horse chestnut tree that lifted the spirits of young Jewish girl Anne Frank, whose story became famous through her diaries, when she and her family were hiding in Amsterdam from the Nazi occupation of Holland. Efforts were made to keep this individual tree going, but age, decay, and finally a storm in 2010 demolished it. However, saplings raised from the seeds of Anne Frank's tree have been widely planted both as a symbol of remembrance of her and of resistance to tyranny.

Key identifiers

Horse chestnut can be identified by its stout shoots, which have a large terminal bud with the side buds in opposite pairs. The buds

> Horse chestnut seeds (conkers) are a **valuable food source** for deer and other mammals

▼ Buds with sticky sap
Shown here is sequence, horse chestnut buds flush or expand in the spring. Shoots may have small crescents of round scars from the vascular tissue that ran up the petiole (or leaf stalk).

Winter buds are ovoid-pointed and protected by resinous bud scales

Buds starting to expand. The dark brown bud scales are at their stickiest at this stage and can trap unwary insects

Leaves emerge but still benefit from "protection" offered by the sticky bud scales from insects

Sticky resin is still present at this stage

▶ Chestnut Tree in Blossom

This painting by French Impressionist artist Pierre-Auguste Renoir captures the beauty of a horse chestnut in spring. Renoir painted several species of trees during his career.

Flowers in bud form will expand within days to produce flowering "candles"

" For luck you carried a horse chestnut and a rabbit's foot in your right pocket. "

ERNEST HEMINGWAY, *A Moveable Feast*, 1964

New leaves are covered in soft long hairs, which are later lost

GROUP: EUDICOTS

FAMILY: SAPINDACEAE

HEIGHT: UP TO 100 FT (30 M)

SPREAD: UP TO 50 FT (15 M)

Leaf Deciduous; broad; five to seven leaflets on long stalk or petiole; up to 8 in (20 cm) long

Fruits Capsules, with one or two seeds enclosed in prickly covering

Bark Reddish to gray-brown; smooth when young; turns scaly and shallowly fissured with age

Other species

**HIMALAYAN HORSE
CHESTNUT**

Aesculus indica

Large deciduous tree
from the northwest Himalaya
with shiny, pointed leaflets.

RED BUCKEYE

Aesculus pavia

Named after its flower color (with only
four petals) and the resemblance of the
base of the seed to a deer's eye.
Deciduous small to medium-sized tree.

RED HORSE CHESTNUT

Aesculus × carnea

Medium-sized deciduous tree.
Originated as an artificial hybrid
between horse chestnut and
red buckeye.

are pointed, brown, and sticky or resinous. The
leaves consist of five or seven large leaflets set at
the end of a long stalk, which clasps the new
stem. The leaflets are obovate (broadest toward
the tip) and wedge-shaped and stalkless where
they meet the leaf stalk (or petiole).

The tree starts to make its new foliage in early
spring when the buds enlarge and become even
more sticky, with the bud scales catching small
flies. The flowers are carried at the end of shoots
in the crown, generally from the end of April to
late May. They are in large panicles, up to 12 in
(30 cm) in length, with a mixture of white,
yellow, and red petals. It is rare for more
than one or two of the individual flowers
to be fertilized, but those that are
become green spiky capsules. These
ripen in late fall, opening

Bees are
an important
pollinator of horse
chestnut trees

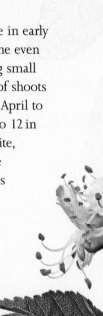

Leaves on the flower
stalk are smaller
and narrower than
typical leaves.

▶ **Conical flower cluster**
Flowers are in long, candlelike clusters
(or panicles) and are composed of many
individual flowers, which are variously
red or yellow tinted on a creamy
white background.

TIMELESS TRADITIONS

Horse chestnut seeds, or conkers, have been used for generations by children in Britain and Ireland for the game of the same name. A hole is drilled through the seed and a string passed through. Players take turns using their conker to try to shatter their opponent's, and the winner is the one whose conker survives.

CHILDREN PLAYING CONKERS

Nectary guides in flowers turn crimson once pollinated, as bees cannot see red

along three valves or sutures to reveal the glossy light brown seeds, which are up to 2 in (5 cm) across.

The species' common name is believed to derive from the resemblance of the seeds to those of the sweet chestnut (see pp.182–183). However, although shiny and similarly bright in color, they are not edible and are mildly toxic to humans and animals, including horses. This is due to the alkaloids in the seed and twigs, the principal one being aescin (or escin), which is useful for its effect on veins and as an anti-inflammatory. It is also used in some cosmetics.

Geographical origins

Horse chestnut is historically native to a small area in northern Greece and adjacent Albania, where it is an uncommon tree. It failed to expand from this restricted area after the last Ice Age—the heavy seeds are reliant on animals to spread them over longer distances. There is a very similar species (Aesculus turbinata) found in parts of Japan, and in the Tertiary period, they probably

formed a single population across Eurasia. More widespread is the subgenus that includes *Aesculus indica*, with species in this group found across Asia from Afghanistan in the West to China and Vietnam, where the seeds can be up to 4 in (10 cm), then with two shrubby species in California and Baja California in the US. The buckeye group, typified by *Aesculus pavia*, is restricted to the eastern US and has flowers with the four petals forming a narrow tube. There is a further, entirely shrubby species in the southeastern US, which is in an entirely different subgenus.

Horse chestnut seeds have been part of various folk beliefs in Britain, northern Europe, and the US for centuries, including that carrying them in a pocket brings good luck, financial security, or even virility in men. Placed around the home, they are traditionally said to repel spiders.

◄ **Leaf-mine larva**

A moth, *Cameraria ohridella*, spends its larval stage eating the thin leaf between the top and bottom surfaces before emerging as a small moth. As a result, the hollowed-out areas of the leaves die and turn brown.

GROUP: EUDICOTS

FAMILY: FAGACEAE

HEIGHT: UP TO 130 FT (40 M)

SPREAD: UP TO 65 FT (20 M)

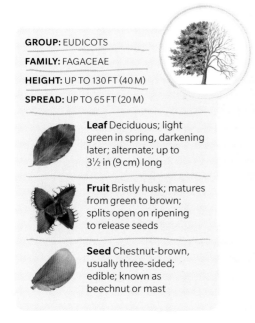

Leaf Deciduous; light green in spring, darkening later; alternate; up to 3½ in (9 cm) long

Fruit Bristly husk; matures from green to brown; splits open on ripening to release seeds

Seed Chestnut-brown, usually three-sided; edible; known as beechnut or mast

◄ Giants of the forest

Beeches often dominate the forest, their leaves forming a thick carpet beneath. This is England's second largest and third oldest beech, in Lineover Wood, Gloucestershire.

► Beech flower

Female beech flowers are small, green, and protected by bracts—modified leaves that surround the flower. These are pollinated by male flowers—small, largely colorless, spherical catkins that scatter their pollen into the wind.

Bract encloses female beech flower

Hairs cover the beech bracts

European Beech

Fagus sylvatica

Few forests are as haunting as those of the beech tree. Its smooth, silver-gray boughs arch like flying buttresses, while its wide-spreading, high canopy extends outward to fill the sky.

The evocative feel of a beech forest is enhanced by the lack of other plants beneath the canopy. The forest floor is largely bare of vegetation, covered only with fallen beech leaves. In comparison, other deciduous woodlands possess a rich and varied flora—the greatest diversity within a temperate woodland is in its herbs rather than its trees. Beech woods are bare because mature beeches have a thick canopy that blocks light and a shallow, spreading root system that competes efficiently with surrounding plants for water and nutrients. The leaves are rich in

lignin, the main component of wood, making them slow to decompose, and the annual shedding of beech leaves has a significant effect on the flora of the forest floor. The thick layer of dead leaves inhibits the growth of herbs and acidifies the soil, perturbing the woodland herbs that prefer neutral or alkaline soils.

Compared to other deciduous trees, beech is hesitant to shed its leaves. The leaves are marcescent, meaning they turn brown in fall but remain attached to the branches for much of the

▲ Medicinal plant

This illustration from the 19th-century *Medicinal Plants* shows the various parts of European beech. Beech bark was used as an antacid and an expectorant—to clear mucus and treat coughs.

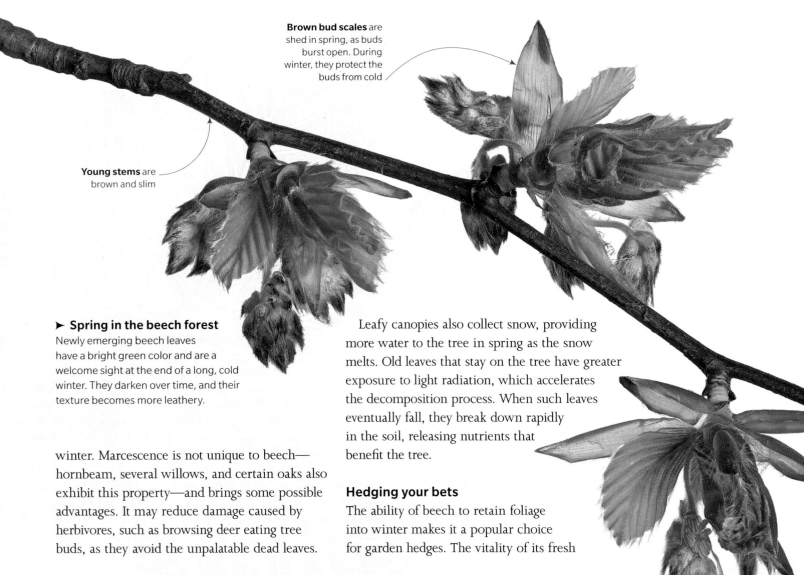

Brown bud scales are shed in spring, as buds burst open. During winter, they protect the buds from cold

Young stems are brown and slim

► Spring in the beech forest
Newly emerging beech leaves have a bright green color and are a welcome sight at the end of a long, cold winter. They darken over time, and their texture becomes more leathery.

winter. Marcescence is not unique to beech—hornbeam, several willows, and certain oaks also exhibit this property—and brings some possible advantages. It may reduce damage caused by herbivores, such as browsing deer eating tree buds, as they avoid the unpalatable dead leaves.

Leafy canopies also collect snow, providing more water to the tree in spring as the snow melts. Old leaves that stay on the tree have greater exposure to light radiation, which accelerates the decomposition process. When such leaves eventually fall, they break down rapidly in the soil, releasing nutrients that benefit the tree.

Hedging your bets
The ability of beech to retain foliage into winter makes it a popular choice for garden hedges. The vitality of its fresh

◄ Dark beeches
Northern Ireland's distinctive Dark Hedges has been used as a shooting location for various popular films and television programs.

MASTING AND MARTENS

Beeches produce seed every year, but the quantity varies greatly. The years when a massive crop is produced are described as masting years, usually occurring the year after a summer drought. Producing a surplus ensures enough food for local seed-eating animals, with some seeds left over to germinate. Masting years also benefit predators like the beech martens (*Martes foina*), found from Spain east to the Himalayas, as they increase the number of seed-eating prey.

BEECH MARTEN

green spring growth also entices gardeners, as do the numerous color forms available, such as the copper beech. The world's tallest and longest hedge is a beech hedge in the Scottish village of Meikleour. It is 1,739 ft (530 m) long and, on average, 98 ft (30 m) tall. It was planted by the heiress of the estates of Aldie and Meikleour,

Silky hairs cover the margins of immature beech leaves to protect them from hungry herbivores

Jean Mercer, and her husband Robert Murray Nairne in 1745. Robert was killed at the Battle of Culloden shortly after, in 1746. It is said that Jean left the trees to grow skyward as a tribute to the soldiers who lost their lives in this battle between England and Scotland.

The Dark Hedges (see opposite page) in Northern Ireland's County Antrim are also made of beech and were planted around 1775 along the driveway of Gracehill House. Unlike the neatly clipped hedge in Scotland, this wind-ravaged avenue of contorted trees is sculptured and dramatic. These charismatic trees have begun to suffer, and fewer than 90 of the 150 originally planted remain. Traffic is now banned along the road through the avenue, as shallow-rooted beech are easily damaged by heavy vehicles.

Climate change

Its shallow root system also makes beech prone to drought or toppling in stormy weather. Climate change is likely to cause more extensive droughts with increasingly violent storms, and European beech will suffer the consequences.

> " The beech can command a great presence, but may at any moment fall flat on its face. "

RICHARD MABEY,
Beechcombings: The Narratives of Trees, 2008

Other species and varieties

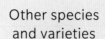

AMERICAN BEECH
Fagus grandifolia

Native to eastern North America; can be distinguished by its toothed leaves and prickly cupules.

WEEPING BEECH
Fagus sylvatica 'Pendula'

Pendulous form of European beech; all parts resemble wild beech except for its weeping habit.

COPPER BEECH
Fagus sylvatica f. purpurea

Purple-leaved variety of European beech; found in the wild several centuries ago and has remained in cultivation ever since.

Leaves are long and slender, deeply veined, and sharply pointed at the tip and have coarsely serrated edges

Long yellow catkins are produced in summer together with male and female flowers

Fall fruits, around 2½ in (6 cm) across, have spiny, greenish-yellow husks that split to release usually one to three chestnuts

▲ **Chestnut fruits**
The sweet chestnut's fruits are easily spotted in their pale green, spiky husks. Despite their fruits' superficial similarity, sweet chestnut is now thought to be only distantly related to horse chestnut, *Aesculus hippocastanum* (see pp.174–177).

Sweet Chestnut

Castanea sativa

Commonly found in parks, streets, fields, and woodlands, this handsome deciduous tree is draped in yellow catkins in summer, and in winter is well known as the provider of one of the simplest seasonal comfort foods.

GROUP: EUDICOTS

FAMILY: FAGACEAE

HEIGHT: UP TO 100 FT (30 M)

SPREAD: UP TO 65 FT (20 M)

Flowers Small and musk-scented, unisexual flowers; clustered along upright catkins

Seed Tough, glossy, brown outer skin protects the softer white seed

Native to warm areas around the Mediterranean and in southwest Asia, the stately sweet chestnut is a fast-growing, deciduous tree that was introduced into northern Europe by the Romans. Trees can live for several hundred years, with older specimens exhibiting impressively gnarled trunks and branches. The oldest known chestnut tree in the world, the Hundred-Horse Chestnut in Sicily, is so named because a legendary queen of Aragon took shelter from a thunderstorm beneath its branches with 100 of her knights. Its trunk is over 187 ft (57 m) in diameter and it is estimated to be between 2,000 and 4,000 years old.

Widely planted as a shade tree in Renaissance Europe, the sweet chestnut is now grown throughout temperate parts of the globe mainly for its edible seeds that are harvested both for human consumption and for animal fodder. Varieties producing single seeds that keep well are preferred by commercial growers.

A winter treat

Chestnuts can be lightly roasted in their skins as a snack and are a popular street food in Europe, Asia, and North America. They are also used in a range of table dishes, both sweet and savory. In Europe, they are particularly associated with midwinter feasts, used to stuff meat, in soups, or as an accompanying vegetable. They are even more popular puréed and sweetened in desserts such as Mont Blanc or as a filling for a Christmas yule log (*bûche de Noël*). Crystallized chestnuts (*marrons glacés*) are a luxury that was greatly enjoyed at the court of Louis XIV at Versailles. Removed from their skins, chestnuts can be pulverized to a flour that is gluten free and which has a long history in Italian cuisine. The flour can also be added to conventional flour in bread making. Ancient Greek authors wrote of its medicinal properties, and in his book *The English Physitian* (1652), English herbalist Nicholas Culpeper recommends blending ground chestnut with honey to treat bronchial complaints.

Other species

CHINESE CHESTNUT
Castanea mollissima

Native to China and similar in appearance to its European relative; has long been cultivated for its edible seeds.

AMERICAN CHESTNUT
Castanea dentata

Imposing species, now endangered in its natural range of North America because of its susceptibility to disease.

" ...apples and oranges were put upon the table, and a shovel full of chestnuts on the fire. "

CHARLES DICKENS, *A Christmas Carol*, 1843

Fall feast
This painting, from around 1490, shows a peasant with a herd of pigs feeding on the rich crop of acorns in an oak wood. The traditional right to feed pigs in this way, called "pannage," continues to this day in some regions of Europe.

GROUP: EUDICOTS

FAMILY: FAGACEAE

HEIGHT: UP TO 100 FT (30 M)

SPREAD: UP TO 82 FT (25 M)

Leaf Deciduous; broadly oval in outline; 3–6 pairs of lobes; alternate; up to 5 in (12 cm) long

Fruit Characteristic acorn, pale green turning brown when ripe; ½–1½ in (15–40 mm) long

Bark Grayish green and smooth on young trees, becoming ridged and fissured with age

▶ Veteran oak
This fine old oak in the Reinhardswald, a former imperial forest in Hessen, Germany, shows the typical spreading crown of an English oak. A storm has snapped its trunk, but new branches have regrown from the stump.

English Oak

Quercus robur

Known as tall, strong, and resilient, there is a mythic quality to the English oak that has made it popular in the country that lends it its common name. In fact, the species' range and history extends across Europe and beyond.

English oak has various historic links to England (and Britain, more widely). It provided the timber for the ships of the Royal Navy, Britain's main instrument of national defense, colonization, and empire. It is the chief timber of Britain's great historic buildings and much of the ornate furniture they contain. The tree was once regarded as sacred, and has been praised in poetry and song. The 18th-century English playwright David Garrick made that connection between the tree and the nation in his poetry: "Heart of oak are our ships, heart of oak are our men."

Lobed leaves, typical of oak

▲ Sacred leaves
In ancient Greek mythology, oak was the sacred tree of Zeus, king of the gods, celebrated in this golden wreath of oak leaves from 350–300 BCE.

There are **450 known species of oak,** mainly in the **northern hemisphere** and **tropical mountains**

The longevity of the oak tree—which can live for centuries—is also part of its power and mystique, as James Montgomery, an early 19th-century poet, acknowledged: "The tall Oak, towering to the skies, the fury of the wind defies. From age to age, in virtue strong, inured to stand, and suffer wrong."

The common name "English oak" is widely used and is somewhat geographically inappropriate for a species that has long been the dominant timber tree across much of Europe. It is found growing from Britain and western Europe to as far east as Turkey and the Caucasus. Its dominance in England is the result of centuries of woodland management: many of the trees were planted commercially, often using varieties from continental Europe. In fact, English oak is not even the only oak species native to England.

Two native oaks

The more correct botanical name is pedunculate oak, which distinguishes it from the other native British species, sessile or durmast oak (*Quercus petraea*). The names relate to the acorns, which grow on a stalk, or peduncle, in the former species, but are stalkless, or sessile, in the latter. The name can be confusing because the leaves are the antithesis of the acorns: the leaves of the pedunculate oak are sessile, while those of the sessile oak have a stalk, or petiole (both species are deciduous).

" Houses and ships, Cities and Navies are built with it. "

JOHN EVELYN, writing about oak timber, *Sylva, or A Discourse of Forest-Trees*, 1664

▶ **Shipbuilding**
These 16th-century Spanish carpenters are building a small, two-masted sailing vessel for Francisco de Orellana, the Spanish explorer who was first to navigate the entire length of the Amazon River.

Other species

SESSILE OAK
Quercus petraea

Another common European oak; can grow even taller than English oak. A sessile oak in the Forêt de Bercé, France was measured at 158¾ ft (48.4 m) in 2012.

ROYAL OAK

When King Charles I was executed in the English Civil War in 1649, his eldest son was not recognized as heir to the throne. Charles II raised an army but was defeated at Worcester in 1651. He escaped and hid at night in an old oak tree in Boscobel Wood, still known as the Royal Oak. In 1660, he returned from exile to reclaim the thrones of England, Scotland, and Ireland, as shown here.

EMBROIDERED SCENE WITH CHARLES II

DOWNY OAK
Quercus pubescens

Native from western France through central Europe to the Caucasus; rather shorter tree with leaves that are hairy when young and have lobes ending in a sharp point.

Fanned tail
aids control
in flight

◄ Oak woods predator
In oak woodlands, little owls hunt the mice and squirrels that feed on the acorns. Sheltered hollows in old oak trunks also provide them with nesting holes.

In Britain, English or pedunculate oak is a tree of high forest, actively managed (coppiced) woodland, and ancient wood pasture. It grows best on soils that are relatively heavy and fertile and can cope with a degree of waterlogging, but its natural range is obscured by wide-scale planting in woods and hedgerows. It is largely absent in the far north. Sessile oak, on the other hand, was much less favored for commercial forestry, so it exhibits a more natural range. It forms woodlands on well-drained, shallow soils that are moderately or strongly acidic, in the north and west of Britain. It is a characteristic species of upland woodlands.

European spread

The distribution in Europe follows a similar pattern, with a northern limit for both species in southern Scandinavia. English oak is the more common, with sessile oak covering a similar range but mainly growing on poorer soils. English oak was planted in greater numbers than sessile oak in commercial forests around Europe because it was believed to grow faster and produce stronger timber. However, that is because it mainly grows on better soils. When planted on poor soils, it grows more slowly than sessile oak and produces less durable timber.

The range of the two species is confused by the fact that they readily hybridize when growing in proximity to one another. It is tricky to tell the hybrid (*Quercus* × *rosacea*) from its parents because its features are so intermediate. Sometimes it can grow without any pedunculate oak nearby, and, in places, it can form pure stands without either parent present.

HUNGARIAN OAK
Quercus frainetto

Found in southern Italy, the Balkans, Romania, and parts of Hungary; tall, domed oak species identified by leaves with 7–9 pairs of deeply cut lobes.

Leaf buds and catkins open together in late spring in clusters at end of young shoots

Young leaves are golden-green as they open, making oaks distinctive amid other trees in spring

Dangling male catkins are yellowish or brownish green, ¾–1½ in (2–4 cm) long; they release pollen in May

► **Spring opening**
English oak leaves open with the catkins in April or May. Inconspicuous female catkins grow at the tip of new shoots on the same tree as male catkins.

The English oak is a long-lived species. It can take 50 years to produce its first crop of acorns and 100 years to reach its full height. However, it can then live for another 300 years if left unmanaged. If it is pollarded (see p.141), the base of the trunk may continue producing branches for 800 years. The tallest British specimen grows in Duncombe Wood in Yorkshire, measured at 134½ ft (41 m) in 2014. Outside Britain, it is beaten by a tree in the Białowieża National Park in Poland, which reached 143 ft (43.6 m) in 2011.

Tree of life

Both oaks are important for the range of other species they support. More than 500 invertebrate species have been recorded feeding on oak leaves, including the purple hairstreak butterfly,

Leaves turn a burnished gold color in fall; a few remain on the tree through the winter

whose caterpillars rely on its leaves. Several insects lay their eggs in the leaves, stimulating them to produce protective galls around the insect larvae. Possibly the best known is a wasp called *Biorrhiza pallida*, which lays its eggs in leaf buds. This stimulates the buds to develop into round galls known as oak apples. The trunk and branches support many lichens and mosses, and a huge variety of fungi benefit from dead oak leaves on the forest floor. European jays and squirrels feed on acorns on the tree in late summer, while rooks, wood pigeons, and mice feed on them when they fall. So many acorns get eaten on the tree or forest floor that the oak relies for its reproduction almost entirely on squirrels or jays, which bury acorns as a winter food supply. If the animals then die, or simply forget where they had buried their food stash, the buried acorns may go on to germinate and grow into new trees.

Uses and traditions

The timber from English oak is hard, strong, and naturally durable. For centuries, it was the timber of choice for building ships, grand houses, and the roofs of churches and cathedrals. It could be wrought into fine furniture or used to make wooden tiles (shingles) for roofs. Coppiced oak branches were made into charcoal, and its young bark was used in leather tanning. It was also used in agriculture: in many parts of Europe, local people still zealously guard their traditional right of "pannage," which allows them to graze pigs in oak forests in fall when the animals can feast on the fallen acorns.

As well as featuring in ancient Greek religion (see p.184), oak trees were also sacred in Celtic religions. In Europe, druids held ceremonies in oak groves and venerated the trees.

> " To my mind, no wood is so awe-inspiring as one filled with old oaks. "
>
> EDWARD STEP, *Wayside and Woodland Trees*, 1904

The **bulkiest English oak** alive in 2014 grew in **Sweden**

Lignin-rich oak heartwood has a rich brown color that polishes well and adds to its appeal in furniture

◄ **Oak furniture**

Oak is one of the most widely used hardwoods in Europe for doors, windows, paneling, furniture, and cabinet making. This magnificent oak inlaid chest was featured in a book titled *A History of English Furniture, the Age of Oak* from 1904.

Live Oak

Quercus virginiana

Also known as the southern live oak, this magnificent, evergreen tree is an icon of the Old South—the states in the southern US that were among the original Thirteen Colonies.

GROUP: EUDICOTS	
FAMILY: FAGACEAE	
HEIGHT: 40–65 FT (12–20 M)	
SPREAD: UP TO 150 FT (45 M)	

Leaf Evergreen; elliptic to roughly oval; leathery, glossy, smooth-edged; alternate; to 5 in (13 cm) long

Bark Dark red-brown with vertical furrows and small surface scales

Found in the southeastern states of the US and in northeastern Mexico, live oak is mainly coastal, spreading farther inland in the southern part of its range. It is a tolerant species, growing in both dry and damp climates (always preferring wet soil), though it cannot survive severe frosts.

Branches are held horizontally from low on the trunk to produce a broad, rounded crown, and the spread of an established specimen often exceeds its height. Yellowish-green, inconspicuous flowers are produced in separate male and female catkins in spring and are followed by typical oak acorns. It is

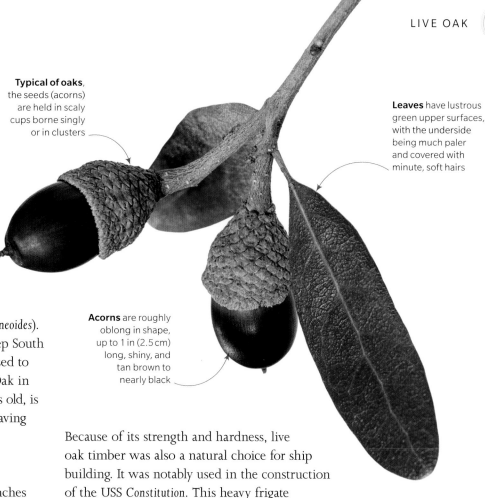

◄ Covered with moss

A ghostly apparition in the early morning fog, this venerable specimen in Fontainebleau State Park, Louisiana, is draped with Spanish moss, a plant that gains all its nutrients from the air.

Typical of oaks, the seeds (acorns) are held in scaly cups borne singly or in clusters

Leaves have lustrous green upper surfaces, with the underside being much paler and covered with minute, soft hairs

Acorns are roughly oblong in shape, up to 1 in (2.5 cm) long, shiny, and tan brown to nearly black

not strictly evergreen because old leaves are shed immediately before a fresh crop emerges in spring.

Live oaks can be long-lived and are majestic in old age, especially when the candelabralike branches are garlanded with Spanish moss (*Tillandsia usneoides*). Many older specimens survive in the Deep South in the US, where they were frequently used to line plantation roads. The Seven Sisters Oak in Louisiana, estimated to be 500–1,000 years old, is the largest certified specimen, the trunk having a girth of around 40 ft (12 m).

Strong branches

Besides Spanish moss, the spreading branches often support other plants, such as ball moss (*Tillandsia recurvata*) and the parasitic mistletoe, and provide shelter for several mammals and birds. Indigenous people extracted an oil from the acorns and used other parts of the tree in medicine and dyeing. The wood makes excellent fuel because of its high density.

Because of its strength and hardness, live oak timber was also a natural choice for ship building. It was notably used in the construction of the USS *Constitution*. This heavy frigate (a type of warship) played a decisive role in the War of 1812, fought between the US and UK, and is the world's oldest ship still afloat. The density and resilience of the live oak timber allowed the ship to withstand enemy cannon fire and led to it being given the nickname "Old Ironsides."

▲ Acorns

Unlike some other species of oak, acorns of live oak mature early in the fall of their first year. They are a valued food source for a variety of wildlife.

> " All alone stood it and the moss hung down from the branches … "

WALT WHITMAN, "I Saw in Louisiana A Live-Oak Growing," poem in *Leaves of Grass*, 1860

BLACK OAK
Quercus velutina

Relatively small, fast-growing deciduous species; readily hybridizes with other members of the genus.

RED OAK
Quercus rubra

Among the largest and most widespread deciduous trees of North America; also planted in Europe. Has deeply cut leaves.

WHITE OAK
Quercus alba

Deciduous tree found in the eastern states of the US; leaves turn orange to burgundy before falling.

GROUP: EUDICOTS

FAMILY: FAGACEAE

HEIGHT: UP TO 70 FT (20 M)

SPREAD: 70 FT (20 M)

Leaf Evergreen; oval with wrinkly edge; green above, gray and hairy below; 1¼–2¾ in (3–7 cm) long

Fruit Acorn, up to 1¼ in (3 cm) long, half-enclosed in cup at base; ripens in late summer

Bark Thick, rough, deeply fissured; dark gray, showing reddish underbark when stripped

◄ **Botanical perspective**

This engraving depicts an idealized cork oak tree, with its round, broadly spreading form. It also shows the tree's leaf; acorn; pendulous male catkins; and small, budlike female flowers.

Cork Oak

Quercus suber

A native species of the western Mediterranean, the cork oak's modern distribution has been shaped by human intervention in the quest to harvest its spongy, fireproof bark. Cork products include bottle stoppers, sports equipment, and more.

Cork oak's **bark** is used as the inner material of **cricket balls** and **badminton shuttlecocks**

The Mediterranean region, with its hot, dry climate, is prone to fire, and the local vegetation has adapted. While many Mediterranean plants regrow from their roots or seeds after a wildfire, cork oak uses a different strategy. Its dead outer bark is a honeycomb of tiny, air-filled cells. Although this outer bark may burn, it insulates and protects the living tissue inside, so the tree can survive and resprout quickly afterward.

Of wine and wildlife

Cork has been harvested for more than 5,000 years, and cork oak grows in forests from Portugal to eastern Italy and North Africa. Within that zone, particularly in Spain and Portugal, orchards of cork oak have been cleared from the natural forest or planted. Glades between the trees are often lightly grazed by sheep or pigs and support a rich ground flora, with nightingales in the trees. The cork oak forests of Portugal and Spain are also home to the Iberian lynx, an endangered species.

Cork cannot be harvested until the tree is 25 years old—a cork oak tree can live for 200 years, yielding 20 crops of cork over that time. Slabs of cork stripped from the trunk are manufactured into wine corks or compressed and bonded into flooring or insulation tiles. Increased use of plastic corks and screw-tops in wine bottles threatens the future of the cork industry and the biodiverse woodlands it supports, but cork remains a useful and renewable material.

▲ Cork cutter at work
Today, machines cut wine corks from the cork oak's bark, but historically these were hand-cut using a sharp knife.

The dead outer bark is carefully removed, using special axes and saws

► Cork harvesting
Once every nine years or so, in managed cork oak woods, the entire outer cork layer is stripped off the trunks of the living trees in large slabs, right down to the red inner bark.

The inner bark immediately begins to regrow new outer bark around itself

Other species

TURKEY OAK
Quercus cerris
Grows in thickets and woods across southeast Europe; its wood is used only as props for vine crops or as firewood because it weathers very badly.

CHINESE CORK OAK
Quercus variabilis
Native to eastern Asia, including China, Japan, and Korea; sometimes cultivated in China for cork production, although it yields much less than cork oak.

GROUP: EUDICOTS

FAMILY: OLEACEAE

HEIGHT: UP TO 30 FT (10 M)

SPREAD: UP TO 25 FT (8 M)

Leaf Evergreen; leathery; borne in opposite pairs; up to 4 in (10 cm) long and 1¼ in (3 cm) wide

Flower Small, white; borne in panicles; fragrant, with four petals and sepals

Bark Silvery gray or darker gray; finely fissured and usually fluted or with crossing ridges

▶ Olive-laden branches

Olive leaves have a short point and a wedge-shaped base. They appear in opposite pairs on silvery gray, scaly shoots, which become brown with age. Each flower cluster usually results in only one fruit.

Lanceolate or obovate leaves are shiny gray-green above and silvery beneath with an untoothed margin

Olive

Olea europaea

Olive is a small, broadly spreading tree cultivated for its edible fruit and flavorful oil. An ancient tree, it features in many myths and is imbued with symbolism.

Olive cultivation can be traced back 5,000 years, making it among the earliest trees to have been grown by humans. The species is probably native to the Eastern Mediterranean region and may have been derived many thousand years ago from its wild form, the botanical variety *sylvestris*, which extends down into Saudi Arabia. Since then, it has been planted all around the Mediterranean, with extensive areas under cultivation from Israel in the east to Spain in the west, along the southern and northern shores. While it is probably best known for its extensive plantations in Italy, where it can be a dominant landscape feature, older trees— up to 2,000 years old—can be found farther east in Iran. Olive has been planted in India; Indonesia; China; and, more recently, in

Australia, New Zealand, and sub-Saharan Africa. It was probably taken over to the Americas by Spanish conquistadors.

The olive is first mentioned in the Bible in the story of Noah. As the waters of the Great Flood subsided, Noah sent out a raven and then a dove in search of land. The raven soared away, but the dove, finding nowhere to settle, returned to

▶ Symbol of peace

An olive branch has become an enduring symbol of peace across many cultures. In Christian mythology, a dove carrying an olive branch signaled an end to the Great Flood—a time of peace.

The inscription on this 4th-century tombstone mentions the Latin phrase *in pace*, which means "in peace"

Oval fruits are up to 1½ in (3.5 cm) long and ripen from green to black or brown over a period of 12 months

the ark. After a week, Noah sent the dove out again, and this time it returned with an olive leaf in its beak (*Exodus* 8, verse 11). As a sign of life on land, the dove's fruitful excursion signified hope, the end of the Great Flood, and a time of peace.

A Greek icon

In Greek mythology, the goddess of war and wisdom Athena and the sea god Poseidon competed for control of a city by each presenting its people with a gift. Athena gifted the people of this city an olive tree, while Poseidon struck a stone with his trident to raise a salty spring. The people embraced the olive tree with its bounties of food, oil, shelter, and timber, rejecting the sea Poseidon had raised. Athena, the victor of the

▶ Olive grove

In a typical olive grove, the trees are managed by frequent pollarding (pruning of tree tops). This encourages the growth of short, vigorous fruiting branches and gives the trees their characteristic gnarled crown structure.

◄ Pressing olives for oil extraction
Earlier, olives were pressed using large millstones. The liquid produced in this process was then decanted into another container to allow the oil to rise to the surface and be separated, as shown in this Roman mosaic.

contest, went on to give this city her name, and so Athens was born. Olive remains a central part of Greek culture.

The olive fruit is a drupe, which is defined in botany as a stone fruit that is surrounded by a fleshy or leathery layer derived from the ovary wall. It is this fleshy layer that is the reason for the olive's commercial importance, as it is used for human consumption and oil production, the latter being the larger of the two industries.

Olive oil is monounsaturated and is considered beneficial for the heart. To make the best grades of oil, the olives are picked when ripe and crushed within 24 hours. Traditionally, large millstones were used to crush olives, stone and

▼ Olive tree plantation
Olive has the ability to withstand hot and dry conditions, such as those of this rural landscape in Tuscany, Italy. It can survive in colder climates but will rarely produce fruit.

> " The olive tree is surely the richest gift of heaven. I can scarcely expect bread. "

THOMAS JEFFERSON (1743–1826), American founding father and third president

all. More modern plants use a hammer process or first remove the stone. The oil is contained within the cells in the flesh, and the purpose of grinding the fruits is to release the small goblets of oil. The pulp is then pressed and, as the oil does not mix with water, it rises to the top of the pulp and can be scooped off. About 80 to 90 percent of the oil can be recovered from a first pressing with more from a second pressing. Cold pressing produces the best-tasting oil, which is called extra virgin, but more oil can be extracted using some heat or chemical additives for a cheaper version.

Oil, food, wood

Once the oil has been extracted, the solid residue, called pomace, can be converted into a biomass fuel for industrial and agricultural use. It can be fed to livestock, especially if the olives have the stones removed before pressing. Depending on the country, 70 to 90 percent of olives are used to make oil and the rest for eating; olives harvested for culinary use can have the stone removed and are often stuffed. The wood from the olive tree is also valued—it is hard, with a fine color and rich texture, and is used for creating carvings, fashioning utensil handles, and making turned bowls.

In 2020, the **European Union** was responsible for **69 percent** of the world's **olive oil** production

Ripe olives are cold pressed to yield extra virgin olive oil

◄ Olive oil
Most olives are used for olive oil production. Apart from its culinary uses, this oil can be used in lamps or as an anointing or massaging oil.

Other species

WHITE FRINGE TREE
Chionanthus virginicus
Small deciduous tree, with 2–8 in (5–20 cm) long leaves; fragrant white flowers borne in lax panicles with 4 or 5 straplike petals; dark blue fruits are ¾ in (2 cm) long.

CHINESE FRINGE TREE
Chionanthus retusus
Deciduous shrub or tree, with oval leaves 1–4 in (2.5–10 cm) long; strongly fragrant snow-white flowers have four strap-shaped petals and appear in upright panicles.

JASMINE BOX
Phillyrea latifolia
Small evergreen tree with variable dull dark green foliage; greenish-white flowers appear in short axillary clusters; small rounded blue-black fruits follow flowers.

Avenue of the Baobabs

This remote dirt road located on the west coast of Madagascar is lined with around two dozen majestic Grandidier's baobabs (*Adansonia grandidieri*), some of which are believed to be many hundreds of years old. The trees are the remnants of a forest that was mostly cleared and have become a popular attraction.

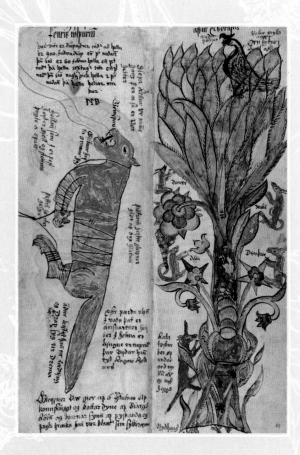

GROUP: EUDICOTS

FAMILY: OLEACEAE

HEIGHT: UP TO 130 FT (40 M)

SPREAD: UP TO 70 FT (20 M)

Leaf Deciduous; pinnately compound with toothed margins; opposite leaves; up to 4¾ in (12 cm) long

Fruits Samaras, often known as keys, each with one long green wing, in large bunches

Bark Pale gray; fissured, but young stems smooth and gray-green, with scars from fallen leaves

▲ **Sacred tree**
In Norse mythology, an ash tree called Yggdrasil lies at the center of the cosmos. In this illustration from an Icelandic manuscript, Yggdrasil is pictured with the wolf Fenrir, son of the god Loki.

Ash leaves can move slightly toward the direction of sunlight

Twigs have smooth bark

Leaves fall when they are still green

Ash

Fraxinus excelsior

As disease threatens its survival, scientists and foresters are working to protect this important tree whose wood has been used in the sky, the sports field, and elsewhere.

Growing in Europe, parts of Asia, and Africa, ash is a tall, elegant, deciduous tree that often grows in groups, creating a rounded canopy. In 1992, dead ash trees were found in Poland, killed by an unknown disease. Dark brown to orange lesions appeared on the foliage, while diamond-shaped lesions developed on the stems and the crown lost its leaves. Many infected ash trees died. Concerns spread as the disease traveled west, reaching the British Isles in 2012. Ash dieback, as the disease became known, threatened the future of this charismatic landscape tree, echoing the catastrophic loss of elms in the 1970s and 1980s caused by Dutch elm disease.

► Sweeping crown
Ash foliage is used as fodder for domestic livestock but also has herbal applications, utilized traditionally in the treatment of constipation, rheumatism, and gout and for weight loss.

▶ Flowers

Ash blooms appear on 1-year-old stems before the leaves in spring. Flowers may be male, female, or bisexual and trees can bear only male or only female flowers. Some trees produce male flowers one year and female flowers the next.

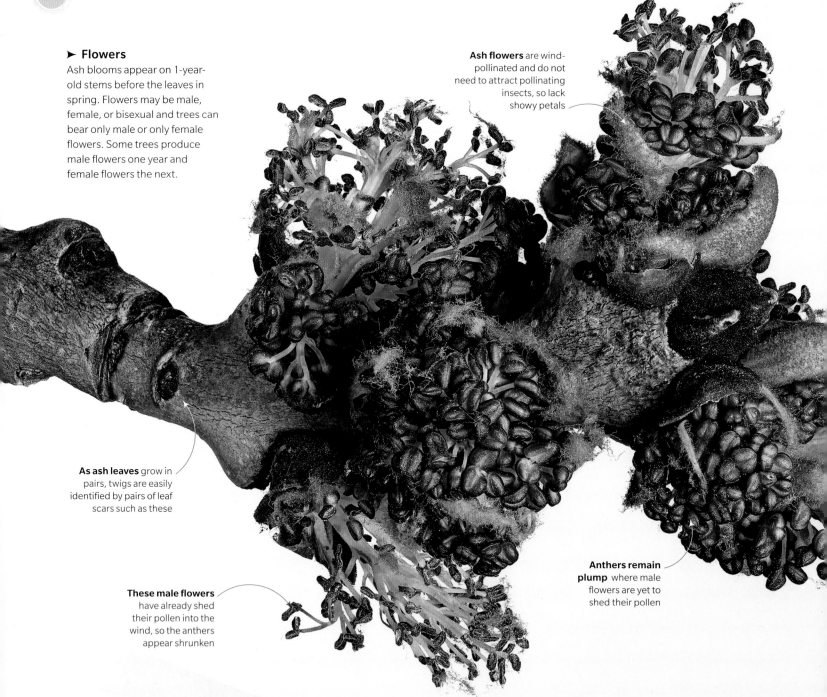

Ash flowers are wind-pollinated and do not need to attract pollinating insects, so lack showy petals

As ash leaves grow in pairs, twigs are easily identified by pairs of leaf scars such as these

These male flowers have already shed their pollen into the wind, so the anthers appear shrunken

Anthers remain plump where male flowers are yet to shed their pollen

Hymenoscyphus fraxineus is the fungus that causes ash dieback. Originally native to Asia, its route to Europe is unknown, though fungal diseases have traveled between continents in shipments of live plants or products such as timber. It continues to cause high levels of mortality in both wild and cultivated ash. Fungal spores are released by reproductive structures that develop on decomposing leaves dropped by infected trees. They spread on the wind, allowing ash dieback to quickly colonize new areas. In Asia, the fungus is found on native ash but does not cause the catastrophic dieback seen in Europe, possibly because Asian ash species have coexisted with the fungus much longer, developing immunity. There is hope that resistance will develop in wild European ash populations, but studies show that fewer than 10 percent of trees exhibit any degree of immunity. Together with emerald ash borer (*Agrilus planipennis*), a destructive insect pest of ash that is invading Europe and North America, ash trees have never been more threatened.

Ash twigs are easy to identify **in winter months,** as their **buds are black** and can appear to be **burned**

Strength and flexibility

In the Irish sport of hurling, teams attempt to score goals by hitting a small ball (the sliotar) between goalposts using a stick called a hurley. Traditionally made from ash wood, the sound of colliding hurleys, the "clash of the ash," resonates with hurling fans around the world. The wood of ash has several physical characteristics that make it sought after for hurley production, including natural strength, flexibility, lightness, and shock absorption qualities. As the sport has increased in popularity, Irish hurley producers have had to import ash wood from mainland Europe to satisfy demand. Ash wood is also preferred when manufacturing snooker cues and baseball bats, and it was a popular choice for tennis racket construction before being superseded by aluminum and then composite materials such as fiberglass. Outside of sports, ash wood has a wide range of uses, especially to make the handles of tools, including hammers and axes. Historically, it was used to build the frames of houses, cars, and aircraft, as well as walking sticks and crab pots.

WORLD WAR II'S "WOODEN WONDER"

During World War II, Britain's defenses relied upon a steady supply of aircraft, but raw materials were in short supply, so Geoffrey de Havilland designed and created a new aircraft with a wooden frame. The DH.98 Mosquito used ash wood for its structural members and served with the Royal Air Force until the 1950s.

BUILDING THE DH.98 MOSQUITO

Growth and life span

Aside from its many physical virtues, ash wood is popular because it is relatively fast-growing, producing usable poles for framing homes within 10 years of coppicing. Rapid growth is a common characteristic among pioneer species, those plants that are first to colonize new territory, and pioneers seldom live long. The oldest recorded ash is around 850 years old, but trees seldom reach more than 250 years of age.

▲ **Ash pump drill**
The wood of ash is very well suited to producing handles for tools, such as this pump drill, which uses a pumping action to drill small holes or for starting fires.

" The ash must be considered as the most economically valuable of all our native trees. "

HENRY J. ELWES AND AUGUSTINE HENRY, *The Trees of Great Britain & Ireland*, 1906

Other species

MANNA ASH
Fraxinus ornus

Native to southern Europe and western Asia; sometimes known as Flowering Ash, as it produces large, showy clusters of fragrant white flowers.

NARROW-LEAVED ASH
Fraxinus angustifolia

Native from Spain and Morocco to Iran; has narrower leaves than common ash and winter buds that are brown, not black.

WHITE ASH
Fraxinus americana

Common in eastern North America; can be distinguished by its distinctive C-shaped leaf scars. Leaves have white undersides.

Wych Elm

Ulmus glabra

A large, striking, deciduous tree, wych elm has a long association with humans from the Mediterranean to Scandinavia and beyond and a plays significant role in the ecology of forests. However, it is probably best known for a deadly disease that threatens to wipe it out.

Despite its name, Dutch elm disease has its origins in Asia. Caused by three fungus species, it first arrived in Europe in the early 20th century, killing some trees but largely causing minor damage. However, in the 1960s, a more virulent strain reached Europe, causing widespread loss of elms across the continent. The fungus is spread by beetles, which penetrate the bark to lay their eggs. Once infected, trees attempt to prevent the fungus spreading by blocking off parts of their vascular system, which causes individual branches to die off. The disease can also spread via interconnected roots or through the use of contaminated tools during pruning.

In England, the common English elm (*Ulmus procera*) was devastated by the disease and few mature trees remain. Dutch elm disease does not kill the roots and English elm survives today by resprouting from the base of otherwise dead trees. When the new shoots reach a suitable size, they

▲ Botanical beauty
At the mill in Bagot's Park, Staffordshire, UK, stood a wych elm that was "more distinguished by its beauty than its size," here illustrated by Jacob Strutt.

► Winged fruit
Elms rely on wind to fertilize their flowers and distribute their seeds; the latter can travel up to 320 ft (100 m) from the parent tree.

GROUP: EUDICOTS

FAMILY: ULMACEAE

HEIGHT: UP TO 100 FT (30 M)

SPREAD: UP TO 80 FT (25 M)

Leaf Deciduous; coarsely hairy with extra lobes at tip; alternately arranged; up to 6¾ in (17 cm) long

Bark Gray to brown; fissured, largely hairless; young stems are stout, slightly hairy

Elm fruits develop from wind-pollinated flowers that appear before the foliage in spring

Fruits are samaras and each has a single seed at the center of the wing

Descendants of the tree under which Penn's Treaty was signed still survive

Penn's peace
In 1683, English settler William Penn brokered a peace treaty with the Indigenous American Lenni Lenape tribe underneath an American elm tree—a relative of wych elm—in what is now Pennsylvania.

Buds are protected by hairy leaf scales, which drop off in spring when the leaves emerge

are once more visited by bark beetles, becoming reinfested with the fungus. Here, wych elm has an advantage: although not immune to the disease, its bark contains a chemical called alnulin, which makes it less attractive to the beetles that spread the disease. However, wych elm is largely unable to resprout from the roots, so an infestation that does occur is often fatal.

Butterflies, burrs, and burls

The loss of any species from its habitat invariably causes a chain reaction where other species that were once dependent upon it also begin to suffer. As elm numbers declined in the UK, so did numbers of the white-letter hairstreak butterfly (*Satyrium w-album*), which only lays its eggs on elm, preferring wych elm. In order to ensure the continued survival of this butterfly, conservationists have experimented by planting non-native elms and the result was an increased population of butterflies, challenging previous assumptions that only native species should be used in conservation projects.

The "wych" in wych elm conjures images of witchcraft, but the name derives from an Anglo-Saxon word meaning "flexible," and the supple branches were suited to making bows. The wood is also rot resistant and popular for building boats, bridge foundations, and cartwheels. Elm wood has an attractive grain and is popular for carving. Trunks often produce swollen woody bosses—those with shoots are called burrs, while those without are burls—that can be harvested to produce the finest veneers.

Other species

CHINESE ELM OR LACEBARK ELM
Ulmus parvifolia

Native of eastern Asia; has proven a tough replacement for European elms. Largely resistant to Dutch elm disease.

DUTCH ELM
Ulmus × hollandica

Hybrid between wych elm and field elm (*Ulmus minor*); occurs naturally across Europe, although it is variable in form.

" One of the noblest of native trees. "

W. J. BEAN, *Trees & Shrubs Hardy in the British Isles*, 1914

GROUP: EUDICOTS
FAMILY: BOMBACACEAE
HEIGHT: UP TO 79 FT (24 M)
SPREAD: UP TO 98 FT (30 M)

Leaf Deciduous; dark green, glossy; five to seven fingerlike leaflets; alternate; to 6 in (15 cm) long

Flower Pendulous; has five white petals; up to 8 in (20 cm) in diameter; sweet-scented

Fruit Green, egg-shaped capsule; covered in yellowish hairs; up to 14 in (35 cm) long

Bark Grayish brown and smooth; becomes folded on older trees; 2–4 in (5–10 cm) thick

Baobab batik
The iconic shape of baobab has inspired many artists. This batik (a pattern created by wax-resistant dyeing) from Mozambique showcases the tree's distinctive swollen trunk encompassing people, plants, and animals.

◄ Fruit harvest
These women use a special tool to harvest the edible fruits from a baobab in the African Republic of Senegal, where it is the official national tree.

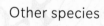

" Wisdom is like the baobab tree; no one individual can embrace it. "

AFRICAN PROVERB

African Baobab

Adansonia digitata

Sometimes called "upside-down trees" due to the rootlike appearance of their branches when leafless in winter, the iconic baobabs store water in their swollen, succulent trunks.

The large, deciduous African baobab makes for a magnificent sight, its massive trunk and high canopy dominating the surrounding landscape. The water reservoir in its barrel-like trunk allows the baobab to survive in well-drained, sandy soils across the dry tropical regions of Africa—from the Cape Verde islands in the northwest, to Sudan in the northeast, and south to the Limpopo province of South Africa. Another six species of baobab are confined to the island of Madagascar, and one is found in scattered sites across northwestern Australia's outback, where it is known as boab.

African baobabs typically grow in regions with moderate summer rainfall and a long, dry winter. They shed their leaves at the start of the dry

Other species

GRANDIDIER'S BAOBAB

Adansonia grandidieri

One of six baobab species found only in Madagascar; endangered species with a massive, unbranched trunk, topped with an umbrellalike crown.

season to reduce water loss by transpiration. The gaunt outline of the leafless tree is celebrated in African legend. It is said that the Great Spirit, who made the world, dedicated a tree to each species of animal. The hyena was so disgusted at being awarded the baobab that it threw the tree away. It landed upside down and has grown that way ever since, with roots replacing its branches.

Naming the tree

French explorer and botanist Michel Adanson first observed the baobab tree in 1749 while on a visit to Senegal in West Africa. He published

4 in (24.8 m) tall in 2013. The most impressive feature, however, is the expansive base to the trunk. Another Senegalese tree, measured in 2021, had a girth of 94 ft (28.7 m) at breast height—4 ft 3 in (1.3 m) above the ground.

The age of baobabs is often impossible to determine. Many have hollow trunks, and the annual rings found on most trees, which can be counted to estimate their age, are almost invisible in baobabs. Instead, scientists use radiocarbon dating to determine their age, and one tree in Namibia is thought to be about 1,275 years old.

Baobab seeds are sometimes colored, sugar-coated, and sold as candy

a scholarly account of the tree on his return home, and the Swedish botanist Carl Linnaeus named the genus Adansonia in his honor. Its species name *Adansonia digitata* is derived from the shape of its leaflets, which resemble the fingers (digits) of the human hand.

Recent research suggests that certain baobab trees found in the mountainous regions of Africa may belong to an entirely different species, *Adansonia kilima*, but this is not widely accepted.

Record holders

The trunks of the baobabs are truly impressive. One record holder in Senegal measured 81 ft

Flowers and fruits

Reproduction of baobabs begins in early summer. Spherical, green flower buds develop on long, drooping stalks that grow from the points where leaves connect to stems. Late in the afternoon, these open into pendulous, white flowers that begin to emit a sweetish scent. The flowers only last 24 hours, soon turning brown and beginning to smell unpleasant. At night, these scents attract fruit bats, who carry pollen from one flower to another, thus helping pollinate them. The scented flowers attract many nocturnal insects. Insectivorous bats feeding on these insects may also play a role in pollination.

Patterns are carved into the dried fruit

▶ Versatile pods

The hard, waterproof shells of the fruit are used to make bowls, fishing floats, and gourds. Dried fruits can be used as rattles—when shaken, the seeds strike the shell to make a rattling sound.

Buds grow on long, pendulous stalks

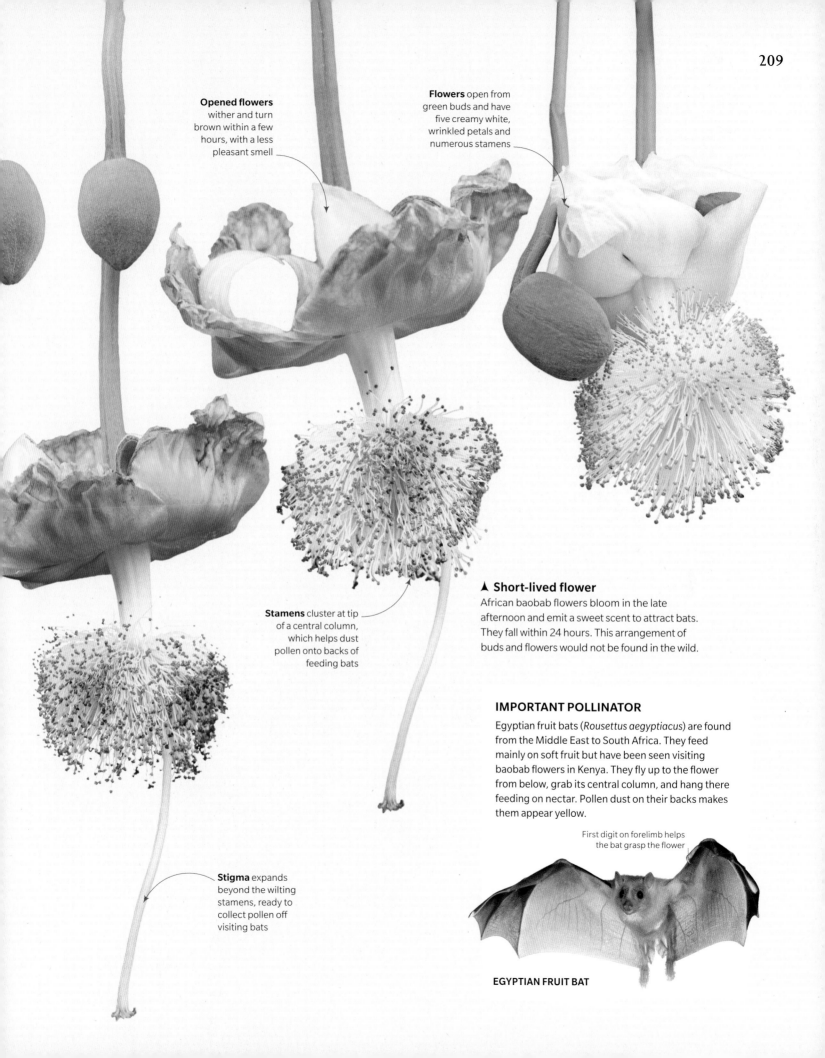

209

Opened flowers wither and turn brown within a few hours, with a less pleasant smell

Flowers open from green buds and have five creamy white, wrinkled petals and numerous stamens

Stamens cluster at tip of a central column, which helps dust pollen onto backs of feeding bats

Stigma expands beyond the wilting stamens, ready to collect pollen off visiting bats

▲ Short-lived flower

African baobab flowers bloom in the late afternoon and emit a sweet scent to attract bats. They fall within 24 hours. This arrangement of buds and flowers would not be found in the wild.

IMPORTANT POLLINATOR

Egyptian fruit bats (*Rousettus aegyptiacus*) are found from the Middle East to South Africa. They feed mainly on soft fruit but have been seen visiting baobab flowers in Kenya. They fly up to the flower from below, grab its central column, and hang there feeding on nectar. Pollen dust on their backs makes them appear yellow.

First digit on forelimb helps the bat grasp the flower

EGYPTIAN FRUIT BAT

The flowers take up to six months to develop into melon-sized fruits with a tough outer casing covered in yellowish brown hair. Inside, numerous kidney-shaped, dark brown seeds are embedded in a white, mealy pulp that is sweet to eat and rich in vitamin C. The fruit hangs on the tree until monkeys come to feed on it, or gets blown to the ground where other animals feed on the pulp. In the process, they discard and spread the seeds.

In the right soil, the seeds germinate quickly. The seedlings look very different from mature trees, with undivided leaves and inconspicuous stems. They are slow to establish and may take 8 to 23 years before producing their first flowers. As a result, the species has never been cultivated, although agronomists, who study plant cultivation, are testing various systems of grafting to see if these can accelerate fruit production.

People and baobabs

Baobabs have great social and economic importance to indigenous inhabitants across their range, with almost every part of the tree put to use. Mature trees are often left as landmarks along traditional, well-traveled routes. Indigenous people from the Kalahari Desert tap an emergency water supply by sucking water from the trunk through hollow grass stems. The fruit pulp is eaten, mixed into oatmeal, or soaked in water or milk to make a refreshing drink. The seeds are used to thicken

> **One baobab trunk** can store more than **1,426 gallons (5,400 liters) of water**, making it 80 percent liquid

▼ Filling stations
Elephants use their tusks to gouge the trunks of baobabs and reach the water inside. In severe droughts, they may even topple over and consume an entire tree.

► Hanging fruit

A baobab is a focal point in the African countryside, providing welcome shade. The dangling fruit earned it the name "rat-tail tree" in the Caribbean, where it was introduced.

soups and are said to make a good substitute for coffee when roasted. Young leaves are cooked as a vegetable.

The fibrous bark can be peeled from the tree, and the inner tissue will continue to produce fresh bark to replace it. The bark is pounded to release fibers that can be used to make ropes, floor tiles, or baskets, or be woven into cloth. The roots produce a dye. The bark, leaves, and fruits all have roles in traditional medicine. It is even said that a decoction of the seeds can provide protection against crocodiles.

Large baobab trees with naturally hollow or excavated trunks have been used by people for centuries for diverse purposes, including as houses, prisons, pubs, stables, and bus shelters. One tree was even converted into a toilet, complete with flushing water.

Sudden deaths

In recent years, some of the oldest and largest baobabs, or their oldest stems, have begun to die out. Researchers believe this sudden decline of Africa's longest-lived tree may be caused by climate change. Higher temperatures and extended droughts may be drying the trees out, with larger trees unable to support the weight of their massive trunks. Their deaths also impact the ecosystem and the animals that they shelter.

" ... the beauty of the baobab ... induced me to pitch my little camp at the side of it. "

SILVESTER MEINRAD XAVIER GOLBERRY, *Travels in Africa*, 1808

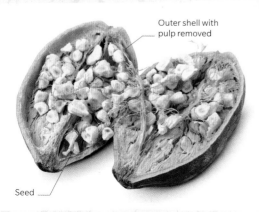

Outer shell with pulp removed

Seed

HEALTHY FRUIT

Baobab is in the same family as durian, famously the smelliest fruit in the world, but also refreshing and rich in vitamin C. The baobab fruit is similarly edible and nutritious, consumed by people across its range in a variety of ways, from soups to refreshing drinks. The fruit contains six times as much vitamin C as oranges, as well as vitamins B1 (thiamine) and B9 (folic acid). It also has twice the calcium of milk and significant amounts of potassium, magnesium, and iron, all key minerals for a healthy diet.

GROUP: EUDICOTS

FAMILY: MALVACEAE

HEIGHT: UP TO 230 FT (70 M)

SPREAD: UP TO 197 FT (60 M)

Leaf Deciduous; divided into leaflets with a palmlike arrangement, 5 to 9 leaflets per leaf; to 3⅛ in (8 cm) long

Flower Small, white to pink, pungent fragrance; appearing before leaves

Bark Green with large thorns when young; smooth and gray at maturity

► **Lone kapok**
When forest is cleared, not every tree is felled. In this illustration of a village in Suriname, a kapok with wide-spreading buttress roots remains, providing shade, shelter, and cotton.

Kapok

Ceiba pentandra

A giant of the rainforest, kapok towers over most tropical trees, so when it produces its silky seeds, they drift a significant distance from the parent.

Also known as silk-cotton or ceiba, kapok grows wild in the hot forests of Central and South America, the Caribbean, and West Africa. This majestic tree, sometimes growing to around 230 ft (70 m) in height, is known for its seeds, which provide silky fibers used as stuffing and insulation.

Kapok grows in challenging conditions. In the warm, humid forests of the tropical lowlands, biomatter such as fallen leaves does not last long. An army of fungi, bacteria, and other organisms work quickly to decompose this rich waste and, as rainfall is regular and torrential, soils are typically poor in nutrients. Trees living in these forests must spread their roots widely in search of essential nutrients. However, a wide but shallow root system cannot bear the weight of a massive tree, so many rainforest species such as the kapok develop broad, flattened structures near the base of their trunks called buttress roots. These act like architectural buttresses, propping up the tree and bracing its weight.

▲ **Thorny trunk**
The short, thick thorns on kapok trunks are a formidable natural defense mechanism against animals that would otherwise eat the tree's bark.

European Linden

Tilia × europaea

With its largely columnar form and sweet-smelling flowers favored by honeybees, European linden has long been popular for planting along avenues and on great estates.

A naturally occurring hybrid, European linden derives from a cross between large-leaved linden (*Tilia platyphyllos*) and small-leaved linden (*Tilia cordata*). It is found growing wild in several European countries and is cultivated in many others. Linden trees are not related to the citrus fruit lime, though lime is another common name for *Tilia*.

European linden flowers produce copious amounts of nectar and are a popular food source for foraging bees. Several instances have been recorded where large numbers of dead bees were found beneath linden trees. The cause of these strange events remains somewhat mysterious. In some cases, the trees were sprayed with insecticide to control aphids, and the bees were unintended casualties. Otherwise, linden trees often carry a heavy burden of sap-sucking aphids, and the honeydew released by the insects creates a sticky mess below, possibly trapping the bees. Another possibility is that bees become addicted to linden nectar and die from starvation once it runs out.

▲ Leaves, flowers, and seeds
Once pollinated, linden flowers develop seed capsules. Each cluster bears a leafy bract that acts like a parachute, allowing the seeds to travel farther.

" ... a fine plant, covered with rich foliage, and growing ... to the magnitude of the first order. "

DAVID LOW on European linden, *On Landed Property, and the Economy of Estates*, 1844

► Honeybee on flower
A wide variety of insects visit European linden flowers, attracted by their fragrance and abundant nectar. Bees such as this often rely on linden nectar and transfer pollen between trees.

GROUP: EUDICOTS

FAMILY: MALVACEAE

HEIGHT: 49–164 FT (15–50 M)

SPREAD: UP TO 49 FT (15 M)

Leaf Deciduous; asymmetrical at base, edges toothed; intermediate in size between parent species; up to 4 in (10 cm)

Fruit Spherical capsules; often sterile with no seeds; in clusters

Bark Smooth, gray, ridged; young stems red to brown

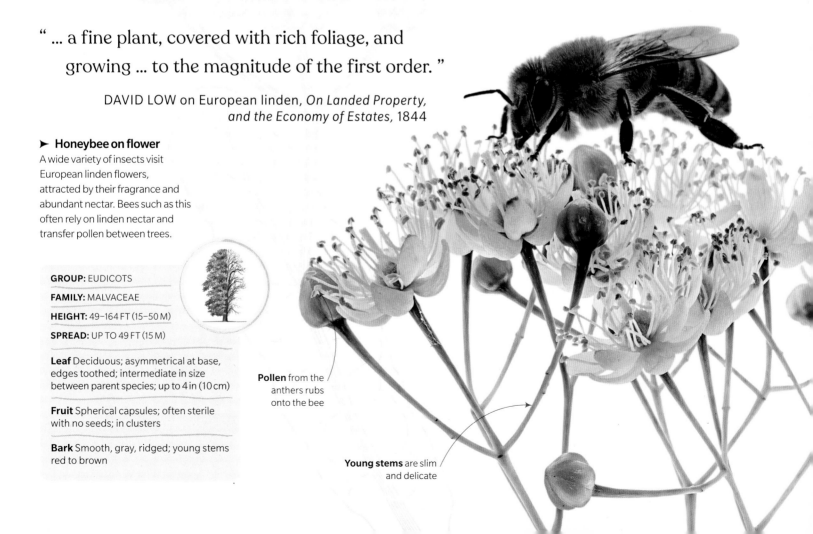

Pollen from the anthers rubs onto the bee

Young stems are slim and delicate

Cacao pods are known as "cherelles"; around three-quarters die before maturing due to various diseases

Fruits are fleshy, wrinkled, and oblong, beginning green but ripening to red, yellow, or purple in different varieties

Trunks are usually weak because they grow, protected from gales, in the forest understory

Cacao trees produce fruit from the age of 4 years

GROUP: EUDICOTS

FAMILY: MALVACEAE

HEIGHT: 13–26 FT (4–8 M)

SPREAD: 13–20 FT (4–6 M)

Leaf Evergreen; egg-shaped, shiny, leathery; alternate; 6–20 in (15–50 cm) long

Bark Rich brown; marked by studs where dead flowers or fruits have fallen

◄ **Trunk fruits**
Unusual among trees, the flowers and fleshy fruit pods of cacao trees grow directly from the trunk and older branches instead of on side shoots (an adaptation described as "cauliflory").

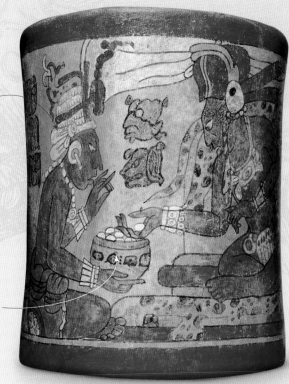

Servant offers a bowl to the dignitary

White foodstuff, possibly cacao seeds or beans

Cacao Tree

Theobroma cacao

Cacao probably originated in montane forests around the source of the Amazon River in the eastern Andes, but it was spread widely across South and Central America by the Mayan and Aztec civilizations.

▲ **Mayan tradition**
The painting on this vessel from around 1,300 years ago is thought to show a scene in a Mayan palace, where servants are serving a dignitary. Mayan drinking vessels such as this were used with their hot chocolate beverage.

This small, evergreen tree has a slim trunk; oblong, leathery leaves that are red when young and later turn dark green; and large fruits—the much-prized cacao pods. Cacao was used to make a drink in Central America and Mexico from at least 1750 BCE. The first civilization of the region, the Olmecs, must have brought the beans from their original range in the eastern Andes. Local agriculture was developed further by the Olmec's successors, the Maya and Aztecs. The tree (which they called Cacau) played a major part in their spiritual lives, as well as providing food and drink. The beans were used as currency and paid as tributes to their leaders, who stored them in huge warehouses. They mixed the roasted beans with maize, chili powder, and spices to make soups and sauces, but mostly they used them in a frothy drink that they called *xocoatl* (the "x" in this case is pronounced as "sh," hence the English word "chocolate").

Spreading popularity

When the Europeans arrived, they were not impressed by the bitter taste of this strange confection. Once exported to Europe, chocolate initially was only drunk by the nobility, but it became more popular with the availability of sugar. Milk was added to chocolate beverages from the mid-17th century, but it was the early 19th

The Mayans believed cacao had been **discovered by the gods** and celebrated this **every April**

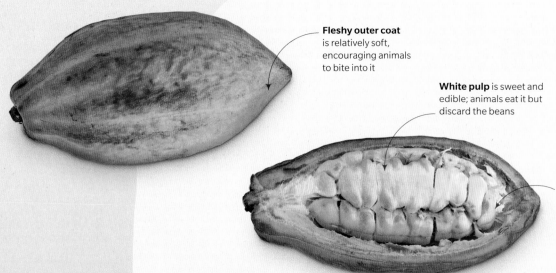

Fleshy outer coat is relatively soft, encouraging animals to bite into it

White pulp is sweet and edible; animals eat it but discard the beans

◄ **Fruit pod**
Technically a berry, the fruit is filled with 20–40 seeds surrounded by a sweet, edible pulp. This attracts monkeys and squirrels, which nibble into the pod, releasing and spreading the seeds.

Seeds (beans) are around 1½ in (4 cm) across and bitter tasting

Varieties

CRIOLLO

First grown by the Olmecs; pale-colored or white bean has a delicate flavor and is said to produce the best-quality chocolate. Less resistant to disease than other varieties.

TRINITARIO

Probably originated as a hybrid between the other two varieties; has a thick, hard husk. Beans are variable, with a less intense aroma than that of Criollo beans.

FORASTERO

Hardy variety from lower-level Amazon forests; mainly grown in West Africa, which produces most of the world crop. Beans require much longer fermentation than Criollo beans.

century before mass production began of the two main modern products: cocoa powder and slab chocolate (the term "cocoa" being simply a misspelling of the Mayan name).

Cacao is grown in open orchards, usually pruned to an accessible height, beneath taller shade trees. It is still widely cultivated in Central and South America, but two West African countries are now the dominant producers. In 2019 and 2020, Cote D'Ivoire grew over half of world crop of 4.6 million tons (4.19 million tonnes) of beans, with Ghana producing 19 percent.

From trees to the world

The production method of chocolate is still rather basic. The harvested pods are split open and the beans are scooped out and piled onto banana leaves or into wooden "sweat boxes." Bacteria and yeasts in the white pulp cause the beans to ferment, and the spent pulp drains away. After five or six days, the beans are removed and dried in the sun for a week. The dried beans are then exported to factories, mostly in the US and Europe, for production. There, the beans are roasted and their seed coats removed. The interiors are then ground into a paste, called cocoa mass. To make cocoa powder, this is pressed to remove a large proportion of the fat (called cocoa butter). For chocolate, extra cocoa butter and sugar are added to the cocoa mass, along with milk powder in most formulations. Today, over 7.2 million tons (6.5 million tonnes) of chocolate is consumed worldwide per year, with a market value of around $208 billion.

INSECT POLLINATION

Flowers grow singly or in clusters from the trunk. They are around ⅔ in (1.5 cm) across, with five white or pink petals, each with a little cup at the base holding a pollen-producing stamen. In some varieties, the flowers can pollinate themselves, but others must be pollinated by tiny midges, which are vital to many commercial cocoa crops.

CACAO FLOWER AND MIDGE

◄ French drinking chocolate poster
This early 20th-century poster promotes drinking chocolate. Made directly from chocolate, this contains a lot more cocoa butter (fat) than hot cocoa, made from cocoa powder.

Whistling Thorn

Vachellia drepanolobium

GROUP: EUDICOTS
FAMILY: FABACEAE
HEIGHT: 20 FT (6 M)
SPREAD: 20 FT (6 M)

Leaf Evergreen; leaflets in two ranks along a straight to curving midrib; opposite; up to ³⁄₁₆ in (5 mm) long

Fruit Seeds produced in narrow pods; edible for humans

Related to the acacias, this thorny, sometimes shrubby, evergreen member of the pea family is native to grassland areas of tropical East Africa. Here, in the conditions that suit it best, it can dominate the vegetation and form forests.

Whistling thorn's short branches radiate out from a central trunk to form an open, spreading crown. The stems are armored with spines, some of which are fused at the base and enlarged into roughly globular galls. These are used by ants for shelter—the ants gain access by digging holes in the galls. The tree's common name alludes to the whistling made by the wind as it blows through these holes, a sound long thought to be supernatural by the people who live in the area. The white or cream flowers are pollinated by bees. The species thrives on so-called "black cotton" soils, which have a high clay content and, as a result, drain

Leaves are grazed by various herbivores

Branches are usually short but can extend outward into a wide crown

▶ Familiar habit
The whistling thorn's characteristically umbrella-shaped habit is a familiar sight on the savannas of parts of East Africa. Its timber is used locally for tools and fencing.

poorly. Trees can withstand flooding and can even regenerate following forest fires, growing from low stumps at ground level— a sort of natural coppicing. Despite its toughness, the whistling thorn tree is seldom encountered outside its natural range apart from in botanic collections. In areas with suitable conditions, it can proliferate to such an extent that it becomes an invasive weed.

Fused stems form a hollow, bulbous swelling (gall) about 1 in (2.5 cm) in diameter

Long thorns are up to 3 in (7.5 cm) long

A home to ants

Several species of ant have been identified living in whistling thorns, though a single tree typically hosts only one species. Not only do the ants rely on the swollen spine bases for shelter, but they feed on nectar produced by glands near the leaf bases. In return, the ants help protect the plant from attack, including from other species of ant. The resident ants may trim the buds at the branch tips to inhibit the tree's spread, so it is less likely to come into contact with a neighboring tree occupied by a different ant species. They also protect the tree from larger animals, including giraffes, which browse the young stems, precisely where the ants tend to congregate. Giraffe calves

are particularly sensitive to the bites and stings of the ants; older animals are more tolerant. Without the defense mounted by the ants, the mammals would strip trees bare.

Locally, it is used as a food source, as the young galls are edible (before they are drilled by ants) and the young seed pods are vegetablelike. The inner bark has a sweetish, if often slightly bitter, taste and can be used as a chew. Commercially, gum from the tree is harvested for processing as gum arabic.

▲ Thorny stem
Whistling thorn has strong defenses. Stems with long, sharp thorns and bulbous swellings harboring stinging ants protect the plant from its natural predators.

> " ... it pipes through the holes like the music of a thousand flutes. "
>
> HELEN COWCHER, *Whistling Thorn*, 1993

Other species

BULLHORN ACACIA
Vachellia cornigera
Grows in Mexico and Central America; its swollen thorns resemble the horns of a steer.

GUM ARABIC TREE
Vachellia nilotica
Species from Africa, the Middle East, and India; exudes gum arabic from its trunk.

SYMBIOTIC RELATIONSHIP

The whistling thorn belongs to a group of plants knows as ant-plants, or myrmecophytes, and the relationship between ant and plant has been widely studied. Neither the ants nor the trees are wholly dependent on the other for survival, but instead they each gain a competitive advantage from the relationship. While the tree shelters and feeds the ants, the ants protect the tree from attack.

ANTS ON WHISTLING THORN

Fluffy, globular flowers are highly fragrant

Finely divided leaves have a feathery appearance

◄ **Profusion of flowers**
With its elegant, airy habit, silver wattle is valued as a street tree and garden ornamental in parts of the Mediterranean and other mild temperate areas.

GROUP: EUDICOTS

FAMILY: FABACEAE

HEIGHT: 65–82 FT (20–25 M)

SPREAD: UP TO 33 FT (10 M)

Fruit Flattened pod; ripens from green to brown; contains several round seeds

Bark Gray-green, darkening to brown with age; vertically striated

Silver Wattle

Acacia dealbata

Known to gardeners and florists in the northern hemisphere as mimosa, this evergreen bears winter flowers that are among the sweetest harbingers of spring.

In its native range of southeast Australia and Tasmania, where it can rapidly reach a considerable size, silver wattle is found from high plateaus to deep valleys, along watercourses, and in drier conditions, where it tends to be more shrubby. Collected by British naturalist Joseph Banks on explorer James Cook's voyage to Australia in the late 18th century, the species was then introduced into Europe in the early 19th century. In some regions, it has proved so successful that it is now classified as an invasive weed. Silver wattle is not generally long lived, seldom achieving an age beyond 40 years.

The soft, twice-divided leaves (technically phyllodes, or expanded leaf stalks) give the whole tree a soft, feathery appearance.

The rounded flowers, a light sulfur yellow in color, are produced in loose clusters, or panicles, up to 4 in (10 cm) long and are highly fragrant. The widely used name mimosa is also the botanical name of a related genus of tropical plants that includes several annuals and perennials.

From timekeeping to timber

Indigenous people put acacias to a number of uses: medicine, soaps, food, as a fuel, and to fashion tools and weapons. For the Wurundjeri people, trees growing alongside the Yarra River east of Melbourne were valued as calendar plants. When the flowers fell into the water, it was time to fish for eels that would congregate to feed on grubs that lived in the flowers.

The timber has limited uses beyond a general appeal to craftspeople. It is sometimes pulped and combined with other materials to create wood composite products. It also produces an edible gum that can be used as a food additive.

> Silver wattle is a **pioneer species**—its seeds are among the **first to sprout** on land cleared by fire

▼ Crowning glory
Young silver wattle trees are upright and slender, with a triangular crown that spreads as they mature. In gardens, they rarely achieve the size of wild plants.

Other species

BLACKWOOD
Acacia melanoxylon

Native to coastal regions of southeast Australia; evergreen species with dark gray to black bark that appears scaly on older trees.

SYMBOLIC TREE
In many eastern European countries and the US, the resilient silver wattle flowers serve as a symbol for International Women's Day. Australia celebrates National Wattle Day on September 1 every year. In addition to heralding the start of spring, this day is a commemoration of the native wattles and what they signified for the people over the years—national pride and diversity.

WATTLE DAY, SYDNEY, 1935

► **Goldfinch and plane seeds**
Although not a main food source for wildlife, the fruit of London plane is eaten by some city birds such as this goldfinch. As a hybrid, London plane's seeds rarely develop fully.

Stiff hairs on seeds aid dispersal by wind

Seeds rarely produce starch-rich embryos; they are nevertheless a source of food

GROUP: EUDICOTS
FAMILY: PLATANACEAE
HEIGHT: UP TO 157 FT (48 M)
SPREAD: 50–70 FT (15–21 M)

 Leaf Deciduous; 3–5 lobes with sharp teeth; alternate; up to 10 in (25 cm) across

 Flower In 2–6 rounded clusters on a single stalk; males and females on separate branches

 Bark Brown, scaly; flakes shed, mainly from upper trunk, to show creamy white wood beneath

London Plane

Platanus × hispanica

Surviving in the harshly artificial environment of cities around the world, one of the most successful urban trees is itself a man-made creation.

The precise origins of the London plane have been lost in time. It is thought to be a hybrid between American sycamore and oriental plane, whose native ranges do not overlap (see p.225). It was first recorded in 1666 in the botanic garden in Oxford, England, where it was described as an intermediate between its parents, both of which grew in the garden. However, because oriental plane is not hardy in the British Isles, some experts suggest that the hybrid is more likely to have originated either in France or Spain, where both parents were growing sometime around 1650, and would then have been introduced to Britain. The scientific name × *hispanica* reflects its supposed Spanish origin.

The modern genetic techniques of DNA analysis would normally be expected to confirm this hybrid status, but the evidence is somewhat equivocal. Some analytical techniques support a hybrid origin; others suggest that it is more closely related to oriental plane and could be a mutated form of that species. Hybrid plants are generally infertile because they contain two different sets of chromosomes, one from each

The **London plane** population in **Johannesburg, South Africa**, is under threat from **beetles**

► **Spreading crown**
The thick branches and dense, deciduous foliage of London plane provides welcome shade along busy city streets in summer. It softens the urban landscape and helps reduce traffic noise.

" It has taken with great kindness to London life, despite the drawbacks of smoke, fog, flagstones, and asphalt. "

EDWARD STEP, *Wayside and Woodland Trees*, 1940

Peduncle or stalk hangs from the tip of a branch or twig, supporting two to six rounded fruiting heads

Fruiting heads develop from globe-shaped clusters of female flowers and swell as the nutlets inside mature

Leaves can resemble those of either of the parent species or be intermediate between them in shape

⋏ Spherical fruit
After pollination by wind, female flowers develop into spiky fruit heads. These slowly break up in winter, releasing the cluster of seeds inside. Each seed has a tuft of stiff hairs, which help it spread in the wind.

parent, which cannot segregate properly in the reproduction process; however, London plane is sometimes fertile. It can therefore reproduce itself and does occasionally self-sow into new sites. On the other hand, its fruits on many trees produce seeds without a viable embryo, which is consistent with it being a hybrid. It may be that both forms have been planted since the 17th century and have become so interdispersed that they cannot be told apart.

Whatever the precise nature of the tree, it is known to be very long-lived, with some of its first-known plantings still flourishing. Two London planes were presented to the Bishop of Lincoln in England in the 1660s, and these trees are both still growing at Buckden Towers in Cambridgeshire. Another surviving tree was planted in 1680 beside the Bishop's Palace in Ely, also in Cambridgeshire. The tallest living specimen is in the Bryanston School Estate in Dorset, England, last measured in 2015 at a height of just under 163 ft (49.67 m).

It is part of an avenue planted in 1749 to mark the centenary of the execution of the English king Charles I of England in 1649. All these trees still grow well, without any signs of senescence (deterioration), so it is possible that the maximum lifespan of the tree still remains to be seen.

Hardy city dweller
By 1811, London plane had become a popular street tree in the rapidly growing city of London, hence its common name. It typically grows

London plane is planted as a popular shade tree in major Australian cities

taller than either parent species, lifting its crown above the worst street-level pollution. Its roots can cope with heavily compacted soil, flagstones, tarmac, and polluted rainwater runoff from city streets. It tolerates regular lopping and pruning, rarely sheds branches, and can withstand most gales. It survived the worst London smogs (fogs filled with smoke and soot) of the last century because its leaves open long after the winter smog season and their glossy surfaces are readily washed by rain. Its bark peels off in large flakes, which may stop the lenticels (breathing pores) on the trunk from becoming clogged with soot. Its leaves absorb small carbon particles, so they help reduce air pollution.

In London, it self-seeds onto walls and bridges beside rivers but never forms pure woods. The heat that leaks from industry and urban dwellings may help it survive because it is less

► Flaking bark
On upper parts of the tree, strips of bark flake off in fall, giving the tree a mottled appearance. This prevents a buildup of mosses and soot.

common elsewhere in the UK. Its golden-brown wood with darker flecks, known as lacewood, was formerly used in veneers.

Because of its tolerance to pollution, London plane is also widely planted as a shade and amenity tree along boulevards and in parks and gardens in many southern European cities, in the main cities of Australia, and in the suburbs of Johannesburg, South Africa. London planes constitute more than 1 in 10 of New York's street trees; the symbol of the New York City Department of Parks and Recreation is a cross between a London plane leaf and a maple leaf.

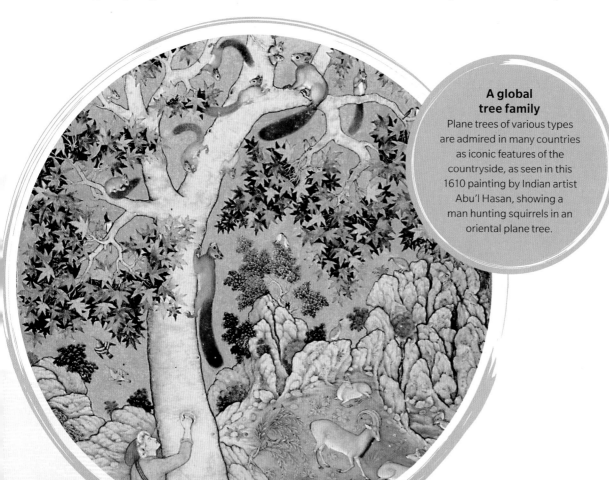

A global tree family
Plane trees of various types are admired in many countries as iconic features of the countryside, as seen in this 1610 painting by Indian artist Abu'l Hasan, showing a man hunting squirrels in an oriental plane tree.

Other species

AMERICAN SYCAMORE
Platanus occidentalis

Native to eastern North America; parent of the hybrid London plane; has leaves with three to five shallow, wavy-edged lobes. Bark peels in thin strips.

ORIENTAL PLANE
Platanus orientalis

London plane's other parent species, native to southeast Europe and western Asia. Leaves have five slender, triangular lobes; bark sheds in large flakes.

A fog hangs over Demerdzhi Mountain in Crimea, Ukraine, cloaking it in an air of mystery. In addition to folktales, the rocky slopes of this mountain are home to a variety of trees, from oaks to yews. Gnarled and spreading with age, this crooked pine (*Pinus sylvestris* var. *hamata*) forms a striking shape against the backdrop of mist.

► Holly leaves
One of the only broad-leaved evergreens in European woodlands, holly has glossy leaves that contrast with its bright red berries.

Each leaf is coated in a glossy cuticle that reduces water loss from leaf pores

Spines around the leaf edges and a tough, leathery texture help deter hungry herbivores such as deer

Holly

Ilex aquifolium

With its dark, evergreen foliage and bright red berries, holly's colors are strongly associated with Christmas in the West, and its branches and likeness are widely used in festive decorations. However, holly's use by humans long predates Christianity.

GROUP: EUDICOTS

FAMILY: AQUIFOLIACEAE

HEIGHT: UP TO 65 FT (20 M)

SPREAD: UP TO 50 FT (15 M)

Flower White, fragrant, with four petals; male and female on different trees

Bark Gray, smooth to wrinkled texture; young stems are green

Holly fruits turn red when ripe

Holly's dark green leaves survive even in snow-blasted winter forests. This compelling image of enduring life has resonated with people across holly's native range in Western Europe, and the tree features in numerous pre-Christian myths and legends. In Ancient Rome, holly wreathes were gifted during Saturnalia, the midwinter festival celebrating the god Saturn. In several Celtic traditions, the seasons play out as a battle between the Holly King and his brother, the Oak King. Evenly matched in strength, the Oak King dominates in summer, but with the arrival of cooler weather, the Holly King takes the crown. As Christianity spread across Europe, pagan festivals were frowned upon but remained popular and were ultimately absorbed into Christian tradition. The holly that decorated homes in winter took on added meaning—prickly leaves are said to symbolize the crown of thorns, while red berries represent the blood of Christ.

Hedges and gardens

Holly is a popular garden plant. It is suitable as a hedge, the prickly foliage acting as a deterrent to intruders. Its leaves are famed for their spiny teeth, but not all leaves are spiny. At ground level, holly foliage is vulnerable to attack by hungry animals such as deer, especially in winter when leaves are scarce, so the lowermost leaves tend to be most spiny. In contrast, the uppermost leaves cannot be

Plain leaves from the top of the tree

Prickly leaves from near the ground

▶ **Varied leaves**
These leaves all come from the same holly tree, but those most exposed to herbivores tend to have more spines than those out of reach of animals.

Holly trees can live for up to 500 years, although most die much younger

Holly and the holidays
Together with ivy and mistletoe, evergreen holly has long been harvested to decorate homes in winter. The attractive leaves and berries are said to bring luck, are sometimes seen as a symbol of eternal life, and are even said to shelter fairies.

▲ The lady and the unicorn
One of a series of six Flemish tapestries representing the senses, this scene is focused on sight and depicts numerous plants, including a holly tree (right).

reached by large herbivores and as a result are largely free of spines. This does not mean they are entirely safe—the larvae of holly leaf miner (*Phytomyza ilicis*) burrow inside holly leaves, causing damage. Wild hollies are typically spiny, but many cultivated varieties are not, while hedgehog holly (*Ilex aquifolium* 'Ferox Argentea') is even more spiny than the wild variety, with prickles on the leaf surfaces as well as the edges.

With its long tradition in folklore and its continued popularity in gardens, holly has traveled beyond its native range. In the Pacific Northwest of North America, *Ilex aquifolium* is

invasive and has several features that make it prone to escape cultivation. Each tree produces thousands of seeds annually, and the red berries are attractive to birds. When cut to ground, hollies resprout from the stump. In addition, any stem touching the ground can root and develop into a new tree. In Washington, hollies were actively planted around Seattle during the 1920s, in order to earn the name "the Holly State." The invasive hollies crowded out native species, so in recent years, efforts have been made to control them. Today, holly can still be found growing wild in 18 out of Washington's 39 counties.

Other species

AMERICAN HOLLY
Ilex opaca

Native to eastern North America; evergreen holly harvested for wreaths just like its European relative. Leaves are not glossy.

LONGSTALK HOLLY
Ilex pedunculosa

Evergreen holly from Japan and China, lacking the leaf spines of European species. Berries are large and hang on long stalks.

HIGHCLERE HOLLY
Ilex × altaclerensis

Derived from a cross between European holly and the Madeira native *Ilex perado*; has larger leaves and fruits than its parents.

Distinctive berries

Bright red berries are holly's finest feature, and the color is especially attractive to birds. Color vision in birds is similar to that of humans, although they perceive more wavelengths at the red end of the spectrum, so plants use the color red to attract birds to their fruits and distribute their seeds. Holly berries are not true berries but are a type of fruit called a drupe. As in other drupes such as cherries and dates, each holly seed is enclosed in a hard outer layer (or endocarp). Not all holly trees produce fruits. Hollies are dioecious, with separate male and female trees, and only females develop drupes. However, a flowering male tree must be present to provide pollen to the female flowers for fruits to develop.

SIMPLE COLORS

Flowers come in many colors, but fruits and berries (such as holly berries) are often red or black. Flowers must be visited multiple times for pollination to occur, and having a unique color ensures the pollinator visits the right flower. Fruits are often eaten by birds, and grow in common colors that are widely recognized.

HOLLY BERRIES WITH GREENFINCH

Branches hardened by exposed conditions

◄ Wind-ravaged
While most often encountered in sheltered woodlands, hollies can survive in more exposed locations, often becoming contorted and wind-pruned.

" But when the bare and wintry woods we see, What then so cheerful as the Holly-tree? "

ROBERT SOUTHEY, "The Holly Tree," 1798

◄ Frankincense resin
The fragrant gum oozes from cuts in the trunk and hardens into tear-shaped droplets that can be collected after 10 days.

GROUP: EUDICOTS
FAMILY: BURSERACEAE
HEIGHT: 5–26 FT (1.5–8 M)
SPREAD: 3–13 FT (1–4 M)

Leaf Deciduous; lime green; oblong, with 6–9 paired lobes; about 4–10 in (10–25 cm) long

Flower Yellow-white; 4–5 spreading petals; around 1½ in (4 cm) in diameter

Fruit Pear-shaped, green; dry capsule containing 3–5 seeds; around ⅜ in (1 cm) long

Frankincense Tree

Boswellia sacra

This small, deciduous desert tree is famous for its sap, which is the main commercial source of frankincense, a popular form of incense that gives the tree its common name.

Frankincense has been traded for around **6,000 years**

This species grows in rocky limestone gullies in the deserts of Somalia and Yemen and on escarpment mountains along the south coast of Oman. In the most exposed situations, the base of its trunk swells, helping it cling to boulders or rock faces.

While *Boswellia sacra* sap is the main source of incense resin, the bark of all 23 species of *Boswellia* produce an aromatic sap, which may repel wood-boring insects. The sap oozes from any gash in the tree trunk, solidifying to seal the wound. Its antibacterial and antifungal qualities help the tree survive, and its protective properties are particularly important in the harsh environments in which it grows.

To extract the resin, the trunk is slashed and the secretion is scraped off the tree or collected from the ground as it drips off. Reddish resin off the bark is considered inferior to pale-colored resin solidified on the ground. Attempts to establish plantations have largely failed, and locals maintain that the best frankincense comes from wild trees. In recent decades, this has led to trees being overharvested. In Oman, trees are heavily browsed by sheep and goats and rarely produce seed, limiting the establishment of new trees.

Besides incense, frankincense is valued in the cosmetics and pharmaceutical industries. Preliminary medical research suggests that it may help treat arthritis.

► Frankincense tree
Frankincense can grow as a low, bushy shrub or a taller tree with spreading branches. Its trunk has a swollen base and papery, peeling bark.

Cylindrical bowl with ibis and snake imagery—symbols of virility and fertility

► Bronze incense burner
This mid-1st millennium BCE incense burner from southwestern Arabia hearkens back to a time when incense was considered precious and its trade was of great importance.

Green Tea

Fig.15.

Fig.16 *Fig.17*

Fig.12

Fig.10 *Fig.11*

Fig.13

Fig.9

Fig.14

Fig.4 *Fig.5*

T *Fig.1.*

Fig.2 *Fig.3.*

Fig.6. *Fig.7.* *Fig.8*

Painted & Engrav'd by J. Miller.   Publish'd according to Act of Parliament Dec 10.ᵗʰ 1771.

GROUP: EUDICOTS

FAMILY: THEACEAE

HEIGHT: UP TO 30 FT (9 M)

SPREAD: UP TO 8 FT (2.5 M)

Leaves Evergreen; oval with toothed margins; shiny, bright green surface; whorled; 2–6 in (5–15 cm) long

Flower Borne singly or in clusters, fragrant, 6–8 white petals; up to 1½ in (4 cm) across

Fruits Oblong capsules; up to 1¼ in (3 cm) long; with one or two chambers, each with one seed

◄ **Botanical detail**
This 18th-century plate shows the botanical features of the tea plant. The flowers have two rings of petals—two to four large, showy petals and smaller, greenish outer ones.

▲ **Tea ceremony**
In Japan, people have been drinking tea since the 8th century CE, initially for medicinal purposes, then as a social ritual, as shown in this 19th-century woodcut.

Tea

Camellia sinensis

A small, evergreen tree or shrub related to garden camellias is the source of the second most consumed drink in the world, after water. The species may have originated in the mountains of Myanmar.

Around 5,000 years ago, some inquiring humans found that, by brewing them in boiling water, the bitter leaves of a low-growing, evergreen tree in their local hills could be made into a palatable and pleasantly invigorating drink. This discovery would go on to be a significant one for humankind—not just in terms of dietary implications, but also cultural and economic ones.

While tea leaves are still chewed raw or pickled and eaten, in parts of Southeast Asia, the Chinese have been using the leaves to make drinks from as far back as 2737 BCE.

Tea cultivation spread rapidly across China and Myanmar, and today, it is impossible to recognize truly "wild" tea plants. Tea was first brought to Europe in 1610 and became a popular drink soon after, brought in bulk from China. In an effort to retain control of this burgeoning industry, China

► **Seed capsules**
The fruit is an oblong or round capsule that ripens from green to brown. It comprises one to three chambers, each with a seed. An oil extracted from the seeds can be used for cooking.

Oblong fruit capsule
splits open to reveal chambers, each with one round seed that is ½ in (1.4 cm) across

Round capsule
with one seed

BOSTON TEA PARTY

In 1773, American colonists in Massachusetts boarded the East India Company's ships moored in Boston Harbor and threw three shiploads of tea overboard in protest of the unfair taxes imposed on tea by the British government. British retaliation to this act of defiance precipitated the American Revolution.

ENGRAVING FROM
THE HISTORY OF NORTH AMERICA (1789)

In 1823, a new type of tea plant was discovered in the rainforest of Assam. Growing in the shade of taller trees, it was considered too tender for cultivation and was crossbred with Chinese tea plants to make them more robust. These hybrids formed the basis of the tea plantations in northeast India and became the main strain planted elsewhere in the tropics over the subsequent century. China tea (*Camellia sinensis* var. *sinensis*) has smaller leaves that produce a lighter, more flowery flavor than those of Assam tea (*Camellia sinensis* var. *assamica*).

Cultivation and production

Tea can grow into medium-sized trees, but only a few are allowed to reach full height to provide seeds for future plantings. The majority are pruned back to a height of about 3 ft (1 m), producing a spreading, flat "plucking table" of stems for hand-picking, which is considered more selective and efficient than using a mechanical harvester.

▼ **Picking tea leaves**
Good-quality tea is hand-picked mainly by female workers, who pluck just the terminal bud and two or three leaves beneath it. Each worker can gather up to 77 lb (35 kg) in a day.

blocked the export of tea plants to other countries. For this reason, in the early 19th century, botanical adventurers from Europe traveled around China, disguised as locals, collecting tea seedlings for the English East India Company's tea plantations in Sikkim and Assam in India.

To produce green tea, the freshly picked leaves are steamed and dried, which locks in their green color and grassy taste. For black tea, the leaves are first "withered" with hot air to remove moisture. They are then rolled and shredded through machinery that ruptures the plant cells before being "fermented" in a warm, dry atmosphere. This induces chemical changes in the astringency and bitterness of the tea, which is then dried and graded for sale. Black tea contains about 2.5 percent of caffeine and green tea contains about 4.5 percent.

Growing tea

Tea grows best in areas with moderate to high rainfall and high humidity all year round. It cannot survive extreme cold. In 2018, nearly 6.5 million tons (5.9 million tonnes) of tea was harvested worldwide. China produced 44 percent, mostly for home consumption, and India produced 23 percent, with other major exports from Kenya and Sri Lanka.

Chinese tea garden
In the 17th century, German Jesuit scholar Athanasius Kircher published this illustration as part of his treatise on China.

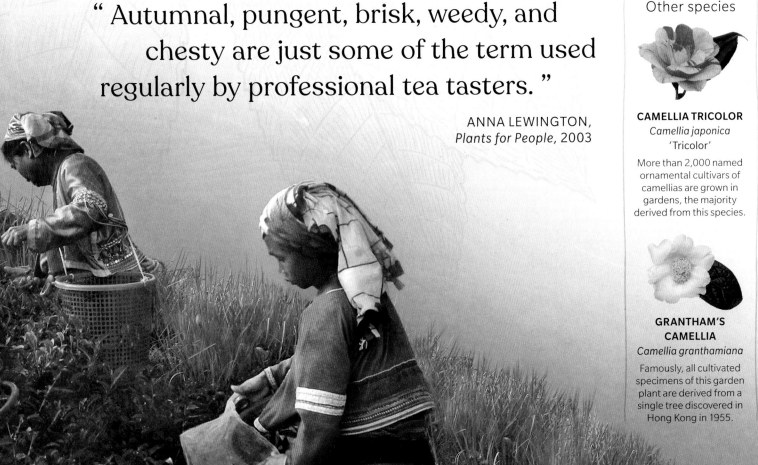

" Autumnal, pungent, brisk, weedy, and chesty are just some of the term used regularly by professional tea tasters. "

ANNA LEWINGTON,
Plants for People, 2003

Other species

CAMELLIA TRICOLOR
Camellia japonica 'Tricolor'

More than 2,000 named ornamental cultivars of camellias are grown in gardens, the majority derived from this species.

GRANTHAM'S CAMELLIA
Camellia granthamiana

Famously, all cultivated specimens of this garden plant are derived from a single tree discovered in Hong Kong in 1955.

Strega Martinazza   Strega Canidia

IL NOCE DI BENEVENTO
Nel' Ballo dello stesso nome. Atto I

Milano presso l'incisore Stucchi   Cost. Giocosi.

GROUP: EUDICOTS

FAMILY: JUGLANDACEAE

HEIGHT: UP TO 100 FT (30 M)

SPREAD: UP TO 50 FT (15 M)

Leaf Deciduous; pinnate, 5–9 pairs of leaflets, one large terminal leaflet; alternate; up to 6 in (15 cm) long

Catkin Male only with numerous small flowers, each with many stamens and no petals

Bark Smooth; gray; developing longitudinal fissures; young stems green to gray

◄ **Benevento walnut**

In Italian folklore, witches would gather under a sacred walnut in the town of Benevento to observe sabbaths. The story inspired the 1812 ballet *Il Noce di Benevento* by Viganò and Süssmayr.

Undeveloped remains of female flowers

Green husk must be removed to access the edible kernels, along with the shell. Husks can stain the skin

Tiny hairs can be seen on the surface of husks

▲ **Green husk**

Walnut fruits develop from small, green female flowers, usually in clusters of two to five at branch tips. An outer green husk encloses the woody shell.

Walnut

Juglans regia

This large, highly prized tree can be known as Persian walnut, Carpathian walnut, Madeira walnut, or English walnut. Its story is inextricably linked to that of humans.

A deciduous tree often found in woodland, riverbanks, and field borders, walnut has striking leaves, a short trunk, and a wide crown. Its valuable nuts and timber have made it an important commodity in human civilizations, and it has been transported so widely that its origin has been obscured. Genetic studies suggest the tree results from a cross between two wild species, most likely in Asia. Today, it can be found in seminatural forests from China through Central Asia to southern Europe; it is cultivated in northern Europe, the Americas, Australia and

New Zealand, and elsewhere. Glaciation has also played a major role in the current distribution of walnut. Walnut trees were once widely spread across Europe and Asia, but during periods of glacial advance in the Pleistocene, their population gradually shifted south to ice-free locales known as refugia. A relatively small walnut tree population may have ended up in present-day Iran; other theories suggest numerous refugia, ranging from China to Spain. Either way,

> **Walnuts** can cause **allergic reactions** in some people, some of which can be **life-threatening**

Other species

BLACK WALNUT
Juglans nigra

Native across much of eastern North America; deciduous tree that produces edible nuts and wood of great commercial value.

BUTTERNUT
Juglans cinerea

Close relative of black walnut, similarly native to eastern North America. Nuts can produce a butterlike oil.

"Wenwan walnuts" are pairs of walnuts collected **in China** and used to **reduce stress**

Male pollen catkins emerge below the branch tips, whereas female flowers emerge directly from the tips

" A thing which I regret ... is that I have never in my life planted a walnut. "

GEORGE ORWELL, "A Good Word for the Vicar of Bray," 1946

▼ Seed dispersal
Walnuts rely on rodents and other animals to disperse their seeds. Some are consumed, but many are hoarded and ultimately forgotten.

walnut began to spread away from such safe strongholds after temperatures began to rise, aided by human intervention. Within its Eurasian distribution, it is essentially impossible to tell whether a given walnut is "native," and the question is largely thought to be redundant.

Walnut is a tree with many uses. The edible kernels are probably the best-known product, eaten raw; used as toppings; or baked into cakes, pies, and baklava. They may be pressed for oil or processed into walnut butter. Kernels can be candied or pickled, and immature fruits with shells yet to

harden are pickled or used to flavor liqueurs. Walnuts have a wide range of medicinal uses and the shells (hulls) produce a dark brown dye. Walnut timber is highly valued, especially the dark heartwood, and it is used to manufacture furniture, gun stocks, musical instruments, and veneer.

Competing species

Walnut trees seldom have grasses growing under their canopies, but few other plants. This is in part because the tree shades out competitors, and its extensive root system outcompetes other plants for water and nutrients. However, another

Squirrels are known to be fond of walnuts as a food source

PISTOLS AT DAWN

When bitter rivals US Vice President Aaron Burr and former Treasury Secretary Alexander Hamilton met in 1804 to settle their differences in a duel, a pair of pistols with walnut stocks were their weapons of choice. Hamilton later died of his wounds. Walnut wood is used in gun stocks, as it is hard and durable.

THE BURR-HAMILTON DUEL

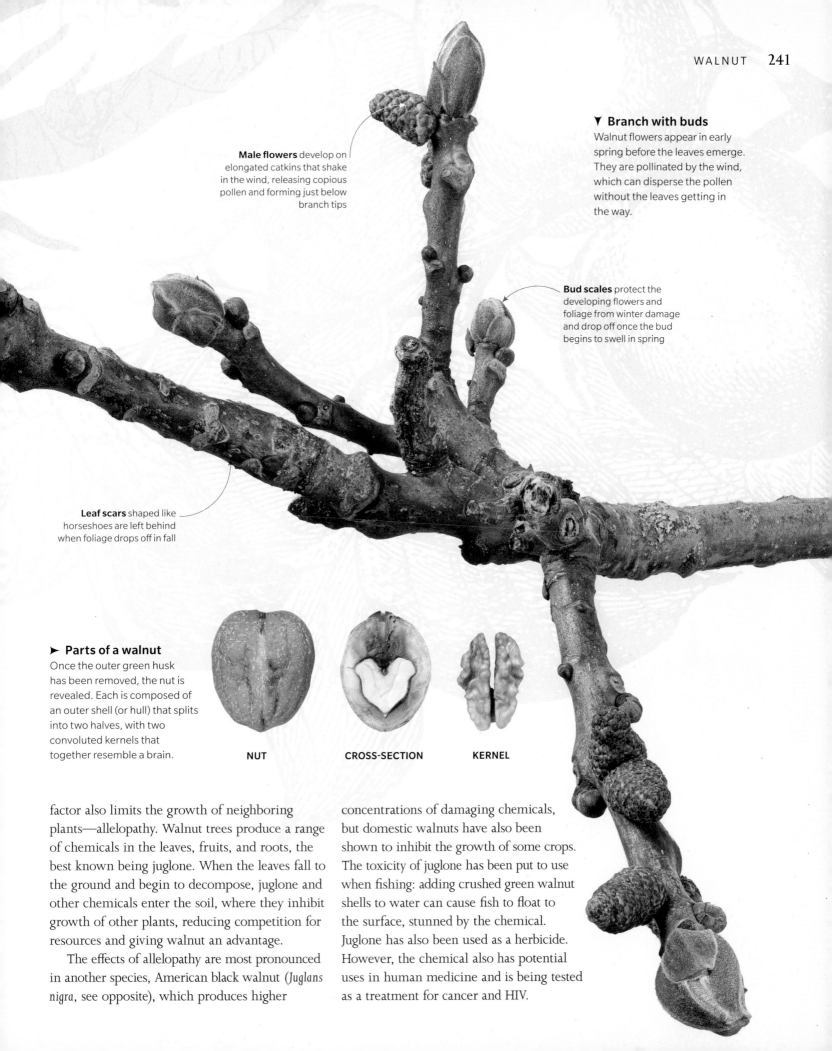

Male flowers develop on elongated catkins that shake in the wind, releasing copious pollen and forming just below branch tips

▼ Branch with buds
Walnut flowers appear in early spring before the leaves emerge. They are pollinated by the wind, which can disperse the pollen without the leaves getting in the way.

Bud scales protect the developing flowers and foliage from winter damage and drop off once the bud begins to swell in spring

Leaf scars shaped like horseshoes are left behind when foliage drops off in fall

► Parts of a walnut
Once the outer green husk has been removed, the nut is revealed. Each is composed of an outer shell (or hull) that splits into two halves, with two convoluted kernels that together resemble a brain.

NUT   **CROSS-SECTION**   **KERNEL**

factor also limits the growth of neighboring plants—allelopathy. Walnut trees produce a range of chemicals in the leaves, fruits, and roots, the best known being juglone. When the leaves fall to the ground and begin to decompose, juglone and other chemicals enter the soil, where they inhibit growth of other plants, reducing competition for resources and giving walnut an advantage.

The effects of allelopathy are most pronounced in another species, American black walnut (*Juglans nigra*, see opposite), which produces higher concentrations of damaging chemicals, but domestic walnuts have also been shown to inhibit the growth of some crops. The toxicity of juglone has been put to use when fishing: adding crushed green walnut shells to water can cause fish to float to the surface, stunned by the chemical. Juglone has also been used as a herbicide. However, the chemical also has potential uses in human medicine and is being tested as a treatment for cancer and HIV.

GROUP: EUDICOTS

FAMILY: ERICACEAE

HEIGHT: UP TO 40 FT (12 M)

SPREAD: UP TO 10 FT (3 M)

Leaf Evergreen; undersides usually covered in white or brown fur; alternate; up to 8 in (20 cm) long

Flowers Color variations include pink, red, and white; appear in April and May

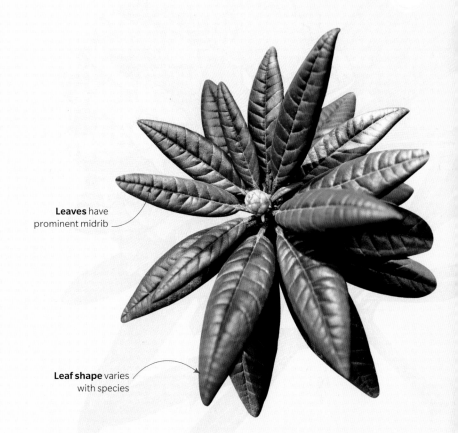

Leaves have prominent midrib

Leaf shape varies with species

◄ **Beauty of Nepal**

The tallest of the rhododendrons, *Rhododendron arboreum* forests are an arresting site when in full bloom in spring, painting the slopes of the Himalayas.

Tree Rhododendron

Rhododendron arboreum

Rhododendrons comprise one of the largest groups of trees and shrubs, with examples found on the highest mountain slopes of Asia, as well as in the gardens of Europe and America. Tree rhododendron is one of the best-known species, noted for its beautiful flowers and its stature.

The tallest of the rhododendrons, and living up to its scientific name *arboreum*, or treelike, the tree rhododendron can reach heights of up to 40 ft (12 m). Native across the Himalayas, when in bloom, it forms dramatic flowering forests, and it has been designated the national flower of Nepal. Tree rhododendron grows mostly at the lower altitudes of its mountainous native range; however, a few hardier subspecies occur at higher elevations.

The name "rhododendron" means "rose tree," reflecting the pink color of its blooms, but flowers of the various rhododendron species come in almost every color. The first recorded flowering of tree rhododendron in cultivation occurred in the south of England in 1826, and a trend for rhododendron collecting followed in the 19th century, with landowners devoting great sums to fill their gardens. This led to a great expansion in plant hunting, especially in China, resulting in many well-known

▲ **Tree rhododendron leaves**

Glossy green with deep veins, tree rhododendron leaves are crowded toward the end of branches. Their bold color and simple shape gives tree rhododendron its distinctive foliage.

Leaves collected and stored in an airtight jar are used in herbal remedies

► **Marsh Northern Labrador tea**

The leaves of the shrub *Rhododendron tomentosum* are collected for various uses, including herbal remedies. It is also called wild rosemary, marsh tea, and marsh rosemary.

Indian Rose bay -
Rhododendron -
Arboreum -

Cultivars

JEAN MARIE

Rhododendron 'The Honourable
Jean Marie de Montague'

Dates from 1921; produces the most intense
scarlet blooms of any rhododendron cultivar.

PERCY WISEMAN

Rhododendron 'Percy Wiseman'

Compact cultivar; owes its small size to its
Rhododendron yakushimanum parentage. Cream
flowers flushed with pink fade to white.

SNEEZY

Rhododendron 'Sneezy'

Small *Rhododendron yakushimanum*
cultivar. New leaves emerge silver; deep
pink red-spotted blooms.

◄ Botanical record
As Westerners traveled the Himalayas, they cataloged any new species they encountered. Painted illustrations, like this *Rhododendron arboreum* by Margaret Cockburn, soon caught the eye of gardeners back home.

► Himalayan view
Rhododendron arboreum blooms early in spring and its flowers are sometimes damaged by frost. Flowers can be pink, red, or white and are flecked inside with dark nectar pouches (nectaries) at the base.

A tree at Mount Japfu in India holds the Guinness World Record for the tallest tree rhododendron, at 108 ft (33 m)

garden plants being introduced alongside these popular shrubs. The collecting craze hugely increased the diversity of garden plants in Britain and other parts of Europe, but also led to a boom in invasive species, including another species of rhododendron, *Rhododendron ponticum*, which threatened a variety of natural habitats and which became the subject of many costly eradication programs.

A tree among shrubs

Many rhododendrons are shrubs or small trees—and often these are the most widely cultivated species in Europe—but rhododendrons have adapted to a range of habitats, with many different growth forms. Within the genus, *Rhododendron arboreum* is one of the most substantial trees, with a columnar, upright habit, and may be either narrow with a single stem or may have many branches growing out from its base. It may take up to 50 years to grow to its full height and width. Its large leaves are stiff and leathery with a glossy, dark green coloration.

Tree rhododendron remains a popular decorative tree grown in gardens in Europe, beloved for its bright blooms and handsome foliage. As with many rhododendrons, the flowers are often large and are quick to attract pollinators, including birds, butterflies, and bees—the showy floral displays of tree rhododendron so beloved by gardeners are entirely for the benefit of animal pollinators.

It is a relatively low-maintenance species for gardeners but is prone to several diseases, including petal blight and honey fungus. It may also be attacked by pests, including caterpillars and aphids.

Within the *Rhododendron* genus are a subset of shrub species known as azaleas. Previously treated as an entirely separate genus, azaleas are mostly deciduous, unusually for rhododendrons.

▼ Hairstreak butterfly habitat
Invasive rhododendron has negative effects in ecosystems but also provides some benefits: bumblebees feed on its nectar, and it is part of the preferred habitat for green hairstreak butterflies.

Distinctive green coloration on underside of wings

Leaves have prominent teeth around the edges and a coarse texture

Male flowers are green with no petals. In bud, each is enclosed within red-tipped sepals

GROUP: EUDICOTS	
FAMILY: MORACEAE	
HEIGHT: UP TO 50 FT (15 M)	
SPREAD: UP TO 26 FT (8 M)	

Leaf Deciduous; egg-shaped, heart-shaped, or lobed; toothed edges; alternate; up to 12 in (30 cm)

Fruit Each mulberry is a syncarp, formed by the merging of numerous small, fleshy fruits

Bark Gray-brown, smooth to furrowed; young stems pale brown with lenticels and leaf scars

◄ Buds and leaves
Mulberry flowers are produced in spring on short catkins. Male catkins are longer than female catkins and can be produced either on the same tree or on separate trees.

White Mulberry

Morus alba

Mulberry is a tree with different personas. It was coveted by royalty as a source of silk, yet its vigorous habit and weedy nature make it a pest in some regions.

Trees with many uses are often transported by people as they migrate, and so it has been with white mulberry. Its exact origins are unclear—China is a likely candidate—but it now grows widely across Europe and Asia and has been introduced to the Americas, South Africa, and Australia. Mulberry leaves can be made into tea; its bark made into paper and textiles; and its fruits eaten, dried, or made into wine. The tree is often grown as an ornamental, especially the weeping mulberry with its drooping branches,

and its extracts are used in Eastern medicine. Its most celebrated purpose, however, is as the preferred foodstuff for caterpillars of the silk moth (*Bombyx mori*). Demand for luxurious silk fabrics has driven the spread of white mulberry around the world.

Source of silk
Silk is the main reason why white mulberry is planted. The relationship between tree and silkworm is ancient, dating back more than

When **male flowers** open, the stamen filaments flex like springs, catapulting the pollen at over **half the speed of sound**

► Mulberry myth
Two ill-fated Babylonian lovers, Pyramus and Thisbe, meet an untimely end under a mulberry tree. Their blood is said to have turned the white fruit of the mulberry black.

► **Stages of fruit growth**
Despite their name, most white mulberry fruits are dark purple or black when ripe. A mulberry syncarp is a collection of multiple small, fleshy fruits, each one derived from a separate flower within an inflorescence.

Female inflorescences bear small, green, petal-less flowers, each topped with a stigma to collect pollen

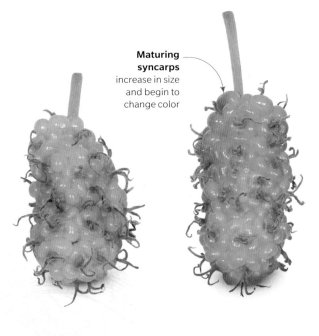

Maturing syncarps increase in size and begin to change color

White mulberry was probably introduced into Europe before **1596**

5,000 years. Silk moths are one of the very few insects to be domesticated and the modern moth differs starkly from its closest relation, the wild silk moth (*Bombyx mandarina*). Domestic silk moths cannot fly and lack any color. Protected from predators, they tolerate living in groups and being handled by people. This characteristic is important, because while wild male silk moths would fly around the forest in search of flightless females to mate with, today's domestic moths need people to facilitate reproduction. Their larvae, the silkworms, feed voraciously on mulberry leaves, ultimately forming a silken cocoon in which to pupate. This cocoon is the source of the fibers used to make silken fabric. Sericulture—the cultivation of silkworms—relies on a steady crop of mulberry leaves as food, and while white mulberry is favored, the silkworms also consume other mulberry species and some related trees.

Live fast, die young

White mulberry trees are noted weeds. Their many uses have ensured that people introduce them widely, but some aspects of their biology make them prone to spread beyond the areas under cultivation. Their small, fleshy fruits are popular food for many birds, which in turn act as effective providers of long-distance seed dispersal. The white mulberry tree is fast-growing and often short-lived, though it will occasionally live up to 500 years. Rapid growth is a useful characteristic in weeds, as it allows them to quickly overshadow their neighbors and compete effectively for light and soil nutrients. In North America, invasive white mulberries have begun to interbreed with the native red mulberry (*Morus rubra*), and the two are difficult to distinguish from each other. Red mulberry

◄ **Cleaning silkworm cocoons**
Silk is derived from the cocoon produced by the silkworm. Cocoons are boiled, killing the silkworm and making the fibers easier to unravel. Each cocoon is built from a single thread up to 2,950 ft (900 m) long.

Stigma remains are visible on the surface of each small fruit and persist until maturity

When ripe, the syncarp is black, although some trees have red or white ripe fruits

leaves usually have a hairy underside, while white mulberry leaves do not. Intermediates with some leaf hairs suggest that introduced white mulberries are now sharing genes with native reds. Studies show that white mulberry trees and their hybrids outcompete native red mulberries, and the long-term future of wild red mulberries is now at risk.

Given the ease with which mulberry species interbreed, it is not surprising that the different mulberry species can be difficult to identify. What makes this harder is that the leaves vary considerably in shape, ranging from unlobed to deeply lobed. The leaves of young plants often look completely different from those of mature plants. The fruits, too, do not aid identification: despite their names, the white mulberry, red mulberry, and black mulberry all produce purple-black fruit when ripe. While certain white mulberry trees do have ripe fruit that is white, they are rare in the wild. Both black and red mulberry trees produce fruits with a sweeter taste than those of white mulberry. The invasive white mulberry, though very useful for producing silk, is not the best choice for a garden mulberry tree.

THE MULBERRY BUSH SONG

This English nursery rhyme, beginning "Here we go round the mulberry bush," is one of several in Europe, with the mulberry sometimes replaced with bramble or juniper. Some historians connect the song to a women's prison in the city of Wakefield, England, where prisoners circled a mulberry tree in the prison yard for exercise. This picture is from British illustrator and painter Walter Crane's *The Baby's Opera* (1877).

ILLUSTRATION OF THE POPULAR SONG

" With time and patience, the mulberry leaf becomes a silk gown. "

CHINESE PROVERB, DATE UNKNOWN

Other species

BLACK MULBERRY
Morus nigra

Similar to white mulberry but with sweeter fruits and smaller stature. Occurs in Europe and Asia; native range uncertain.

RED MULBERRY
Morus rubra

Sparsely distributed across eastern North America. The tallest of the three mulberries; has distinctly hairy leaf undersides.

Sacred Fig

Ficus religiosa

Celebrated as the tree beneath which the prophet Buddha attained enlightenment, the sacred fig tree from the forests of northern India, Nepal, and Pakistan has been widely planted in tropical regions. However, it relies on a species of wasp to set seed and spread naturally.

GROUP: EUDICOTS
FAMILY: MORACEAE
HEIGHT: UP TO 100 FT (30 M)
SPREAD: UP TO 100 FT (30 M)

Leaf Evergreen; broadly oval or almost triangular; alternate; 4–6 in (10–15 cm) long, including tip

Bark Gray; smooth texture; develops fluting and buttressing as it matures

In its native forest habitat in the foothills of the Himalayas, the veteran sacred fig (known locally as "Bodhi" or "Peepul") is an impressive tree. It is usually evergreen, but it can shed its leaves during droughts. Its life begins when a bird perches on the branch of another tree to eat a fig fruit. As the bird pecks at the sweet flesh, it scatters a few seeds, or the seeds pass through its gut and out in its droppings. The seed then germinates and the seedling begins life as an epiphyte, growing on the host tree.

Strangler figs

The young tree soon sprouts aerial roots that dangle down to the soil below. As the fig tree develops, the hanging roots encircle the trunk of the host tree, restricting its growth, while the branches and leaves smother the host's foliage, so it can no longer photosynthesize and eventually dies. The aerial roots then coalesce together to form the massive trunk of a free-standing fig tree, which can extend up to a diameter of 10 ft (3 m) in maturity. Some lower roots spread outward at an angle, forming a buttress that props up the tree during storms.

Sacred figs can also grow like typical trees, from seeds germinating in the soil, but some other species of fig always begin life as epiphytes. Because fig trees do not penetrate

or parasitize the host tree but simply smother it, they are also known as "strangler figs" or "curtain figs."

Welcome shade

It is easy to imagine why humans, when they began to clear the forests, might have left this distinctive, wide-spreading tree standing as a landmark and a welcome source of shade. Buddhists believe that, in the 6th century BCE, the Buddha attained enlightenment beneath one such tree. The tree in question, in Bihar, India, is long dead. However, legend has it that in 288 BCE, a Sri Lankan princess, who had converted to Buddhism, took a cutting from the tree and planted it back home in Anuradhapura. A massive tree still grows there and is claimed to be the oldest living human-planted angiosperm (flowering plant) in the world. Sacred figs are also revered by Hindus, who believe that the god Vishnu—responsible for the preservation of the Universe—was born under it.

Sacred figs are widely planted in and around Hindu and Buddhist temples. The species has been introduced to other tropical countries with a Buddhist tradition, including Myanmar, Thailand, Vietnam, and southern parts of China. In the Middle East, the Philippines, and

> # " Among the trees, I am the *ashvattha* (sacred fig tree) "
>
> LORD KRISHNA, *Bhagvad Gita,*
> 1st century CE

◄ Fig gatherers
This modern copy of a 19th-century BCE painting from an Egyptian tomb shows workers gathering edible figs (in this case, *Ficus carica*).

▲ Ancient figs
These sacred figs in Hsipaw, Myanmar, are at least 200 years old. Their fluted trunks formed from merged aerial roots that grew from seedlings perched on long-dead tree hosts.

Flask-shaped syconium (fruiting body) filled with sweet flesh and seeds

▲ Cultivated figs
Edible figs come from varieties of common fig, first cultivated in Jericho around 9400 BCE.

Other species

COMMON FIG
Ficus carica

Cultivated varieties of this low-growing shrub yield edible figs; can produce fruits without pollination by wasps.

Nicaragua, it is planted in parks and as an avenue or roadside tree. In the US, it is cultivated in southern California, Florida, and Hawaii (which has a substantial Buddhist community). The sacred fig tree cannot spread in most of the countries to which it has been introduced because it is unable to set seed there. This stems from the fact that the fig species have evolved distinctive flowers, adapted to a unique system of pollination. As in all figs, the tiny flowers, both male and female, of sacred figs are hidden inside a hollow, oval chamber called a syconium. This unripe, fruitlike growth is formed from the swollen base of the inflorescence. The syconium eventually forms the fig fruit, and the flowers develop into the massed seeds inside the fruit. First, though, pollination has to occur.

Elongated leaf tip speeds runoff of water, minimizing damage in rainstorms

A sacred fig tree in **Anuradhapura, Sri Lanka,** is believed to be **2,300 years** old

Unique pollination

For pollination, the 750 different species of fig rely on around 650 species of wasp in the family Agaonidae, colloquially referred to as fig wasps. Certain fig species can be pollinated by several species of fig wasps, but most rely on just one. They can only form their fruits after pollination by their specific wasp, and, in turn, the wasps can only lay eggs in the

syconium of their associated species of fig. The one exception is cultivated varieties of common fig (*Ficus carica*), which humans have selectively bred to be able to set seed without being pollinated.

Sacred wasp

The sole pollinator wasp for sacred fig is a species called *Blastophaga quadraticeps*. This wasp is not found in most countries where the tree has been introduced, so the fig trees cannot produce ripe fruits there. Two exceptions are Israel and Florida. Somehow, the pollinator wasp has reached Israel and become established alongside sacred figs, allowing the trees to produce ripe fruits bearing seeds that can be dispersed by local birds. In Florida, too, sacred figs occasionally produce ripe fruits. *Blastophaga quadraticeps* wasps have never been recorded there, so it is possible that the fig wasp that pollinates the native Florida strangler fig (*Ficus aurea*) can also pollinate the introduced species.

A useful tree

The sacred fig tree has various herbal and other uses. Its bark and leaves are used to treat diarrhea and dysentery, and its leaves are used in a poultice for boils and as an antidote against venomous bites. Tannins from its bark are used to dye cloth, and its wood—although generally considered to be of low quality—is used in the manufacture of miscellaneous items such as crates, bowls, and spoons.

Distinctive leaf shape is recognizable as that of sacred fig

Square railing around trunk indicates a sacred tree

◄ Offerings to the Bodhi Tree
This 2nd-century CE temple carving from southern India shows worshippers making offerings of water to the sacred Bodhi Tree.

Flexible leaf stalk

Egg-shaped leaves have 5–7 pairs of veins on either side of a midvein

FIGS AND THEIR WASPS

Pregnant fig wasps enter unripe syconiums to lay their eggs. In the process, they deposit pollen picked up earlier, fertilizing female flowers. Male wasps hatch first, impregnating the unhatched females before dying off. Once hatched, pregnant female wasps gather pollen from mature male flowers and escape, in search of another syconium to lay their eggs.

Fig wasps squeeze in and out through opening near tip of fig (ostiole)

Male and female flowers line inside of syconium

The wasp lays eggs within some female flowers, transferring pollen to stigmas from her forelegs

FIG WASP POLLINATION

▲ Sacred fig foliage

The leathery, oval leaves of sacred fig start off pinkish, turning coppery, and then dark green. Tiny flowers are produced inside green, flask-shaped vessels called syconia, which, upon pollination, ripen into edible fruits.

High-altitude haven
The highest mountain range in the world—the Himalayas in Asia—is home to trees such as oaks, pines, and firs. Not only do such trees thrive in harsh climes, but they support a variety of local fauna as well. Himalayan natives such as deodar cedar (*Cedrus deodara*) provide food and shelter to more than 600 species of birds.

GROUP: EUDICOTS

FAMILY: MORACEAE

HEIGHT: UP TO 100 FT (30 M)

SPREAD: UP TO 330 FT (100 M)

Leaf Evergreen; hairy stalk; dark green, broadly oval, leathery, downy underneath; alternate; up to 8 in (20 cm) long

Flower Tiny and enclosed in figlike "syconium"

Bark Fluted, gray, smooth, downy when young

Other species

FLORIDA STRANGLER FIG

Ficus aurea

"Strangler" found in mangrove swamps from Florida and the Caribbean south to Panama.

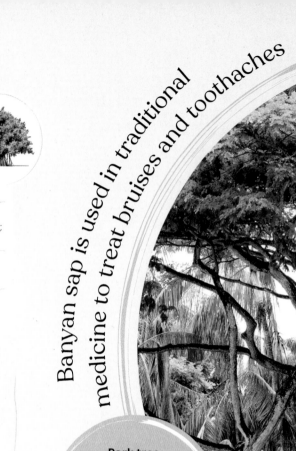

Banyan sap is used in traditional medicine to treat bruises and toothaches

Park tree
This large banyan grows in a public park in Singapore City. Banyans are often planted in tropical regions, mainly for the dense shade they offer.

Banyan

Ficus benghalensis

This evergreen tree has a claim to be the world's largest tree. As its branches grow outward, it puts down aerial roots that become new trunks, eventually forming huge patches.

Like sacred fig (see pp.250–253), banyan usually begins life as an epiphyte—growing in the branch of another tree. As it grows, it sends out aerial roots that reach down to the soil and supply nutrients to the growing tree. Eventually, it smothers and strangles its host tree and then continues growing without competition. Some of the aerial roots become trunks, and their spreading branches continue the process of expansion. It is said to be the only species in which a single tree can eventually form a forest. The largest known specimen, growing in Andhra Pradesh, India, has a canopy that covers an area of 4.7 acres

(1.9 hectares). It would take nearly nine minutes to walk around its perimeter at a standard walking speed.

Indian icon

Banyan is native to monsoon forests and rainforests at elevations of 1,640–3,940 ft (500–1,200 m) from India to Malaysia. Its fruit is edible but is mainly eaten when other foods are not available. India's national tree, the banyan is considered sacred by Hindus and Buddhists and is often grown near temples.

▼ **Dusky leaf monkey**
The leaves and fruit of banyan trees provide a source of food for various animals, including this species of monkey.

Rainbow Eucalyptus

Eucalyptus deglupta

GROUP: EUDICOTS

FAMILY: MYRTACEAE

HEIGHT: UP TO 250 FT (75 M)

SPREAD: UP TO 125 FT (38 M)

Leaf Evergreen; oval when young, turning lance-shaped; opposite; up to 6 in (15 cm)

Flower Tiny, like a powder puff, with many white stamens in small clusters

A member of the diverse eucalyptus genus, this looming evergreen is best known for the vivid coloration that can be seen when its bark peels.

There are more than 500 eucalyptus species, the vast majority in Australia and Tasmania. They are generally tall, slim, elegant trees, often with stringy bark, and leaves that vary in shape between juvenile and adult trees. Rainbow eucalyptus is one of the few species in the genus that grow elsewhere—its native range is humid, tropical forests with high rainfall in Indonesia, Papua New Guinea, and the island of Mindanao in the Philippines (leading to an alternative common name, Mindanao gum). This makes it the only eucalypt indigenous to the northern hemisphere.

This fast-growing tree, named after the kaleidoscope of colors revealed as the bark peels from its trunk, tends to be less colorful when grown outside the tropics. It is widely cultivated elsewhere for wood pulp used in paper production. It is also planted as an urban street or shade tree, but its shallow roots and brittle branches make it susceptible to storm damage. It is invasive in Florida and Hawaii.

In the right conditions, a rainbow eucalyptus can grow up to 6 ft (1.8 m) in a single year

Leaves turn dark green later in life; they are pinkish when young

▶ Eucalyptus oil
Aromatic oils found in rainbow eucalyptus leaves have a fruity smell and were used in traditional medicine.

▲ Colorful giant
Bark peels in strips off the trunk, revealing underbark that can be green, blue, purple, or bronze-red, depending on the degree of weathering.

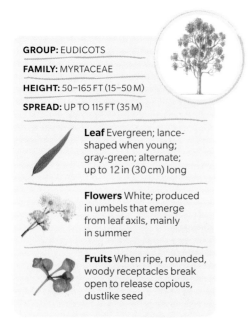

GROUP: EUDICOTS

FAMILY: MYRTACEAE

HEIGHT: 50–165 FT (15–50 M)

SPREAD: UP TO 115 FT (35 M)

Leaf Evergreen; lance-shaped when young; gray-green; alternate; up to 12 in (30 cm) long

Flowers White; produced in umbels that emerge from leaf axils, mainly in summer

Fruits When ripe, rounded, woody receptacles break open to release copious, dustlike seed

▲ **River red gum bark**
The bark is smooth and white or cream with patches of yellow, pink, or brown. Loose slabs of bark near the base were used in canoe building.

River Red Gum

Eucalyptus camaldulensis

Endemic to most of Australia, and with the widest natural distribution of any eucalyptus, river red gum is a distinctive evergreen that is one of the most iconic of all Australian trees.

Found growing near many watercourses across inland Australia, where they provide welcome shade, eucalyptus trees such as river red gum are dense, upright, and spreading. They are fast growing and rapidly become large: trunks of some specimens have a circumference up to 16 ft (5 m). Estimating the age of any particular specimen is difficult, but some may be as much as 1,000 years old.

As with other eucalypt species, river red gum's juvenile leaves differ from older ones. Roughly oval and gray-green as they emerge, they lengthen and narrow as they age, usually turning a more definite green. Clusters of white flowers are produced mainly in summer but can also appear at other times in warmer areas.

The species name *camaldulensis* derives from a private botanical garden near Naples in Italy—Hortus Camaldulensis di Napoli (or Camaldoli gardens)—where head gardener Friedrich Dehnhardt grew and studied the tree, writing the first botanical description of it in 1832. (The trees he grew were cut down in the 1920s.)

While the apparently dry sites in which it occurs may suggest it is drought-tolerant, *Eucalyptus camaldulensis* can thrive only where

▶ **River red gums in floodwaters**
The floodplain of the Murrumbidgee River, New South Wales, provides a perfect habitat for these trees, which need regular floods for growth. They are managed for timber production and provide a breeding ground for animals.

there is adequate underground water or in areas where flooding occurs often enough to replenish the water supply. It prefers clay soils that tend to stay moist even during hot, dry weather and is often a dominant species in grassy woodland adjacent to a large, permanent body of water.

In periods of drought, trees can shed up to two-thirds of their leaves, reducing their demand on the available water and preventing wilting. After a wet spell, the full canopy is restored. If particularly stressed, trees can shed entire branches and, in extreme cases, an entire tree may collapse, apparently with no warning.

Australian export

River red gum is now sometimes cultivated in parts of the world that enjoy a similar climate to its native Australia, both as a timber crop and for soil stabilization. It is used in agroforestry in places such as Sudan, where it protects crops from blowing sand. On marshy ground, it helps drain the soil and so manage potential breeding sites for mosquitoes. With its elegant form and attractive bark, it is often planted in avenues and gardens, but in South Africa, Jamaica, Spain, and some warmer states of the US, it is classed as an invasive species due to its propensity to spread by seed.

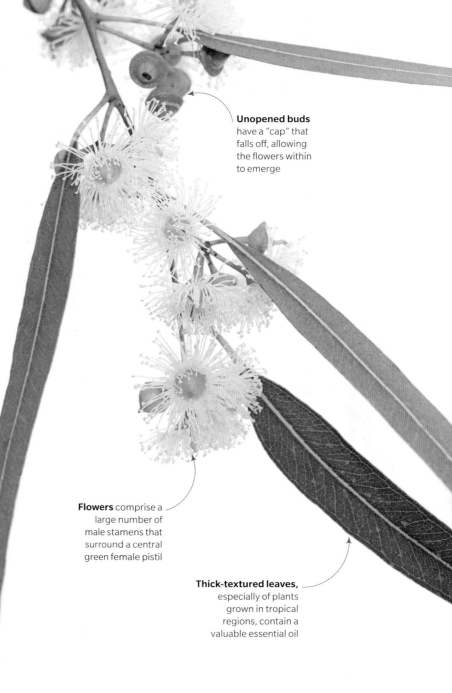

Unopened buds have a "cap" that falls off, allowing the flowers within to emerge

Flowers comprise a large number of male stamens that surround a central green female pistil

Thick-textured leaves, especially of plants grown in tropical regions, contain a valuable essential oil

▶ Flowering river red gum
Delicate white flowers are a perfect nectar source for bees and are produced even on very young trees. In suitably warm climates, river red gum trees can flower and set seed at any time of year.

GIANT EUCALYPTUS TREE

Many eucalypts, including *Eucalyptus camaldulensis,* are capable of growing to a considerable size. Felling a mature tree is a skilled operation, as illustrated in this engraving. To bring the tree down safely, the woodcutter must first make an angled cut to one side of the trunk before cutting on the opposite side, thus creating a central "hinge" that allows the tree to fall in the desired direction.

FELLING A EUCALYPTUS, PRINT

River red gum's **scientific name** comes from an **Italian monastery** where **a specimen was grown in the 1800s**

Its common name alludes to its wood, which is always a brilliant, almost blood red when cut. The color is caused by chemicals in the tree that form a natural biotic on exposure to the air, as was realized by Indigenous people who used it in their medicine. Essential oil extracted from the leaves is a powerful antiseptic and can also be used as disinfectant. These compounds protect the tree from disease and pest attack and make the timber extremely durable. For this reason, it has been used for fence posts and piers that need to withstand moisture. Indigenous people have various names for the tree, including *aper*, *kunjumarra*, and *ngapiri*. They used the wood to craft canoes, bowls, shields, and other utensils.

Red gums and ecology

River red gum trees are host to a number of species and play a valuable part in the ecosystem of any area where they occur. Mature trees sometimes develop cavities in the trunk—though these can take centuries to form—that become home to many animals, including bats and carpet pythons. The superb parrot (*Polytelis swainsonii*) is one of several species of birds that nest in its branches, while the flowers are an important food source for honey bees.

Where river red gum trees grow next to rivers and streams, their tendency to shed branches can become a positive benefit to some fish species, particularly river blackfish, which take shelter in any branches that fall into the water.

▲ Koala food
Eucalyptus leaves, such as those of the river red gum, form the mainstay of koalas' diet. While they are toxic to most animals, koalas have bacteria in their guts that metabolize the toxins and make the leaves safe to eat.

" ... there's always a bulky Red Gum here or somewhere else ... muscling into the eye, as it were ... "

MURRAY BAIL, *Eucalyptus*, 1998

Other species

TASMANIAN BLUE GUM
Eucalyptus globulus

Smooth-barked, fast-growing species known to reach heights of 180 ft (55 m); young plants are used in garden beds.

MOUNTAIN GUM
Eucalyptus dalrympleana

Striking species with gray-brown to red-brown bark that peels to reveal fresh, creamy white bark beneath.

SPINNING GUM
Eucalyptus perriniana

Small eucalyptus with white bark and silver leaves that appear to spin in the wind, hence the common name.

Flowers grow in large panicles; each flower has 10 stamens, of which usually only one is fertile

► **Ripening fruits and nuts**
Only a few flowers produce the fruit. This consists of the yellow, orange, or crimson enlarged base (the cashew "apple") and the "nut" that holds the kernel.

GROUP: EUDICOTS

FAMILY: ANACARDIACEAE

HEIGHT: 46 FT (14 M)

SPREAD: UP TO 39 FT (12 M)

Leaf Evergreen; hairless, thick, leathery; elliptic to obovate in shape; spiral; up to 8½ in (22 cm) long

Seed Kidney-shaped with a hard coat containing a single oily seed around ¾ in (2 cm) in length

The cashew "nut" has a double shell, which contains an acrid oil and the oily kernel

The fleshy cashew apple, about the size of a small pear, develops from the flower stalk and can be eaten

Cashew

Anacardium occidentale

A medium-sized evergreen, the cashew tree is native to northeast Brazil and southeast Venezuela. In the 1500s, the Portuguese took cashews to Goa, and today it is grown worldwide within the tropics, with Ivory Coast and India being the largest producers of the nut.

The **largest living cashew tree** grows in **Natal, Brazil**, and covers almost 2 acres (0.75 hectares).

The evergreen cashew tree, with its bushy branches and leathery leaves, is grown mainly for its nuts—some 4.4 million tons (4 million tonnes) are produced each year. Other parts of the tree have commercial uses, too.

The cashew tree grows up to 46 ft (14 m) tall; modern dwarf varieties, which reach just 20 ft (6 m), have been introduced to make picking easier. These also come into economic production earlier than wild varieties.

The cashew fruit is made of two parts—the swollen stalk and calyx that forms the cashew "apple" and the nuts (containing the seeds) that dangle below the apple. As the fruit ripens, the apple enlarges and becomes brightly colored.

or by heating, the oil can be used to treat timber infested with termites, for example. It is also used in varnishes or modified to form resins, which are used in epoxy materials with such purposes as fire retardants.

The fleshy apple can be eaten raw or used in cooking, such as curries. It may also be trodden or pressed to give a juice that can be fermented to make alcoholic drinks or used to flavor drinks. Cashew apples are easily bruised, so are only used locally.

Cashew timber is used for boat building, for construction, and as charcoal. The bark gives a yellow dye.

▲ Artist's rendition
This botanical illustration shows a flowering shoot with alternately arranged leaves. Details of various parts of the flower, fruit, and "nuts" are illustrated in the inset drawings.

" The cashew tree is handsome in appearance and dimensions ... "

US DEPARTMENT OF AGRICULTURE, *Foreign Agriculture: A Review of Foreign Farm Policy, Production, and Trade,* 1946

The nut has a hard double layer and encloses the mature seed. Between the layers is a honeycomb structure with spaces that are filled with an acrid oil called anacardic acid. This oil is a natural defense from being eaten before the nut has had a chance to fall to the ground and germinate. To make the nut edible, the poisonous oil has to be eliminated by a process of steaming, drying, and roasting. Poorer-quality or broken nuts are pressed to produce cashew nut oil, a dark yellow oil used in cooking or on salads.

The acrid oil from the between the layers of the nut has an industrial use, however. Once extracted from the nut, either by using solvents

► Giant cashew tree
This cashew in Pirangi do Norte, Brazil, is recorded as the largest in the world, with its branches extending around 164 ft (50 m) from its trunk and covering an area of many thousands of square feet.

GROUP: EUDICOTS

FAMILY: ANACARDIACEAE

HEIGHT: 100 FT (30 M)

SPREAD: 50 FT (15 M)

Leaves Evergreen; oblong-lanceolate with arching veins; alternate; 4–12 in (12–30 cm) long

Fruit Drupe 2–6 in (5–15 cm); green, purple, or yellowish skin; sweet, juicy pulp around large seed

Bark Gray-brown; becomes furrowed and cracks into small square gray plates with age

◄ In art and culture

Mango trees are a popular motif in art, culture, and literature from around the world. In this Indian miniature from around 1850, a prince meets with a princess under a mango tree.

Flowers grow in large, upright, and softly hairy panicles from the bud terminating the shoot

► Leaves and flower buds

This mango tree blossom was photographed in California. Mango trees are widely cultivated outside their native range, and there are several hundred cultivars.

Mango is the **national fruit** of India, Pakistan, and the Philippines, and is the **national tree** of Bangladesh

Shiny, dark green leaves have numerous lateral veins and wavy margins

Mango

Mangifera indica

This large, evergreen tree with deep green leaves and a wide spread is a familiar sight in warm climates across the world. It is best known for its sweet, fleshy fruits, which can be consumed in a variety of ways.

Mango fruits are extremely versatile and are edible at various stages of their development. When fully ripe, the flesh becomes very juicy and almost falls off the seed, leaving some fibrous bundles. At an earlier stage of ripeness, the flesh is more succulent and can be cut off the stone, or peeled and cut into squares, and when unripe, the fruit is not sweet but can be used to make chutneys and pickles. The skin of the mango is full of antioxidants and other useful compounds and the seed is also edible and is rich in vitamin C. The kernel or embryo (see p.266) is kidney-shaped, similar in appearance to a cashew kernel but much larger. Mature kernels are hard and bitter to the taste, but immature ones, which may be harvested when the unripe fruit is used for

Leaves are set alternately on the shoots but often cluster toward the tip

RELIGIOUS SIGNIFICANCE

The mango tree and its fruit have strong associations in religion. In Hinduism, the mango is regarded as a symbol of prosperity and happiness and is used in a number of religious ceremonies. In Buddhism, it is said that Gautama Buddha rested under a mango tree, while in Jainism, it is associated with the goddess Ambika.

BURMESE PAINTING OF BUDDHA

30–70 species are found. Mango may be native across India, but it is more likely that it originally came from the northeast of India along the border with Myanmar.

Mango does not tolerate frost, especially when young, and requires a subtropical and nearly frost-free climate. It can form a tree to 100 ft (30 m) but is more often seen in rural India as a broad-spreading tree whose evergreen branches provide shade during the heat before the monsoon and make a distinctive feature of the landscape. When a tree's fruiting days are over, its timber remains. The wood is somewhat vulnerable, as it has no natural resistance to fungal or insect attack and it is not widely traded. However, it can be used for making furniture, flooring, and certain musical instruments.

In bloom

The flowers of the mango tree are carried in large, multibranched panicles with stalks that are softly hairy and reddish brown in color. The individual flowers are small, measuring around $\frac{1}{8}$ in (4 mm), but are carried in such large numbers that when a tree is in full flower, the leaves are nearly hidden. An unusual feature of the mango flower is that only one of the five stamens matures to provide pollen, while the other four are sterile and minute.

The flowering time of the mango tree is dependent on the climate. In southern India, it starts flowering in December, with the fruit ripening three or four months later. However, in northern India, in regions such as the Punjab, flowering occurs in March or April and the mangoes ripen in July to August. The "Neelum" form can produce two crops a year in favorable southern locations.

▼ Inside seeds

The mango's seed is large—around 4 in (10 cm) in length—with a pale, gray-brown, furrowed coat. It forms around a sixth of the weight of the fruit.

Kernel or embryo contains nutrients and can be dried and powdered to use in cooking

chutneys, have a more pleasant taste and can be used in cooking. With mature fruits, the kernel is extracted from the seed case, dried, roasted, and ground. The resulting flour is called *guthli* and is a good source of protein, carbohydrates, and minerals; several medicinal uses are claimed for it, including reducing cholesterol and curing diarrhea. An oil or butter can be extracted from *guthli* that has a melting point of around body temperature, making it useful for moisturizing the skin. The oil contains roughly equal amounts of saturated and unsaturated fats, including 3–4 percent omega-6 fatty acids. Mangiferin, a chemical compound in the leaves and bark, is extracted for pharmacological uses. Urushiol, an irritant, is present in the skin or peel of the fruit and can affect some people, especially those who have been sensitized by exposure to poison ivy or poison oak or who have previously reacted to other members of the Anacardiaceae family to which *Mangifera* belongs.

The genus *Mangifera* is mainly found in Southeast Asia, from Myanmar to the Philippines, and in New Guinea, where most of the

Other species

PAHUTAN
Mangifera altissima
Species from Southeast Asia with fruits that are very sweet but smaller and more fibrous than those of *Mangifera indica*.

KUWENI
Mangifera odorata
Hybrid of mango and bachang; unknown in the wild. Planted in Southeast Asia; yellow-green fruits ripen to green.

BACHANG
Mangifera foetida
Native to Southeast Asia; also known as horse mango. Ripe fruit is edible but has a fetid smell; the sap in unripe fruits can cause skin blisters.

" Mango among fruits is as
        the Ganges among rivers. "

BENGALI PROVERB,
from *Cultural History of Bengali Proverbs*, 2010

▲ **Under the
mango tree**
Open-grown mango trees
in rural India, such as this,
typically have a wide
spread, providing shade
that is appreciated by both
people and cattle during
the heat of the day.

West Indies Mahogany

Swietenia mahagoni

Several species are known as mahogany in the timber trade, but this is the first one to be widely exploited for its durable, beautiful wood.

GROUP: EUDICOTS

FAMILY: MELIACEAE

HEIGHT: UP TO 82 FT (25 M)

SPREAD: 40–60 FT (12–18 M)

Leaf Semievergreen; 2–6 pairs of shiny green, oval leaflets; opposite; 4–6½ in (10–16 cm) long

Cone Brown, woody capsule up to 5 in (12 cm) long, held upright on a thick stalk

West Indies mahogany is native to the Bahamas, Cayman Islands, Cuba, Dominican Republic, Haiti, Jamaica, and southern Florida. Its timber has been exploited for over 500 years. As a result, its surviving populations have been severely depleted, and in most places it is considered "commercially extinct" because no large trees worth harvesting are left. Today, plantations in Indonesia, India, and Bangladesh are the last remaining source of "genuine mahogany." In Florida and many Caribbean islands, the species is instead planted as a shade tree along pavements, in parks, and in gardens.

Sought-after wood

This species was the first mahogany species imported to Europe, around 500 years ago. It was highly regarded for ship building because its timber is strong and resistant to decay. It holds its

Spanish Armada
The Spanish used mahogany to build a fleet of formidable, sturdy, fast ships for the invasion of England in 1588.

> " Mahogany was once the most sought-after cabinet wood in the world. "

JOHN K. FRANCIS, US Department of Agriculture Forest Service, 1991

shape well and was used by Spanish conquistadors to repair their ships in the Caribbean in the 16th century. The lustrous, richly colored wood was also used in high-quality furniture and cabinetwork by makers such as Chippendale and Hepplewhite in England.

The trees are semievergreen, shedding their leaves in droughts or cold spells. They are monoecious, meaning they have separate male and female flowers on the same plant. The flowers, which appear in spring, are small, with five greenish-white, waxy petals. After fertilization by bees and moths, the fruits develop slowly, usually with just one maturing on each leafy shoot. They are large, oval, woody capsules the size and shape of a large potato. They take over a year to mature, then split at the base into five thick valves, releasing large numbers of winged seeds, which are dispersed by the wind.

When mahogany populations in the Caribbean were exhausted, they were replaced in the timber trade by big leaf, Honduran, or Brazilian mahogany, a tree once common in the Amazonian rainforest; however, this has also been overexploited. Most large trees have been felled, and those that survive today are undersized, young trees.

Body made of mahogany

▶ 1972 Gibson Les Paul Custom
This guitar has a big-leaf mahogany body. West Indies mahogany timber is also used to make instruments on rare occasions.

◀ Mahogany forest
West Indies Mahogany grows mostly in moist, lowland forests (as seen here in Florida), but in Jamaica, it is found at altitudes up to 4,900 ft (1,500 m).

Other species

BIG LEAF MAHOGANY
Swietenia macrophylla
Provides the most valuable timber in South America; found from southern Mexico, across Central America, to the Amazon.

PACIFIC COAST MAHOGANY
Swietenia humilis
Overexploited for furniture making; now rare in remote forests, but common along city streets in Central America.

GROUP: EUDICOTS

FAMILY: MELIACEAE

HEIGHT: 49–131 FT (15–40 M)

SPREAD: UP TO 82 FT (25 M)

Leaf Mostly evergreen; pinnate; 5–9 pairs of leaflets; alternate, terminal missing; 7¾–15¾ in (20–40 cm) long

Fruit Ovoid-oblong drupe with bittersweet, fibrous pulp; ripens to greenish yellow

Bark Midbrown; cracks into squares and oblongs, revealing reddish underbark

Leaves are long and gently curled with jagged edges

Flowers have five petals and grow in auxiliary panicles of up to 300, which are shorter than the leaves

◀ **Brown-headed barbet in neem tree**
This bird is found in open and lightly wooded country throughout most of India. It feeds on fruits and insects and nests in holes in trees.

▶ Mughal illustration
This 17th-century Islamic miniature depicts a prince and his wife on a terrace with a neem tree in the background. The tree is a familiar sight on many parts of the Indian subcontinent.

" Thou charm'st the wanderer's woe away/With soothing shade. "

ELSA KAZI, "The Neem Tree" poem, early 20th century

Neem

Azadirachta indica

This large, elegant tree is evergreen except in dry, arid conditions, where the leaves fall in winter before the new ones develop with the rains.

The original distribution of neem is uncertain, as it has been planted and naturalized for a long time. It is found from southern Nepal south to Sri Lanka, and from Pakistan east across most of India, possibly as far as Myanmar; it is thought to be native somewhere in this range. However, as human populations have dispersed, it has been more widely planted in tropical and subtropical regions, and in a few regions—such as parts of sub-Saharan Africa and the Northern Territories, Australia—it has become a weed.

Ecologically, it is tolerant of a wide range of soils, including saline (salty) ones, and it can withstand low rainfall. This has made it useful for improving arid soils. The tree, including the seeds, contains a range of natural chemical compounds, and the dried foliage can be used to line drawers to deter insects. The seeds can be crushed and then soaked to produce an "insecticide," which is sprayed onto foliage, not directly killing the insects but repelling them and stopping their egg-laying. It has been used in traditional medicine in India, where the young leaves, shoots, and flowers are also used as cooking ingredients and are fried or made into a soup.

▶ Oil, fruit, and leaves
Various parts of the neem tree have uses in hair and skincare products, as well as in natural insect repellent.

Seeds take the form of small brown kernels

Other species

SENTANG
Azadirachta excelsa
Found from Malaysia to Vietnam and Papua New Guinea; a larger tree with off-white flowers and slightly pink-tinged bark.

Arabica Coffee

Coffea arabica

Consumed worldwide, coffee is one of the most valuable traded commodities. It is produced from the seeds of a compact, low-growing tree with lush, dark green foliage native to Ethiopia.

There are many legends about how the stimulating effects of the seeds of this tree were first discovered in Ethiopia. It is known for certain that coffee drinking spread early on to the Arabian Peninsula (hence "arabica coffee"), and by the 15th century, the drink was popular across the Islamic world. In the early 17th century, coffee reached Europe, where commercial coffee houses soon sprang up. A few coffee seeds were taken to India, then to Sri Lanka and Indonesia. From Indonesia, some plants were taken to the Caribbean and Central and South America.

Coffee plants can produce fruits without cross-fertilization from another coffee plant, making it easy to spread them around the world under taller shade trees (often fruit trees). Newer varieties can grow in the open, allowing this "sun coffee" to be planted at higher densities in large plantations. These can be harvested by machines, which collect unripe fruit along with the ripe, producing coffee of a lower quality.

Coffee production

The total production of arabica coffee in 2020–2021 was 102 million of the 132 lb (60 kg) bags in which coffee is traded, or 6.75 million tons (6.12 million tonnes). Brazil produced 49 percent of this total, although

Glossy leaves are quite leathery and robust but cannot tolerate frosts

Arabica coffee originated in southwest Ethiopia and **still grows wild** in surviving forests there

> " Coffee should be black as hell, strong as death, and sweet as love. "
>
> TURKISH PROVERB

from a few original plants. Arabica coffee is mainly grown in cooler, elevated areas of the tropics and subtropics, typically 3,300–6,600 ft (1,000–2,000 m) above sea level. Brazil is the biggest producer of coffee, followed by Colombia and Ethiopia. In most countries, coffee is grown on small family farms, often as part of a mixed system with other crops. The trees are usually pruned to shoulder height to make it easier for pickers—who often work long hours on low wages—to collect the ripe fruit. Traditional varieties grow best under partial shade, so they are planted at relatively low densities

Ornamentation uses an Asian copper-gold alloy

◄ Coffee urn
This decorated, three-legged Vietnamese coffee urn from the 18th century has multiple taps to dispense coffee.

GROUP: EUDICOTS	
FAMILY: RUBIACEAE	
HEIGHT: UP TO 26 FT (8 M)	
SPREAD: UP TO 16 FT (5 M)	

 Leaf Evergreen; stalked, elliptical with a pointed tip; opposite; up to 6 in (15 cm) long

 Flower White; star-shaped, with a tubular base; long anthers and five spreading lobes; fragrant

 Fruits Green turning orange, then red; fleshy; each fruit contains two seeds (beans)

 Bark Pale gray on trunk; green young branches become brown and fissured when older

◄ **Managed coffee bush**
Cultivated coffee bushes are pruned to a height of around 5 ft (1.5 m) to make harvesting easier. Side stems are removed to ensure a single productive stem.

Fleshy fruits or drupes have one or more stony seeds

Other species

ROBUSTA COFFEE

Coffea canephora

Discovered in the forests of the Democratic Republic of the Congo in the late 19th century; taller tree, produces cheaper coffee with a more bitter taste.

Coffee house
This lively Ottoman coffee house was painted in the 16th century. Such coffee houses attracted learned people and became popular centers for literary and social activity. By the following century, similar houses sprang up in Europe, bringing people together to discuss politics and commerce.

Brazilian drinkers accounted for almost half the country's production. The Dutch drink the most coffee in the world, followed by the Finns, Canadians, and Swedes.

Robusta coffee is produced from a different species, *Coffea canephora*. This is better adapted to wet equatorial climates and is typically grown in warmer areas and at lower elevations than arabica. It produces a lower-quality coffee, with a more intense (robust), woody flavor. It is mainly used in instant coffee and for blending with arabica to add body. It is also selected for espresso coffee because it produces more crema (the foam on top of an espresso). Nearly

74 million bags of Robusta coffee were traded in 2020–2021, with Vietnam, Brazil, Indonesia, and Uganda as the main producers. More than 100 million people worldwide depend on these coffee crops for their livelihood.

Extracting the beans

Inside the coffee fruit, a fleshy pulp surrounds a parchment enclosing two seeds (the green coffee "beans"), each with a silvery outer coat. After harvesting, two possible processes can be followed. In the dry production process, the fruits are dried in the sun and the pulp, parchment, and seed coat are removed in hulling machines.

▲ **Roasted beans**
Coffee "beans" are the roasted seed of the tree and are only popularly referred to as beans because of their beanlike appearance.

In the wet process, which produces milder coffee with a better flavor, the pulp is first removed mechanically from the fruits. The beans are then washed and left to ferment in water for 12–24 hours, during which time the characteristic aroma and taste develop. The beans are dried in the sun for a week or so, then put through polishing machines, which remove the parchment and seed coats.

Instant coffee is made by brewing the beans under pressure to make a concentrate, which is spray-dried or freeze-dried into soluble granules. For decaffeinated coffee, water, steam, or solvents such as methylene chloride or ethyl acetate are used to remove caffeine from green beans. Typical brewed coffee contains around 0.3 percent caffeine, which acts as a short-term stimulant but also increases heart output, stimulates digestive juices, and is a powerful diuretic.

Consumer choice

People who want to be ethical consumers of coffee have several options available to them. "Shade grown" coffee offers better working conditions for pickers, and the shade trees benefit local insects and birdlife. Organic coffee is often grown under shade in wooded farm environments, but the organic credentials need to be carefully checked. Fairtrade coffee bypasses conventional dealers to buy directly from farm cooperatives at better prices. The Rainforest Alliance certification also tries to improve livelihoods for coffee growers while ensuring environmental sustainability.

▲ Coffee trade
For two centuries, coffee was exported in sacks weighing 132 lb (60 kg), as seen in this 1900 photo. Today, 1.10-ton (1-tonne) polypropylene "super-sacks" are being used.

Roasting hugely adds to the value of imported coffee beans

> " Without my morning coffee, I'm just like a dried-up piece of a roast goat. "
>
> PICANDER, in Johann Sebastian Bach's *Coffee Cantata*, c.1735

ROASTING COFFEE BEANS

Coffee beans are exported green. They are roasted in hot air by the wholesaler at their destination. The roasting determines the flavor and aroma of the coffee. Higher temperatures produce darker roasts with stronger tastes. Roast varieties range from light cinnamon roasts to bitter, dark Italian and French roasts.

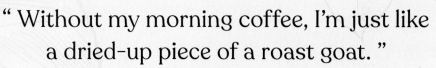

| GREEN | CINNAMON | LIGHT | MEDIUM | DARK |

Cinchona Tree

Cinchona calisaya

Indigenous South American tribes have long used the bitter bark of the cinchona tree from the Andean rainforests to treat fevers. European colonists discovered that one of the main active ingredients, quinine, was especially powerful against malaria. It is still widely used to flavor tonic water.

GROUP:	EUDICOTS
FAMILY:	RUBIACEAE
HEIGHT:	UP TO 50 FT (15 M)
SPREAD:	UP TO 26 FT (8 M)

Leaf Evergreen; oblong to lance-shaped; opposite; up to 6 in (16 cm) long

Bark Thin; grayish brown with many shallow fissures; contains several bitter alkaloids

When Jesuit missionaries first visited Peru in the early 17th century, many succumbed to malaria. Indigenous tribal doctors treated them with the powdered bark of the cinchona tree, a small evergreen tree or shrub with tubular flowers that is native to the Andes. By 1639, cinchona bark had been exported to Europe; it was another 50 years before it became accepted as a treatment to kill the *Plasmodium* parasite that spreads malaria and ease the fever it causes.

In 1820, French chemists Joseph Caventou and Pierre-Joseph Pelletier were the first to extract an active alkaloid—which they called quinine—from dried cinchona bark. At that time, malaria was a major problem in the British and Dutch colonies in India, Sri Lanka, and Java, so botanists were sent to South America to collect cinchona seeds, although the resulting cultivated trees produced poor quinine yields.

There are around 23 species of cinchona native to mountainous tropical forests in Central America and the western Andes. All contain quinine, but to varying degrees, which causes problems in

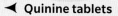

◄ Quinine tablets
Quinine is a rather basic chemical, so many medical preparations were developed to aid its effectiveness.

Hydrochlorides were commonly used with quinine in antimalarial drugs

cultivation. The trees are related to coffee (see pp.272–275), and the alkaloids in the bark probably deter grazing animals, just as the bitter caffeine in coffee beans does.

Today, the taxonomy of cinchona species is confused by this history of cultivation and hybridization, but *Cinchona calisaya* is the main commercial species. Since the 1950s, quinine has been largely replaced in the treatment of malaria by synthetic drugs, including chloroquine.

The word **"quinine"** is derived from the Amerindian word *quinaquina*, meaning **"bark of barks"**

► Harvesting cinchona bark
Cinchona bark was once harvested from wild trees, their inner bark carefully peeled and then sun-dried. Today, medical quinine comes mainly from plantations in Indonesia and Zaire.

◄ Cinchona tree
This 19th-century illustration shows the features of a cinchona tree, including the peelable bark, which is dried and powdered for use.

Emerald forest

The only tropical rainforest in the US National Forests System, El Yunque is a verdant haven nestled in the northeast corner of the Caribbean island of Puerto Rico. Spread over rolling mountains and enjoying rain all year round, this lush forest has more than 240 varieties of tree and over 150 species of fern.

▼ Rainforest giant

The Brazil nut is a huge rainforest tree, reaching a height of 164 ft (50 m). It can live for 1,000 years, but records show that some are as much as 1,600 years old.

Crown is high and rounded

Leaves fall during the dry season

GROUP: EUDICOTS

FAMILY: LECYTHIDACEAE

HEIGHT: UP TO 164 FT (50 M)

SPREAD: UP TO 66 FT (20 M)

Leaf Dry-season deciduous; oblong, copper-colored to bright green; alternate; 6¾–18 in (17–45 cm) long

Fruit Large, spherical, dark brown woody capsule, 3–6 in (8–15 cm) in diameter

Bark Thick, gray-brown, and resinous, with deep, narrow, vertical cracks

Agouti
These large rodents, related to mice and squirrels, weigh up to 13 lb (6 kg) and have bodies up to 30 in (76 cm) long. They live at ground level and are the only mammal with strong enough teeth to crack open Brazil nut fruits. They are key to the dispersal of Brazil nuts (see p.283).

Brazil Nut

Bertholletia excelsa

The edible nuts sold as "Brazil nuts" are not nuts, nor even fruits. They are the seeds of a giant tree that towers above the rest of the rainforest, across the huge basin of the Amazon River in Brazil and neighboring countries.

As well as Brazil, the tree's range in the Amazon forest includes parts of Bolivia, Peru, Colombia, the Guianas, and Venezuela. It grows at low densities, mainly in unflooded forests, on soils that are poor in nutrients.

The fruit of the Brazil nut tree is a large, spherical, brown capsule the size of a grapefruit but with a hard, woody exterior, reminiscent of a coconut. It can weigh 1–5½ lb (0.5–2.5 kg). Rather than splitting to release its seeds, it falls to the ground intact. Human collectors gather them off the ground, ignoring other possible methods of collection that might

risk bombardment from the heavy, falling fruits. A sharp machete is needed to open the shell. Each capsule holds up to 25 seeds. The three-sided seeds are packed neatly

> " Extremely persuasive ... for the preservation of the globally significant Amazonian ecosystem. "
>
> E. SMALL & P. M. CATLING ON THE BRAZIL NUT TREE
> "Blossoming Treasures of Biodiversity," *Biodiversity*, 2005

Fruits have hard outer shell

Stems are woody and forked

" It is not unusual to meet a worker who has been injured by a falling fruit. "

Insight Guides: Amazon Wildlife, 1990

▼ **Amazon native**
Brazil nut trees' future is tied to the fate of the rainforest, as they depend on its ecosystem for seed dispersal via agoutis and for pollination by local bees.

like the segments of an orange. It is these seeds that are marketed as "Brazil nuts." Each seed has a hard, woody exterior, with white, edible flesh inside. Brazil nuts are marketed shelled (with the woody coat removed) or left unshelled to be tackled by consumers with nutcrackers.

Nut-cracking agoutis

The Brazil nut has evolved its impenetrably hard-shelled fruit to stop animals from accessing its large, oil-rich seeds. Capuchin monkeys, giant Amazonian squirrels, and macaws can break open the hard shells to reach the seeds, but do so only in small quantities because of the effort involved. However, the dispersal of Brazil nut seeds depends on a remarkable coevolution between the tree and a rodent called the agouti (see p.281).

The vast majority of the fruits fall, unopened, to the forest floor. There, the agouti has evolved uniquely to take advantage of the feast inside the fruit. Powered by massive jaw muscles, its chisel-sharp incisor teeth are strong enough to crack open the shell, then push into the crack and wedge it apart, revealing the seeds. The seeds are so rich in oil and protein that two or three are enough to sustain the agouti. It buries the rest of the seeds as a food store, singly or in small caches, in the surrounding forest. It usually fails to find most of its caches, and the undiscovered seeds germinate

12–18 months later. The large energy content contained in the seeds ensures that the saplings establish quickly, outcompeting other species around them. When a forest tree falls, this may open up a sunlit gap in which the sapling can rapidly grow into a full-height tree.

Bee partnership

The complex structure of the Brazil nut tree's flower is key to another remarkable animal interrelationship. The flower's petals tightly protect its interior, and a curled hood encloses the anthers and nectaries. Only one species, an insect called a Euglossine bee, has a body heavy enough to open the flower and a tongue long enough to reach the sweet nectar supply. In the process, pollen from the anthers is dusted onto the bee's back, which it carries to the next Brazil nut flower it visits, enabling pollination. The Brazil nut tree only flowers for a short period; at other times, the bees feed mainly on orchid flowers. As a result, attempts to grow Brazil nut trees in plantations have mostly failed because there were no orchids for the bees to feed on when the Brazil nuts were not flowering.

Fruits can hold up to 25 seeds

Hard shell protects seeds from most animals

▲ **Cannonball fruit**
The Brazil nut fruit is the size of a cannonball and almost as hard. A sharp machete is needed to open the fruit and find the seeds ("nuts") inside.

Mascot made from Brazil nuts

POSTER ADVERTISING BRAZIL NUTS

THE BRAZIL NUT INDUSTRY

Brazil nuts have been exported to Europe since the 17th century and are consumed raw, roasted, salted, or in confectionery. They are the only internationally traded nut that is still collected almost entirely from the wild, and they provide a major source of income for thousands of Indigenous people in Amazonia. In 2019, it is estimated that 42,440 tons (38,500 tonnes) of Brazil nut kernels (shelled or unshelled) were traded, with a total value of $343 million.

Oval pinnules grow in 14–24 pairs, up to ½ in (12 mm) in length

Leaves are set in opposite pairs on the shoot, with around 16 pairs of pinnae, divided into small pinnules

GROUP: EUDICOTS

FAMILY: BIGNONIACEAE

HEIGHT: 33–66 FT (10–20 M)

SPREAD: 33–66 FT (10–20 M)

Leaf Deciduous; bipinnate; opposite; 12–18 in (30–45 cm) long with many small pinnules or leaflets

Bark Thin and gray-brown in young trees, becoming brown with fissures or small scales

◄ Blooms and foliage

The jacaranda's purple blooms have made it famous worldwide, and it is a popular decorative tree in cities. Each of its leaves carries around 200–400 tiny leaflets, or pinnules. This structure lends the tree's foliage its notably fernlike appearance.

▲ Tree-lined road

Jacaranda trees line a road in Harare, Zimbabwe; their purple flowers are starting to fall and will give way to a haze of green leaves.

Jacaranda

Jacaranda mimosifolia

A deciduous tree native to South America, jacaranda presents a glorious sight when covered with its violet-colored, long-lasting flowers. It is also notable for its massed, fernlike foliage.

Jacaranda, also known as blue jacaranda, is one of 50 or so species in the genus *Jacaranda* and is well known as a truly stunning tree when in full bloom. Medium to large spreading trees explode into color, laden with their pale lilac or purple-blue flowers. The flowers develop on the bare branches before the leaves, in panicles of up to 50 blossoms. The blooms can last for up to a couple of months, and toward the end of this period, the new leaves start to expand. Such majestic displays require a warm, temperate to subtropical climate,

and it is in these climates that the tree is most widely planted. The main regions where it is grown include the southern US, the Caribbean, along the Mediterranean coast in Europe, Australia, and southern Africa.

Climate requirements

Mature jacaranda trees can tolerate temperatures as low as around 19°F (−7°C), although young trees tend to be more susceptible to frost and, if

Branches and twigs are soft and easily damaged

▲ Fruit and leaves

The fruit of the jacaranda usually develops in late summer and resembles a dry, brownish pod.

New leaves emerge toward the end of the extended flowering period as the first blooms drop their corollas

▲ Streets of Johannesburg
Avenues of jacaranda trees in full bloom line the suburbs of Johannesburg. Although not native to South Africa, it has been adopted as a popular local feature in the city.

damaged by it, may be cut to ground level before sprouting again. In cooler climates, flowering is much more sparse, and in these areas, the tree may be planted decoratively more for its distinctive, fernlike, feathery foliage, which is composed of hundreds of very small leaflets on each leaf. Even in climates where it does flower well, there are periods after flowering when its foliage can be appreciated as a decorative feature.

Fruit, seeds, and wood
Jacaranda fruit takes the form of a hard, woody, flattish capsule that opens at its apex to release its seeds. The seeds themselves are small and surrounded by a very thin wing to aid dispersal by the wind. The timber produced by the tree is whitish or pale gray with a straight grain; it is usually knot-free and is relatively

► New blooms
Fragrant, trumpet-shaped flowers grow from buds on the end of the previous year's shoots. When they fall from the trees in large amounts in cities, they tend to decompose into a sludge on pavements and roads, to the inconvenience of local residents.

soft, which makes it good for turning on a lathe. The wood dries well, but can also be used in its "green" state.

When planted as garden trees, jacarandas need ample space, as well as full sunlight, and they thrive on light sandy soils. While they need regular weekly or fortnightly watering, they grow best if they can dry out between waterings. They are often planted as grafted plants, as these tend to flower earlier, and can be selected for more intense colors. In colder regions, where their culture can be manipulated, they can be grown as

Jacaranda grows wild in parts of **Bolivia and Argentina,** where it is listed as **vulnerable to extinction**

" The jacaranda attracts the eye by the lightness of its double-feathered leaves ... "

J. B. VON SPIX AND C. F. P. VON MARTIUS, *Travels in Brazil,* 1824

Spreading panicles grow
to 12 in (30 cm) long with
around 50 individual flowers

JACARANDA OBTUSIFOLIA
Jacaranda obtusifolia

Shrubby tree from tropical
Venezuela and Colombia;
notable for its large,
obtuse leaflets.

JACARANDA CRYSTALLANA
Jacaranda crystallana

Shrub or small tree
that is native to Brazil
and is known mainly
for its purple,
frilly flowers.

JACARANDA CUSPIDIFOLIA
Jacaranda cuspidifolia

Small tree from
Argentina, Brazil,
Bolivia, and Paraguay;
usually less than 26 ft
(8 m) in height, with
purplish-blue flowers.

bonsai trees. In cooler climates, jacarandas
can be also be used as summer bedding for
their foliage alone—they may shed around
24 in (60 cm) of foliage by fall.

Exam tree

In parts of the southern hemisphere, jacaranda
flowering sometimes occurs around the same
time that students take their exams. In universities
with jacaranda trees on their campuses, this has
led to some informal folklore associated with
the tree. In parts of Australia and South Africa,
"purple panic" refers to the campus jacarandas
blooming as students begin a last-minute rush
to finish their studying before exams. Another
legend states that if a bloom falls on a student's
head, a good exam result is certain. One such
campus tree, a large and much-loved jacaranda
at the University of Sydney, Australia, made
news worldwide when it fell in 2016.

Multilobed stigma
on the style

▲ Inside the flower
Jacaranda flowers have a curiously lobed stigma
on the end of a style, while their overall, outer
shape is somewhat tubular. They are pollinated
by various bee species.

GROUP: EUDICOTS

FAMILY: EUPHORBIACEAE

HEIGHT: UP TO 130 FT (40 M)

SPREAD: UP TO 72 FT (22 M)

Leaf Deciduous; compound with three boat-shaped leaflets; alternate; 12–24 in (30–60 cm) long

Seed Egg-shaped, with a grayish, glossy shell with brown marbling; ¾–1½ in (2–4 cm) long

Euphorbiaceae (Acalypheae)

Hevea brasiliensis Müll. Arg.

▲ **Botanical detail**
This 19th-century illustration shows various features of the tree, including the three-lobed fruits, which, when ripe, explode to expel their seeds.

Rubber Tree

Hevea brasiliensis

Native to the Amazon, the rubber tree helped trigger the Industrial Revolution, bringing wealth to some but huge cruelty to indigenous workers who collected the sap.

A number of species in the spurge family (Euphorbiaceae) have a milky latex in their stems and leaves that is caustic or toxic to discourage insects. Three species of *Hevea*, of which rubber is one, take this a stage further. When their latex makes contact with the air, it turns into a sticky gum that may completely clog the mouthparts of an attacking insect. The sap also seals any natural wounds in the trunk. *Hevea brasiliensis*, native to Brazil, produces this latex in the greatest quantity.

Useful sap

The ancient Mayans and Aztecs knew the qualities of this sap, which they used to make rubber balls and homemade shoes. In Europe, it was seen as a curiosity until 1839, when the American Charles

Goodyear discovered that mixing sulfur into the sap and heating it (a process called vulcanization) produced a much harder-wearing material. Vulcanized rubber helped fuel the Industrial Revolution and led to the "rubber boom" in the Amazon region of Brazil from 1879 to 1912.

Huge fortunes were made by the European rubber barons, who built magnificent mansions and even funded the 1896 Opera House in Manaus, Brazil. To produce this income, they forced local indigenous men to gather the rubber sap, in a practice of systematic brutality and slavery that wiped out more than

The latex that comes from the **trunks of rubber trees** consists of **around 30 percent rubber**

▲ **Collecting sap from rubber tree trunks**
Early in the morning, when the sap is rising fastest,
workers in this Cambodian plantation make a
series of slanting cuts into rubber tree trunks.

90 percent of the native population in some areas.
In 1873, the English forester Henry Wickham
acquired 70,000 seeds from Brazil and brought
them to Kew Gardens, London, England. While
the gardeners there got relatively few seeds to
germinate, they produced enough seedlings to
send to Singapore, where failed coffee growers
were persuaded to plant the new crop. The Asian
plantations became hugely productive and the
Brazilian industry collapsed. Most of the world's
natural rubber today comes from Asia.

RUBBER PRODUCTION

The Brazilian rubber industry never
recovered from the advent of Asian
plantations, which benefited from
being free of a fungal leaf blight
disease that was endemic in South
America. In 2020, plantations in
Indonesia and Thailand accounted
for more than half of the total
world production of natural rubber
(14.3 million tons/13 million tonnes).
Another 15.9 million tons (14.4 million
tonnes) was made synthetically from
petroleum using a process developed
in the US during World War II.

**RUBBER SHEETS HANGING ON
BAMBOO POLES**

GROUP: EUDICOTS

FAMILY: LAMIACEAE

HEIGHT: UP TO 148 FT (45 M)

SPREAD: UP TO 60 FT (18 M)

Leaf Deciduous; long-stalked, undivided, untoothed, oval; opposite; up to 12 in (30 cm) long

Fruit Globe-shaped; wrapped in an inflated bell of sepals, with fleshy interior and central stone

◀ **Trunk and canopy**

A straight trunk, often wider at the base, rises to the canopy of the monsoon forest. The gray bark encases a layer of white sapwood and rich golden heartwood.

Teak

Tectona grandis

Teak is one of the world's most sought-after timbers, its price inflated by increasing scarcity in the wild. It is famed for its strength and durability, which is partly a mechanism for survival in the monsoon forests of Asia.

Tropical forests support a high diversity of species, and these areas provide the ideal habitat for teak, where it is surrounded by other species that help support it. However, not all species are benevolent; in tropical climates, trees such as teak often produce large quantities of toxic chemicals in their tissues to protect themselves against pathogens and wood-boring insects. These toxins continue to protect the timber after the tree is felled, making the wood much more durable. As a result, wooden sculptures, beams, doors, and coffins made of teak remain in prime condition in Indian and Persian temples that are more than 1,000 years old.

Teak timber is regarded as virtually imperishable if kept indoors. It is also resistant to decay and corrosion in the harsh conditions of saltwater, so it is a preferred timber—along with mahogany (see pp.268–269)—for constructing the wooden hulls, decking, and bridgehouses on ships. The toxins in the timber also repel the naval shipworm (*Teredo navalis*), a marine clam that is known for tunneling into underwater piers and pilings in saltwater and is a major cause of damage to wooden boat hulls.

Typical Burmese headdress carefully carved from the wood

Fine detail is less susceptible to damage when carved from a hardwood such as teak

▲ **Traditional wooden carving**

The physical strength of teak timber lends itself to intricate carving, like these winged figures on a door panel in a monastery in Myanmar (Burma).

A **teak tree in Kerala, India,** grew to **156 ft (47.5 m)**. It was estimated to be **450–500 years old**

Teak is native to the Indian subcontinent, Myanmar, Thailand, Laos, Cambodia, and Vietnam. It grows in monsoon forest, which, unlike rainforest, is not subject to rainfall all year round but instead has one period, or sometimes two periods, of very high rainfall, called the monsoon. In response to these conditions, teak is deciduous: it sheds its leaves during the dry season, from around November, and then it regrows them when the heavy rains return, usually in May.

Prize of the forest

Teak is a characteristic tree species in two types of monsoon forest. Moist teak forest is defined by a rainfall of 80–95 in (200–240 cm); dry teak forest has a lower rainfall of 40–80 in (100–200 cm). Teak itself only constitutes 1 in 10 of the trees in either forest type, but each has a completely different set of associated species. The species relies on other trees to protect it from high winds and gales. Despite its substantial height, it has a very superficial root system that is easily torn up in a storm.

The roots often penetrate no deeper than 20 in (50 cm) into the soil, but they can radiate up to 50 ft (15 m) from the trunk.

Commercial plantations of teak have been established throughout its natural range and also in other countries, including Indonesia (especially Java), Sri Lanka, Brazil, Costa Rica, and the countries of western Africa, from Côte d'Ivoire to Tanzania. It is also widely planted as a decorative tree in various tropical parks and gardens.

The economics of teak plantations mean that the trees are generally harvested after around 30 years, so they produce a smaller gauge of timber. As a result, most teak is still obtained unsustainably and destructively from natural, old-growth forests. Because there are no more than two to four trees per acre of forest (five to ten per hectare), loggers often fell dozens of surrounding trees to get at the one highly valued teak tree, leaving behind a damaged forest in which new teak trees struggle to grow.

Protected species

Because the extensive logging and deforestation associated with the teak industry were leading to problems such as landslips and devastating

Clusters of flowers develop in June at end of a much-branched inflorescence

> " Teak furniture will keep its color ... Exposure to the elements turns the wood a pleasing gray."
>
> AMERICAN WOODWORKER MAGAZINE, 1997

Pollen sheds from stamens before the stigma is mature, ensuring cross-fertilization

◀ **Teak in flower**
The flowers of teak are small and white, borne in loose clusters above the leaves. Their fragrance attracts bees for pollination, although they can also be wind-pollinated.

A TEAK FOREST OF BURMA

floods, the King of Thailand passed laws in 1988 effectively banning logging in his country. This encouraged a rapid increase in logging in adjacent Myanmar, much of it located along the border with Thailand and relying on illegal importation of teak across the border.

Myanmar now provides around a quarter of the world's teak. In 1990, approximately 57 percent of the country was covered in forests, mostly of teak. Due to excessive logging, almost a sixth of the surviving forest had been cleared by 2005. Although a notional ban on teak extraction was introduced in 2014, Myanmar continues to be a major teak producer.

Scarcity value

The future of teak remains uncertain due to the problems created by its commercial value. Despite the high price that results from its scarcity, teak is still highly prized for the manufacture of products such as high-quality furniture, doors,

window frames, staircases, and outdoor decking. Ideally, the companies that produce these items should provide information about the provenance of the teak used and ensure that it comes from sustainably managed plantations; however, in reality, it is often left to individual consumers to check whether or not this is the case.

▲ Colonial poster
In the British Empire era, when this poster originated, Burma (now Myanmar) had vast forests from which scattered teak trees could be extracted using elephants.

TEAK INSPIRATION

The golden-brown heartwood of unseasoned teak turns a richer, chestnut-brown color when it is matured and seasoned (dried for use). Its firmness and stability has always inspired artists to work with the wood. This curvaceous lounge chair was conceived by Grete Jalk, a Danish furniture designer. It is created from two sinuously carved wooden shapes bolted together.

TEAK LOUNGE CHAIR, 1963

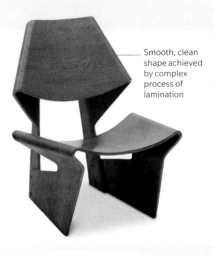

Smooth, clean shape achieved by complex process of lamination

► **Macadamia blossoms**
Macadamia flowers are borne in long, narrow clusters, known as racemes. Each raceme can comprise 100–300 flowers, which develop into several nutlets.

GROUP: EUDICOTS

FAMILY: PROTEACEAE

HEIGHT: UP TO 40 FT (12 M)

SPREAD: UP TO 33 FT (10 M)

Leaf Evergreen; leathery, with a saw-toothed edge; growing in whorls; 3–9½ in (8–24 cm) long

Bark Rough and brown; coarse heartwood inside is pink to reddish brown

Long, narrow, glossy leaves grow in whorls of 4 or 5

Flowers mature from green to creamy white or pink

Macadamia

Macadamia tetraphylla

This medium-sized evergreen tree, also known as Queensland macadamia or rough-shelled macadamia—to distinguish it from its smooth-shelled relative—is native to Australia.

The macadamia seed contains the **highest level of oil** found in a nut—up to **75 percent** of the seed's total weight

This species of macadamia has long spikes of pinkish-white flowers and seeds with thick, hard, bumpy shells, hence its name. Its partner, the smooth-shelled macadamia (*Macadamia integrifolia*), is so closely related that the two were once regarded as a single species. However, the latter has white flowers and a smooth seed coat and is more frequently grown in plantations. Both species have a small native range in subtropical rainforests near the coast of southern Queensland and northern New South Wales in Australia. Commercial growers discovered that the hybrid

Bee pollination
Macadamia flowers are often visited by bees, who are important pollinators for the trees. Some farmers of macadamia nuts place beehives among their macadamia trees to help ensure pollination.

between the two macadamia species was more productive than either of its parents. The hybrid is probably now the most common cultivated form.

Aboriginal Australians have probably eaten the nuts since they first arrived on the continent, but it was only when the tree was taken to Hawaii that its crop potential was fully recognized. Macadamia was introduced to the islands in 1882, and eventually became the third most important crop there, after sugar cane and pineapple. From Hawaii, the tree was introduced to California and countries such as Mexico, Zimbabwe, Malawi, and South Africa.

Half a century ago, Australians finally began their own plantations. In the late 1990s, they overtook Hawaii in their production of macadamia nuts, but South Africa is still the main producer, with a harvest of 62,280 tons (56,500 tonnes) in 2018, compared to the 16,535 tons (15,000 tonnes) produced in Australia.

Oil-rich seeds

The oil-rich seeds are eaten raw, salted, or roasted and are added to ice cream, bakery products, and confectionery. The oils are also used to moisturize and revitalize the skin. Rough-shelled nuts generally contain less oil and more sugar than the smooth-shelled species, so they taste sweeter but tend to char when roasted or baked. Consequently, most commercial macadamias used in cooking are from *M. integrifolia*, and those of *M. tetraphylla* are usually sold raw.

Other species

SMOOTH-SHELLED MACADAMIA
Macadamia integrifolia
Species distinguished by its smoother, more spherical seed and broader leaves, which are found in whorls of three.

GYMPIE NUT TREE
Macadamia ternifolia
Native to Queensland; small, evergreen tree that grows up to 20 ft (6 m) tall; produces very bitter, inedible nuts.

Fibrous husk
surrounds the seed

Oval seed
with rough, pitted coat

▶ **Nuts and leaves**
The two species are difficult to tell apart from each other, and especially from the hybrid. The leaf shape and pitted seed coats suggest this is the rough-shelled macadamia.

Bitter Orange

Citrus × aurantium

Maybe not as well known as its edible fruit-bearing relatives—sweet orange, grapefruit, lemon, and lime—bitter orange is nonetheless a valuable member of the citrus family. This compact evergreen with a rounded crown makes a pleasing addition to parks and gardens.

Botanical jargon can often seem at odds with colloquial usage, and the fruits of bitter orange and other *Citrus* species are an example of this. From a botanist's perspective, a true berry is a fleshy fruit derived from a single ovary that does not split open and in which the seeds are not enclosed within a leathery core (as in apples) or a hard stone (as in peaches). Using this definition, many common berries such as raspberries and strawberries are not berries at all, while bananas and cucumbers are true berries.

Citrus fruits are also berries, although it is hard to consider oranges or lemons as such. These berries have their own designation, hesperidium—a type of berry with peelable, leathery rind and flesh divided into segments, each containing numerous juice-filled vesicles. Hesperidia are unique to *Citrus* species. Their outermost skin, or flavedo, is rich in essential oils and when scraped off is known as zest.

► Street tree, Seville
Grown commercially in many countries, bitter orange is a widespread street tree in the Spanish city of Seville. Its thick-skinned fruits are widely known as Seville or marmalade oranges.

The white pith, or albedo, is usually disposed of, though it contains antioxidants. Inside the skin, each segment represents one of the chambers (or carpels) of the floral ovary. While all citrus fruits are segmented, not all split apart readily for eating. Some are cut in half, while mandarins are typically eaten one segment at a time.

Spain and beyond
The fruits of the bitter orange tree are unpalatable to humans but have various uses and are cultivated in warm regions around the world. Essential oils from the fruits are used as solvents and flavorings and in perfumery and herbal medicine. However, the most famous use came from the Spanish city of Seville, noted for its numerous bitter orange trees. Seville oranges'

◄ Pink's marmalade
This 1890 advertisement shows oranges flying from Seville to England to reassure consumers of an authentic, good-quality marmalade.

Leaves have slightly toothed margins and are a source of fragrant essential oils

Seville oranges ripen in winter, turning from green to orange. They are aromatic and have a tart taste

The first commercial marmalade was produced in Dundee, Scotland, in 1797

Smooth brown bark; the stems bear sharp thorns up to 3¼ in (8 cm) long

GROUP: EUDICOTS

FAMILY: RUTACEAE

HEIGHT: UP TO 26 FT (8 M)

SPREAD: UP TO 13 FT (4 M)

Leaf Evergreen; lance-shaped, with winged petioles; alternate; 2¾–4 in (7–10 cm) long

Fruit Roughly spherical; orange skin; thick pith layer; small segments with large pips

Packed for export

Bitter oranges were the first oranges cultivated in Europe. Now largely replaced by sweet oranges, they remain common around the Spanish city of Seville, from where most are exported to the UK. This 1889 painting shows fruit packers in Andalusia, Spain, readying oranges for the English market.

More than 14,000 bitter orange trees line the streets of Seville

Fragrant white flowers
are ¾ in (2 cm) across and can be borne singly or in clusters

peel contains large amounts of pectin, a natural gelling agent, making them the perfect ingredient for marmalade.

It is believed that the first commercial marmalade was produced in Dundee, Scotland, in the late 18th century. Scottish merchant John Keiller bought a shipment of bitter oranges cheaply from a Spanish shipmaster looking to sell his cargo before it went bad. John's wife, Janet, used these to make a marmalade, as she had with other oranges, with one difference—she added pieces of peel. This new, gelatinous type of marmalade became popular via the family shop and went into large-scale production in 1797.

Bitter oranges are rich in vitamin C (ascorbic acid), an essential substance produced in the body by most mammals, but not humans, apes, monkeys, and some bats and rodents. Without vitamin C, humans develop scurvy, a debilitating condition that can lead to death.

Citrus fruits have long been prescribed to prevent scurvy; lemons and limes were most often used, despite containing less vitamin C than oranges.

A hybrid family

Bitter orange probably originated in Asia as the product of a cross between pomelo (*Citrus maxima*) and mandarin (*Citrus reticulata*). Wild citrus species only occur in Asia and Australia, but the parentage of the many cultivated forms grown worldwide is complex. Wild citrus readily hybridize with one another. In most plants, such hybrids are sterile and unable to produce fertile seed. However, some citrus hybrids can produce fertile seeds via a process called apomixis. This results in seedlings that are genetically identical to the mother plant, and such trees can therefore persist and spread with the help of humans.

▲ Orange blossom

Essential oils are extracted from bitter orange fruit peels, and petitgrain oil from the tree's leaves. Flowers from varieties such as *amara* are the source of neroli oil, used in perfumes and cosmetics.

Other species

CITRON
Citrus medica
Parent to many citrus fruits; native to the foothills of the Himalayas; yellow fruits have a thick layer of pith.

KUMQUAT
Citrus japonica
Native to China, although long cultivated in Japan; tolerant to cold; fruits are eaten whole, including peel.

KAFFIR LIME
Citrus hystrix
Shrub with leaves bearing winged petioles almost as big as the actual leaf blades; leaves and zest are used in cooking.

Sweet oranges are also derived from a cross between pomelos and mandarins. When sweet orange is crossed with pomelo (one of its parents), the result is grapefruit. Lemons derive from bitter orange and citron (*Citrus medica*), while sweet limes have citron and either sweet or bitter orange in their ancestry. The parentage of citrus fruits can have significant health implications for the consumer; pomelo and its hybrid, grapefruit, can increase the effects of medications. These fruits inhibit enzymes that break down drugs in the bloodstream, resulting in a much higher than anticipated dose and potential overdose. With the drug simvastatin, taking one pill with grapefruit juice is equivalent to taking 12 pills with water; users of such medications are now advised against consuming grapefruit and other related citrus fruits.

> " A wise bear always keeps a marmalade sandwich in his hat in case of emergency. "
>
> MICHAEL BOND, *A Bear Called Paddington*, 1958

▶ **Plants in the plaza**
Seville Cathedral was built on the site of a mosque, which included a courtyard for ritual cleansing before entry. It is now planted with bitter oranges and known as *Patio de los Naranjos*, or orange tree courtyard.

Red Mangrove

Rhizophora mangle

Rooted in mud in the intertidal zone of tropical seas, dense coastal thickets of red mangroves provide a defense against storms, floods, and even sea-level rise. They are named after the bright red color of the wood under their bark.

▼ Tidal forest

Red mangrove is the most widespread and salt-tolerant of 55 species of mangroves. Aerial roots prop up its trunk against storms and provide "breathing straws" at high tide.

GROUP: EUDICOTS

FAMILY: RHIZOPHORACEAE

HEIGHT: UP TO 40 FT (12 M)

SPREAD: 20–30 FT (6–9 M)

Leaf Evergreen; leathery, oval, dark green above, lighter below; opposite; 2½–5 in (6–12 cm) long

Flower Bell-shaped, with four creamy petals that fall off, leaving four green sepals

Fruit Green berry; germinates while still attached to tree, growing long hypocotyl "root"

Mangroves are highly adapted to an intertidal habitat. They grow on relatively sheltered coasts where mud can accumulate. Slender trunks and stiltlike aerial roots grow out of the mud, anchoring the tree and helping dissipate energy from the waves. They also stop mud from being washed away in storms.

Roots submerged in mud are unable to absorb oxygen from the waterlogged soil of mangrove swamps. However, the mangrove's aerial roots are covered in pores (lenticels) that open and close with the tide. When the tide falls and the lenticels are exposed to air, they open, allowing the tree to absorb oxygen and replenish its oxygen stores. When the tide comes in, the lenticels close, and the plant uses stored oxygen.

Saltwater causes other problems, too. Plant cells are surrounded by a permeable membrane, meaning that water can flow through it in both directions. When two solutions of different concentrations meet on either side of a membrane, the two concentrations equalize. Salt enters the root tissues, and water from the tissues flows out into the sea. Salt is damaging to plant cells, so mangroves must either keep

Leathery fruit,
up to 1¼ in (3 cm)
long, can float

▲ Rooting fruit
The fruit of red mangrove germinates on the tree. If the fruit falls from the tree at low tide, its stakelike root penetrates the mud and automatically "plants" the seedling.

Other species

SPOTTED MANGROVE
Rhizophora stylosa

Adaptable, hardy mangrove species growing in parts of Asia, Australasia, and the Pacific. Able to grow in colder climates than red mangrove.

ASIATIC MANGROVE
Rhizophora mucronata

Grows along the coasts of tropical and subtropical regions in East Africa and the Indo-Pacific; rich in chemical compounds and has various uses in traditional medicine.

◄ Living sanctuary
The sheltered waters around mangrove roots provide a home for a huge variety of ocean life, including plankton-feeders such as tentacled polyps and bottle-shaped tunicates.

▼ Delicate flowers
Small, sweetly scented flowers are produced mainly in the wet season in equatorial regions and in spring to early summer in subtropical regions.

salt out, get rid of excess, or adapt to live with it— or a balance of all three. Red mangroves pump salt into their older leaves, which then fall, removing excess salt. Red mangrove is the most salt-tolerant of all mangroves, growing farthest from the shore, where the trees are submerged more deeply and for longer. It is found in West Africa and in tropical and subtropical America and was introduced in Hawaii for coastal protection.

Self-planting fruits
Red mangrove reproduces in two ways. Its fruit germinates while still attached to the tree and a long, rootlike structure, called a hypocotyl, grows downward. When the fruit is ripe, it falls from the tree. If the tide is out, the hypocotyl acts like a stake. It plunges into the mud, and the seedling establishes close to the parent tree. If the tide is in, the fruit can float, ready to plant itself when

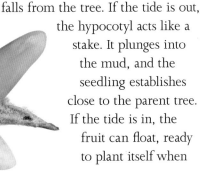

Each bell-shaped flower has four creamy yellow petals about ¾ in (2 cm) long

the tide retreats. If currents carry it out to the saltier open ocean, it becomes more buoyant. The water stops the fruit from scorching in the sun, and the green hypocotyl begins to photosynthesize, providing energy for the fruit to survive for up to a year until it reaches a shore.

The leaf litter from mangroves supports a huge community of marine creatures. Despite that, over half of the world's mangrove forests have been destroyed in recent decades to make way for aquaculture or development, leaving coasts unprotected.

TIDAL SUPPORT
The spindly red mangrove trunk relies on aerial stilt (prop) roots to hold it up against tidal surges and storms. These roots branch off the tree as much as 6 ft 6 in (2 m) up the trunk, at about the highest point the tides can reach. Pores in their surface help absorb oxygen, which is stored in their spongy interiors.

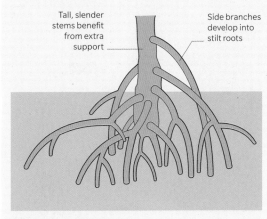

Tall, slender stems benefit from extra support

Side branches develop into stilt roots

AERIAL STILT ROOTS

" If there are no mangroves, then the sea will have no meaning. "

MAD-HA RANWASII, Thai fisherman and village headman, 1992

Spectacular swamp dweller
Native to the southeastern US, where it flourishes in damp or wet soils, swamp cypress (*Taxodium distichum*) is a sight to behold. Often found with its roots submerged in swamps and bayous, this statuesque conifer has heavy, upswept branches with bright green foliage that turns a stunning plum or orange-brown in fall.

CHAPTER 4

Gazetteer

Trees can be seen and enjoyed in many different settings. The following pages offer a miscellany of information—places to see them, ways of identifying them, and more.

Garden Trees

Whether native or introduced, wild species or cultivated hybrid, trees have made their homes in formal and informal gardens around the world. Below is a selection of trees that grow well in gardens and are not featured elsewhere in this book.

Agonis flexuosa

Common name: Western Australian peppermint
Type: Deciduous

Native to Western Australia, this small, sturdy tree resembles weeping willow. Its slender leaves emit a peppermint scent when crushed.

Albizia julibrissin

Common name: Pink silk tree
Type: Deciduous

Attractive, medium-sized tree with a broad crown and frondlike leaves, native to parts of Asia. Notable for the fluffy pink stamens that protrude from its flowers.

Arbutus unedo

Common name: Strawberry tree
Type: Evergreen

Small, shrublike tree native to the Mediterranean and western Europe.

Notable for its red, strawberrylike fruits that ripen from the previous year's flowers.

Brachychiton acerifolius

Common name: Flame tree
Type: Deciduous

Endemic to the east coast of Australia; a large, striking tree with a pyramidal habit that can be distinguished by its bright red, bell-shaped flowers.

Carica papaya

Common name: Papaya
Type: Deciduous

Native to the American tropics, this tree is cultivated around the world for its fruit, the papaya. It has deeply lobed, palmate leaves and it flowers at night.

Catalpa bignonioides

Common name: Indian bean tree
Type: Deciduous

Medium-sized tree native to the US with a spreading habit and white, trumpet-shaped flowers. Its large pale green, ovate leaves reach 10 in (25 cm) in length.

Cercis canadensis

Common name: Eastern rosebud
Type: Deciduous

This large shrub or small tree is native to eastern North America. It has a short trunk, spreading branches, and striking pink blooms that appear in spring.

Cornus florida

Common name: Flowering dogwood
Type: Deciduous

This popular ornamental tree is native to eastern North America and northern Mexico.

It is well known for its showy flowers, whose "petals" are actually bracts.

Corylus avellana

Common name: Common hazel
Type: Deciduous

Native to Europe and western Asia, hazel is cultivated for its hazelnuts, which are a useful food source for wildlife. It is often coppiced and can form part of hedgerows.

Cryptomeria japonica

Common name: Japanese cedar
Type: Evergreen

A large conifer with a conical habit. Native to Japan, its dense foliage changes through yellow, bright green, and blue-green throughout the year.

Davidia involucrata

Common name: Handkerchief tree
Type: Deciduous

A medium-sized, fast-growing tree native to China, with a spreading habit and ovate leaves. Notable for its small flowers that are surrounded by two large white bracts.

Gleditsia triacanthos

Common name: Honey locust
Type: Deciduous

A small tree with a bushy habit. The small pinnate or bipinnate leaflets vary from yellow to green through the year. Considered invasive outside its native US.

Grevillea robusta

Common name: Silky oak
Type: Evergreen

A fast-growing shrub or tree with a bushy habit and distinctive, olive green, fernlike leaves. Native to eastern Australia.

Smooth-edged leaves

Red fruit grows on long stems

DOGWOOD LEAVES AND FRUIT

TULIP TREE FLOWER

Laburnum anagyroides

Common name: Common laburnum or golden rain

Type: Deciduous

A small tree with a spreading habit, known for its beautiful dangling clusters of golden yellow flowers. Its seeds are extremely poisonous.

Liquidambar styraciflua

Common name: Sweet gum

Type: Deciduous

A conical tree with a bushy habit, native to North America. The maplelike leaves are spectacular in fall, with vibrant hues of orange, red, and purple.

Liriodendron tulipifera

Common name: Tulip tree

Type: Deciduous

Named for its attractive, tulip-shaped flowers, this large, spreading member of the magnolia family is native to North America.

Maclura pomifera

Common name: Osage orange

Type: Deciduous

Native to south-central US; a small tree or large shrub, sometimes used as a hedge. It has distinctive, orange-sized fruit with bright green, wrinkly skin.

Metrosideros excelsa

Common name: New Zealand Christmas tree

Type: Evergreen

A coastal, spreading tree endemic to New Zealand with dark green leaves. Easily recognized by its striking flowers with their tufts of blazing red stamen.

Nothofagus antarctica

Common name: Antarctic beech

Type: Deciduous

A hardy, conical tree with a columnar habit; native to parts of South America. The small, sweet-smelling leaves are dark green, turning yellow to orange in fall.

Nyssa sylvatica

Common name: Tupelo

Type: Deciduous

An elegant, small to medium tree with a bushy habit; native to North America. The glossy, ovate leaves turn intense shades of red and yellow in fall.

Ostrya virginiana

Common name: American hop-hornbeam

Type: Deciduous

A small, slow-growing tree with a spreading habit. Native to North America, the tree is notable for its fruit that closely resemble hops.

Parrotia persica

Common name: Persian ironwood

Type: Deciduous

A wide-spreading tree or large shrub with a bushy habit and flaking bark, native to Iran. The ovate leaves turn purple, orange, and red in fall.

Persea americana

Common name: Avocado

Type: Evergreen

Cultivated in temperate regions for its edible fruit, the avocado. This small tree or shrub has a bushy habit and rounded crown. It is native to Mexico.

Robinia pseudoacacia

Common name: False acacia or black locust

Type: Deciduous

A medium-sized, ornamental tree with a bushy habit, native to the US and considered invasive in some parts of the world.

The pea-type flowers are usually white and are arranged in racemes.

Stewartia pseudocamellia

Common name: Deciduous camellia

Type: Deciduous

A small, deciduous tree whose leaves turn a pleasing orange in fall. Its flowers are white and it has flaking bark. Native to Japan and Korea.

Styphnolobium japonicum

Common name: Japanese pagoda tree

Type: Deciduous

A large tree with a rounded, bushy habit; dark green pinnate leaves; and hanging pea-shaped flowers arranged in racemes. Native to China, it was introduced to Japan.

Zelkova serrata

Common name: Japanese zelkova

Type: Deciduous

Native to East Asia, this large tree has a spreading habit and is often used in bonsai. The leaves are lanceolate with a serrate margin.

AVOCADOS ON TREE

Must-see Forests and Woodlands

From tropical rainforests to mixed broadleaf woodlands and dense swathes of conifers, a vast range of arboreal life can be found in different forests around the world. The following pages contain a small selection of such areas.

NORTH AMERICA

Bryce Canyon National Park

Location: Utah
Best time to visit: June–October

Bryce Canyon is located in southwestern Utah, where the arid climate commonly features around 200 days of freeze-thaw temperatures each year. It is known for its ponderosa pine forests, which occur in the middle elevation zones of this mountainous area. Together with distinct zones of pinyon and juniper forest at lower levels and mixed spruce, fir, and aspen forest at higher altitudes, the park's diversity of floral zones supports a high level of biodiversity. Habitats range across 2,130 ft (650 m) of elevation and contain more than 100 species of bird, dozens of mammals, and more than 1,000 plant species. Notable fauna include porcupine, elk, mule deer, pronghorn, black bears, bobcats, and endangered species such as the Utah prairie dog, California condor, and southwestern willow flycatcher. Named after their "ponderous" (heavy) wood, ponderosas at Bryce Canyon may reach 130 ft (39 m) in height and can live for more than 500 years. Their bark is said to smell like vanilla or butterscotch. The national park itself is named after Bryce Canyon, a series of amphitheaterlike rock formations that feature the highest concentration of "hoodoo" outcrops anywhere in the world. Looking like totem poles, these eroded rock spires tower up to 150 ft (45 m) in height. They are created by the scouring effect of ice and water, which wear away the softer pink-, orange-, and white-banded sandstone beneath their hard limestone caps.

BRYCE CANYON NATIONAL PARK, UTAH

Sequoia and Kings Canyon National Parks

Location: California
Best time to visit: late June–late October

Sequoia and the neighboring Kings Canyon National Parks comprise a continuous protected area of 1,350 sq miles (3,500 sq km). They are home to the world's largest extant tree. Around one-quarter of this area is old-growth forest characterized by giant sequoia (also known as giant redwood); at 275 ft (84 m) high and 36 ft (11 m) across at the base, the immense specimen known as General Sherman is the star attraction. Estimated to be up to 2,700 years old, its bole volume is greater than that of any other living tree—taller trees and broader trees exist, but none that combine both characteristics. The temperate climate supports chaparral scrubland and woodlands of blue oak and interior live oak at lower elevations. It rises to montane meadows and mixed evergreen forests of Colorado white fir, red fir, ponderosa pine, and sugar pine, with foxtail and whitebark pine at high altitude. Sequoia National Park contains Mount Whitney, which at 14,505 ft (4,421 m) in height is the highest summit in the US outside of Alaska. The expansive wilderness is home to animals such as black bears, coyotes, mountain lions, and more.

Great Bear Rainforest

Location: British Columbia, Canada
Best time to visit: late August to mid-October (salmon runs)

Part of the largest coastal temperate rainforest in the world, Great Bear Rainforest stretches over 24,700 sq miles (6.4 million hectares) of protected mountains, glaciers, rivers, lakes, and fjords. With 22 ft (6.65 m) of rainfall per year, the region's lush vegetation includes western red cedar, some of which have been dated to 1,000 years old or more, and Sitka spruce growing to 295 ft (90 m) in height. A diversity of habitats provide a home for an array of wildlife, from cougars and grizzly bears, to humpback whales, orca, sea otters, and sea lions. The region's most celebrated resident is the kermode ("spirit") bear, a subspecies of the black bear in which 10 percent of cubs have a distinctive white coat. While closely managed logging is permitted in certain areas, 85 percent of the park is protected (amounting to around 70 percent of the old-growth forest). First Nations groups are involved as full stakeholders in planning, conservation, and economic diversification.

BRANCHES IN CATHEDRAL GROVE, VANCOUVER ISLAND

Cathedral Grove

Location: Vancouver Island, Canada
Best time to visit: March–May

Vancouver Island, a landmass the size of Denmark located off Canada's Pacific coast, is home to part of the last remaining virgin temperate rainforest in the northern hemisphere. Macmillan Provincial Park spans both the island's wetter climatic zone (characterized by western hemlock) and its drier zone (known for Douglas fir). The best examples of Douglas fir are found in Cathedral Grove—the most accessible area of old-growth forest on the island. This now-protected remnant of an ancient ecosystem contains 800-year-old Douglas firs that measure around 250 ft (75 m) in height and 29 ft (9 m) in girth; the largest known specimens were 400 ft (122 m) in height but were cut down following the emergence of industrial logging methods after World War II. Cathedral Grove also contains western hemlock; grand

fir; and western red cedar, a species that plays a key part in the belief systems of First Nations people. Strips of bark were removed from western red cedars—some of which have been dated to 1137 CE—for practical, cultural, and spiritual purposes. Macmillan Provincial Park is home to birds such as woodpeckers and owls, as well as mammals such as deer, elk, black bears, and cougars. The Cameron River, which flows adjacent to Cathedral Grove, contains various species of trout.

LATIN AMERICA

Yasuni National Park

Location: Ecuador
Best time to visit: December–February, August–September (avoid rainy seasons)

Designated a UNESCO Biosphere reserve in 1989, Yasuni National Park has one of the highest levels of biodiversity in the world. This

richness is partly thanks to its unique geographical characteristics, spanning the equator and containing both the Andes Mountains and the Amazon Rainforest. Located in the northeast of Ecuador, 190 miles (305 km) from the capital city, Quito, Yasuni's flora is 99 percent old-growth,

primary rainforest. It is notable for the deciduous ceibo tree, which can grow up to 150 ft (45 m) in height and features flanged buttress roots that stabilize the trunk in the often shallow, wet soil. Other tree species include red cedar, mahogany, peanut, flowering jacaranda, palm, balsa, and sangre de grado ("dragon's blood tree"), the red sap of which is used for traditional medicine. Animals including tapirs, giant armadillos, jaguars, ocelots, anacondas, giant anteaters, giant otters, sloths, harpy eagles, and pocket monkeys (the world's smallest primate) all make their home here. The park's watercourses contain piranhas, catfishes, anacondas, crocodiles, and turtles.

Huerquehue National Park

Location: Chile
Best time to visit: October–April

The Huerquehue National Park is a 30,888-acre (12,500-hectare) reserve of mountains, rivers, and 20 lakes and lagoons. It forms part of the Valdivian temperate rainforest, an ecoregion characterized by a dense bamboo and fern understory, with larger

RIVER BEND IN YASUNI NATIONAL PARK, ECUADOR

LAGUNA CHICA, HUERQUEHUE NATIONAL PARK, CHILE

Los Haitises National Park

Location: Dominican Republic
Best time to visit: November–May (avoid hurricane season)

Los Haitises National Park is one of the most biodiverse regions of the Caribbean. It incorporates 620 sq miles (1,600 sq km) of protected mangroves, subtropical rainforest, limestone hills, subterranean cave systems, and scattered keys (islets) around Samaná Bay in the northeast of the Dominican Republic. Taking its name from the Indigenous Taino word for highland or mountain, Los Haitises features limestone karst geology, in which water erosion has carved a landscape of caverns, sinkholes, waterfalls, outcrops, and rocky keys. Extensive mangrove forests predominate in coastal areas, where red, white, and black mangrove can be found. The largest specimens can reach 80 ft (24 m) in height, although a canopy of around 20 ft (6 m) is more common. It is not the size of these saltwater-adapted group of plants that is their most striking feature, however, but their dramatic aerial prop roots. The mangrove roots in Los Haitises provide protection for a range of

evergreen and deciduous flowering tree species, that spans Argentina and Chile. Prevailing westerly winds blowing off the Pacific Ocean maintain moderate temperatures and high rainfall, providing an ideal climate for a host of giant ferns, mosses, lichens, and climbing plants. The park's most notable tree species is the coniferous monkey puzzle tree, which thrives at elevations above 3,300 ft (1,000 m) and can reach 130 ft (40 m) in height. Despite being the national tree of Chile, it is an endangered species due to logging, grazing, and forest fires. Fauna include Andean condors, pudus—the world's smallest deer—and kodkods (an endangered wildcat).

Monteverde Cloud Forest Reserve

Location: Costa Rica
Best time to visit: January–May

Cloud forest is a type of evergreen montane forest characterized by persistent cloud cover that usually lies at canopy level. The Monteverde Reserve constitutes one of the most species-rich habitats in Central America and is one of three protected areas of cloud forest in Costa Rica. Cloud forests typically contain a high proportion of endemic species because their unique ecosystems and often inaccessible mountainous terrain inhibit population dispersal. The damp, humid conditions in which they grow make the trees of the cloud forest the ideal habitat for the growth of climbers and epiphytes—plants such as mosses, lichens, and ferns that grow on the surface of a larger plant. Another epiphyte, the orchid, is present in the reserve in greater numbers than anywhere else in the world— more than 500 individual species have been identified. One of the reserve's most notable trees, the strangler fig (Ficus species), is also an epiphyte. Its roots grow around the trunk of a host tree, spreading and thickening until the host is enveloped and

choked. The host decomposes in the humid conditions, leaving a hollow structure that can be big enough for a human to climb inside. The Monteverde Reserve is also home to the colorful quetzal bird and is one of the last places in which all six of the wild cat species in Central America—jaguars, ocelots, pumas, oncillas, margays, and jaguarundis—reside.

MONTEVERDE CLOUD FOREST RESERVE, COSTA RICA

aquatic species during spawning and infancy—including shrimps, crabs, smalltooth sawfish, manatees, and turtles—while the branches provide nesting areas for egrets, herons, cormorants, and roseate spoonbills. Inland, tree species include West Indian mahogany, ceiba, musk wood, and cigar-box cedar.

EUROPE

Casentinesi Forest National Park

Location: Tuscany, Italy
Best time to visit: September–November (fall displays)

Spanning the watershed of the northern Apennines—the mountainous spine of Italy—Casentinesi forest national park covers an area of around 140 sq miles (370 sq km). This makes it one of the largest forested areas in Europe; it is not a single forest, but a collection of reserves that have been carefully managed over the centuries. The national park encompasses a transitional landscape between the high-altitude climate of the alpine foothills and the Mediterranean climate of the rolling hills of Tuscany. This results in a unique combination of 28 defined habitat types. Fir trees, beech, and mountain maple predominate at higher altitude, where meadows flower during the summer months; the submountain belt contains a host of different species, including hornbeam, Turkey oak, chestnut, ash, elm, lime, yew, holly, and reforested areas of black pine. Fall displays in these dense areas of mixed woodland are noted for their array of color and shade. At lower levels, the warmer temperatures encourage the growth of the rare cork oak and holm oak. The scale of this protected wilderness has allowed the return of animal

CROOKED FOREST TREE TRUNKS, POLAND

species that had been lost to the area, such as golden eagles and wolves, while healthy populations of roe and fallow deer, wild boar, and European mouflon are also present. The alpine newt and endangered northern spectacled salamander are also resident.

Crooked Forest

Location: Gryfino, Poland
Best time to visit: May–June

Located near the town of Gryfino in northwest Poland, the Crooked Forest is a scattered collection of unusually curved Scotch (or Scots) pines. They are thought to have been forced into their odd, curved-trunk configuration as saplings. Surrounded by naturally growing, straight-trunked pines, the curved trees may originally have been grown for timber for the

construction of ships, furniture, musical instruments, sleds, or carts. While human intervention in their growth cannot be proven, a similar practice occurred in 19th-century England to create curved "compass timbers" for ships, while Indigenous people in North America are known to have manipulated "trail trees," bending a branch to act as a way-marker for route finding. Based on the Gryfino trees' age, it is thought that the saplings were forced into their curved positions prior to or during World War II. The mass population transfers during that conflict may have left the specimens abandoned and unused for their intended purpose, allowing subsequent growth to continue vertically and giving the crooked trees the spectacular, graceful curves of their mature form.

Wistman's Wood

Location: England
Best time to visit: May–September

Wistman's Wood in southwest England is an unusual example of upland oakwood due to its small English oak trees. Around 15 ft (4.5 m) in height, the stunted oaks are thought to date from a cooler climatic period around 500 years ago that limited their growth and led to their contorted forms: some main branches are twisted and weathered, while others lie prostrate on the granite boulders that litter the surrounding moor. Younger specimens dating from a warmer period are markedly taller and straighter in habit. Due to its altitude of around 1,300 ft (400 m) above sea level, the wood contains other high-level tree species, including rowan, hawthorn, hazel, and holly. Epiphytes such as mosses, the common polypody fern, and the bilberry, more commonly situated on the forest floor, can be found growing in shallow depressions in the dwarf oaks' prostrate limbs. Wistman's Wood is one of only two places in the UK where the rare horsehair lichen can be found and is also home to a population of adders (Britain's only native venomous snake), grazing cattle, and wild ponies.

Jasmund National Park

Location: Germany
Best time to visit: April–September

The largest continuous beech forest on Europe's Baltic Sea coast, Jasmund National Park is located on the northeast tip of Rügen island in northern Germany. It is classed by UNESCO as the northern terminus of an extensive Ancient Primeval Beech Forest, which is centered on the Carpathian Mountains in Ukraine. It is a World Heritage Site that contains unbroken stands of ancient beech trees, some up to 700 years old; they owe their survival to the steep cliffs that border the island and the inaccessibility of the forest's interior. The woodland encompasses a rolling landscape of hills, wetlands, hollows, lakes, and river valleys before capping the vertiginous 525-ft- (160-m-) high white chalk cliffs that tower above the waters of the Baltic Sea. The beech-forest canopy of tightly packed crowns prevents direct sunlight from reaching the forest floor, creating a sparse understory of shade-adapted plants and mushrooms. Other tree species in the reserve include black alder (confined to watercourses and swamps), European crab apple, wild service tree, and yew, while protected orchids can also be found, such as lady's slipper and bloom-in-the-meadows. In addition, the forest also provides a habitat for bird species, including the white-tailed eagle, kingfisher, house martin, and peregrine falcon.

AFRICA

Central African Rainforest

Location: Central Africa
Best time to visit: September–October

After the Amazon, the equatorial rainforest of central-west Africa is the next-largest continuous tract of rainforest in the world. Covering 695,000 sq miles (180 million hectares), it encompasses the Congo river basin and spans six countries, including Cameroon, Gabon, Republic of the Congo, and Democratic Republic of Congo (DRC). It hosts valuable timber species such as sapele, iroko, and African mahogany. Individual specimens tend to be taller but less densely clustered than rainforest elsewhere in the world due to the presence of large herbivores such as gorillas and the African forest elephant, who trample and feed on smaller competing specimens. The area of rainforest within DRC is thought to contain the richest concentration of plant species—including relatives of impatiens and begonias—and is home to the bonobo, an endangered species of great ape; the okapi (forest giraffe); chimpanzees; leopards; and hippos. Corruption issues and conflict in the region mean that roads and infrastructure can be poor, and travel in the area can be dangerous.

Bwindi Impenetrable Forest

Location: Uganda
Best time to visit: June–September

Bwindi Impenetrable Forest National Park is a tropical, old-growth rainforest in southwestern Uganda. Around half the global population of the critically endangered mountain gorilla lives in 14 kinship groups within its boundaries. Thought to have been the continuous site of rainforest habitat for more than 25,000 years, it takes its name from its rugged landscape of steep ridges; narrow valleys; and lush, dense undergrowth of bamboo, ferns, and vines. The forest's altitude zones—ranging from 3,900–8,400 ft (1,190–2,560 m) above sea level—are home to more than 220 tree species (10 of which are endemic). These include the evergreen East African yellow wood; at higher altitudes; deciduous African mahogany; and *Newtonia buchananii*, which can grow to 130 ft (40 m) in

AFRICAN FOREST ELEPHANT, CENTRAL AFRICA

FOREST INTERIOR. BWINDI IMPENETRABLE FOREST, UGANDA

height, at lower levels. This range of habitats supports more than 100 ferns and a rich diversity of small mammals, birds, butterflies, reptiles, and moths. As well as the mountain gorilla, primates in the forest include red-tailed monkeys, chimpanzees, L'Hoest's monkeys, blue monkeys, the black-and-white colobuses, and baboons.

Spiny Forest

Location: Madagascar
Best time to visit: April–October

The Spiny Forest (also known as spiny thicket, desert, and deciduous thicket) is a unique Afrotropical ecoregion. It contains a range of species that have adapted to the very low rainfall of southwestern Madagascar and a high proportion of flora and fauna that are endemic to the region. The Didiereaceae family is dominant among the floral species, having adapted small leaves and spines for reduced surface area and less water loss; they are similar to cacti but are woody in composition with long tap roots and waxy leaves, unlike their succulent New World cousins. The region is marked by distinct zones of vegetation: emergent tree species such as *Alluaudia ascendens*, which can reach 30 ft (10 m) in height, can be found in the east of the spiny forest, while dwarf species are more common in the west. Overall, the forest canopy is mostly 10–20 ft (3–6 m) high. Notable trees include six endemic species of baobab, known as *reniala* ("mother of the forest") in Malagasy. These trees' capacity for storing water in their immense, cylindrical trunks has led to another name: "bottle trees." The spiny forest is home to six species of primates, including the charismatic ring-tailed lemur or maki, Verreaux's sifaka, and the regionally endemic *Microcebus griseorufus*. The region's vegetation and wildlife are poorly documented and largely unprotected against the pressures of charcoal production and maize and cattle farming.

Quiver Tree Forest

Location: Namibia
Best time to visit: June–July (flowering)

One of Namibia's national monuments, Quiver Tree Forest contains around 250 quiver trees, some of which are around 300 years old. It is one of the only places in the world where such a high concentration of naturally growing specimens of this tree exists. The trees flourish among local dolerite rock formations, which anchor their extensive root systems and allow the plants to grow in close proximity to one another, giving the impression of a forest. A member of the aloe family, the quiver tree is a slow-growing succulent plant indigenous to southwest Africa that can grow to more than 30 ft (10 m) in height.

Its bright yellow flowers bloom in June and July—when the abundance of nectar attracts a range of avian, insect, and mammalian life—and in times of drought or disease, it is capable of self-amputation, when the plant jettisons limbs in order to survive. Its name reflects the practice of the indigenous San people, who hollowed out its branches for use as quivers, while its roots are used in traditional medicine to treat asthma and tuberculosis.

QUIVER TREE FOREST, NAMIBIA

ZHANGJIAJIE NATIONAL FOREST PARK, CHINA

 ASIA

Yakushima Island National Park

Location: Japan
Best time to visit: August–September

Situated off the coast of southwestern Japan, Yakushima Island National Park encompasses the islands of Yakushima and Kuchinoerabujima and was granted UNESCO World Natural Heritage status in 1993. Featuring vegetation from both subtropical and cool temperate zones, Yakushima's laurel-covered foothills feature evergreen Japanese pieris, Yakushima rhododendron, and Chinese banyan, rising to mixed coniferous and deciduous woodland. In turn, this gives way to shrub and dwarf bamboo at higher levels. The Shiratani Unsuikyo ravine contains yakusugi, or Japanese cedars, some of which are more than 1,000 years old—a specimen named Jomonsugi is

thought to be more than 7,000 years old. The island is home to a range of wildlife, from the Japanese macaque and Japanese deer to loggerhead turtles, which lay their eggs at Nagatahama beach on the northwest of the island between May and July. The smaller island of Kuchinoerabujima is marked by active volcanoes, hot springs, and sulfurous gases and is home to the endangered erabu flying fox, a nocturnal species of fruit bat.

Jiuzhaigou Valley National park

Location: Sichuan, China
Best time to visit: July–October

Located at the intersection of three high-mountain valleys in western China, Jiuzhaigou Valley national park consists of primarily deciduous broadleaf woodland. It is home to sumac, birch, maple, honeysuckle, azalea, and endemic rhododendron and bamboo, as well as needle-leaved evergreens,

such as hemlock and spruce, at higher altitudes. Notable among the region's conifers is the dragon spruce, an endemic species that thrives from 8,530–12,140 ft (2,600–3,700 m). The area has a subtropical to temperate monsoon climate, with annual rainfall of 30 in (761 mm), an abundance of glacial streams, and a unique geology (with high

concentrations of calcium carbonate). These combine to create the crystal-clear lakes for which the area is known, with shimmering waters in blue, emerald green, and turquoise shades. Notable fauna includes a small population of the endangered giant panda, golden snub-nosed monkeys, Sichuan takins, forest musk deer, blue sheep, snow leopards, and Duke of Bedford's voles. Lying at elevations of 6,560–15,630 ft (2,000–4,764 m), the region's snow-capped mountains are characterized by multitiered waterfalls, which turn to ice during the winter months of January and February, often colored blue-green by the chemical composition of the water.

Zhangjiajie National Forest Park

Location: Hunan Province, China
Best time to visit: April–May, August–October

China's first national forest park, Zhangjiajie was given UNESCO World Heritage status in 1992. Densely vegetated thanks to its year-round subtropical humid climate, the park is characterized by towering quartzite sandstone pillars, which were formed by freeze-thaw action and the

SASAN GIR, INDIA

weathering effect of the trees and plants that cling to their vertiginous sides. The forests of Zhangjiajie are home to protected tree species the dove tree and dawn redwood and contain other trees, including the endemic Wuling pine, Chinese nutmeg, rhododendron, ginkgo, red and white magnolia, and Chinese yew. Rare wildlife includes the clouded leopard, pygmy slow lorises, white cranes, macaques, pangolins, giant lynxes, red-footed falcons, cuckoos, giant salamanders, and tiger frogs. The area's extensive network of caves, rivers, lakes, and gorges can be accessed via extensive infrastructure constructed by the park authorities; this includes a 1,070 ft (326 m) outdoor elevator, cable cars, and a 1,410 ft (430 m) glass footbridge across a canyon 980 ft (300 m) deep.

Sasan Gir

Location: Gujarat, India
Best time to visit: December–March

Sasan Gir national park is located in an arid, dry ecoregion in northwest India, in which scrub and savannah predominate. It was founded in 1965 to protect the endangered Asiatic lion, and it contains a range of deciduous, semievergreen, and evergreen trees. These include teak, the dominant tree in the eastern portion of the reserve; flame of forest, a slow-growing species known locally as dhak; ziziphus, a relative of buckthorn; the evergreen jamun; ebony (known locally as tendu); and acacia. Banyan trees, with their characteristic immense aerial prop roots that mature into thick, woody trunks, are found in smaller numbers. Seasonal rivers and reservoirs provide water sources for a wide range of wildlife, from mugger crocodiles, porcupines, jungle cats, leopards, and mongooses, to the endangered Bonelli's eagle,

Indian eagle-owls, brown-capped pygmy woodpeckers, and the Indian pitta.

AUSTRALASIA

Daintree Rainforest

Location: Australia
Best time to visit: June–October

The 460-sq-mile (1,200-sq-km) Daintree Rainforest on Australia's northeast coast is thought to be the oldest extant rainforest in the world. It is thought to have been the site of a continuous rainforest for 110 million years and has a diverse and complex ecosystem of plant species, as well as one of the highest populations of primitive flowering plants anywhere in the world. Notable trees include the fast-growing blue quandong, also known as the blue marble tree or blue fig, which can grow to 100 ft (30 m) in height with a canopy 26 ft (8 m) across. It flowers in fall and winter, yielding small blue fruit (after which the tree is named) in spring. Other species include burrawang palm and wild ginger, which can grow to 20 ft (6 m) in height. Coastal mangroves provide a habitat for saltwater crocodiles, while avian species include great-billed heron, azure kingfisher, and cassowary, a 5¾-ft- (1.75-m-) tall flightless bird that plays a key role in seed dispersal. Daintree's high humidity creates the perfect conditions for the giant tree frog, which is the largest frog species in the world at up to 5½ in (14 cm) in length.

Tarkine Rainforest

Location: Tasmania
Best time to visit: December–February

The Tarkine region is located in northwest Tasmania and consists of coastal heathland, sand dunes, mountains, grassy woodland,

DAINTREE RIVER, NORTH QUEENSLAND, AUSTRALIA

and Australia's largest temperate rainforest. Although unprotected as a conservation area, the Tarkine is a mosaic of different habitats. It features wet sclerophyll forest containing eucalyptus trees of 100 ft (30 m) or more in height and wetlands in which nonvascular species (including mosses and liverworts) predominate. Notable trees include leatherwood; celery-top pine; sassafras; Huon pine (some thought to be 3,000 years old); and the immense beech myrtle, which can live for more than 400 years. Its wildlife is varied, with platypuses, echidnas, wombats, bandicoots, and possums, as well as carnivorous predators such as the Tasmanian devil, spotted-tailed quoll, and eastern quoll, for which the Tarkine is one of the last remaining strongholds. The world's biggest crayfish (the giant Tasmanian freshwater crayfish) is found here, growing up to 3 ft (1 m) in length and 13 lb (6 kg) in weight. The Tarkine is also noted for its rich Aboriginal archaeology, with extensive collections of stone artifacts, middens, rock shelters, burial grounds, and petroglyphs.

Waipoua Forest

Location: New Zealand
Best time to visit: December–March

Waipoua Forest is located on the northwest of New Zealand's North Island and forms a portion of the most extensive remaining tract of old-growth subtropical forest in the country. The kauri tree first appeared in the super-continent of Gondwana more than 100 million years ago and coexists alongside faster-growing species here by growing in poor soil, such as ridges and higher, sloping ground. Seedlings grow in the forest among manuka (tea tree) scrubland or in forest clearings where light levels are highest, developing a tapering trunk and conical crown as adolescents. As the tree matures, the bole thickens and lower branches are shed, giving the adult specimens their distinctive wide, straight, clean trunk. Waipoua is home to kakariki and kaka forest parrots, as well as the carnivorous pupurangi snail. Tāne Mahuta ("king of the forest") is the largest living kauri, estimated at 2,300 years old.

Urban Forests and Parks

As the world's cities grow ever larger, urban parks and forests offer vital oases for those seeking refuge from city life, as well as the chance to see a variety of tree species. Presented here is a small selection of notable parks from around the world.

Central Park

Location: New York City
Best time to visit: April–June, September–November

Nestled in the heart of Manhattan, America's first landscaped public park provides the people of New York City with a much-needed green space, especially in the city's stifling summer heat. Central Park's walkways, meadows, and woodlands are lined with 18,000 trees, almost 1,000 of which are evergreen. The 843-acre (341-hectare) park is home to 170 different species of tree, including sugar maple (*Acer saccharum*), sweetgum (*Liquidambar styraciflua*), green ash (*Fraxinus pennsylvanica*), and swamp cypress (*Taxodium distichum*). In fall, these trees fill the landscape with their vibrant foliage colors, making this season a popular time to visit. Central Park is home to two main species of cherry tree: the yoshino cherry (*Prunus × yedoensis*) and the Kanzan cherry (*P. serrulata* 'Kanzan'). The 35 yoshino cherries were a gift to the US from Japan in 1912, and their pale pink blossoms provide an attractive backdrop to the reservoir in early spring. Cedar Hill and the 4-acre (1.6-hectare) Arthur Ross Pinetum, which contains more than 600 pine trees across 17 different species, offer a pleasing wash of green in winter.

At the center of the park are three wilder woodland areas known as the Ramble. Designed to have the look and feel of upstate New York landscapes such as the Catskills, the Ramble's 36 acres (14.5 hectares) are densely packed with trees and other plants. There are twisting pathways, a pond, a stream, bridges, a cave, and rock outcroppings, and it is considered one of the best places in the park for birdwatching. The Ramble's Tupelo Meadow provides a popular display of fall foliage. Particularly notable is the three-stemmed black tupelo (*Nyssa sylvatica*) that can be found at the meadow's edge, whose three trunks stretch to more than 79 ft (24 m) high and whose canopy spreads to 56 ft (17 m) wide.

South Mountain Park and Preserve

Location: Phoenix, Arizona
Best time to visit: March–May, September–November

The largest municipal park in the US, South Mountain Park and Preserve spreads over 16,000 acres (6,500 hectares) and contains a vast network of trails that cover more than 50 miles (80 km). This popular hiking, biking, and horse-riding area provides sweeping views of the city of Phoenix and the Sonoran Desert. At 2,330 ft (710 m), Dobbin's Lookout is the highest point of the park and provides panoramic views of the surrounding landscape, including Camelback Mountain.

Typical of the Sonoran Desert, sprouting from between the park's sand and granite boulders are palo verde trees (*Parkinsonia* spp.), which offer splashes of bright yellow blooms during their short flowering seasons, and mesquite trees, alongside desert plants such as prickly pears, barrel cacti, and ocotillo. South Mountain is also home to the elephant tree (*Bursera*

CENTRAL PARK, NEW YORK CITY

GOLDEN GATE PARK, SAN FRANCISCO, CALIFORNIA

microphylla). This rare, small tree thrives in the arid desert. Its short, thick trunks, and branches that resemble the trunks of elephants are well adapted to store water.

Golden Gate Park

Location: San Francisco, California
Best time to visit: March–May, September–November

The creation of Golden Gate Park began in 1870 on a vast area of sand dunes, which stretched east for 7 miles (11 km) across the San Francisco peninsula from the Pacific Ocean. Horse manure was added to the sand to transform it into stabilized soil in which trees and plants could thrive. The park's first formal structure, the Conservatory of Flowers, opened in 1879; now it also includes the San Francisco Botanical Gardens; the California Academy of Sciences; the de Young Museum; the Music Concourse; and a paddock containing a small herd of grazing bison, looked after by the San Francisco Zoo. Today, the park spans a total of

1,017 acres (412 hectares), which includes 680 acres (275 hectares) of forest, 130 acres (53 hectares) of meadows, and 33 acres (13 hectares) of lakes. Evidence of its earliest trees can be seen in its Monterey cypress (*Cupressus macrocarpa*), Monterey pine (*Pinus radiata*), blue gum eucalyptus (*Eucalyptus globulus*), giant sequoia (*Sequoiadendron giganteum*), and coast redwood (*Sequoia sempervirens*) trees. There are several commemorative and symbolic tree plantings across the park. The Redwood Memorial Grove features 39 redwoods that were planted as saplings in 1930 to pay tribute to the soldiers who lost their lives in the Spanish–American War and World War I. Another, the Arch of Colonial Trees, includes a tree from each of the original 13 states along a 450-ft (137-m) curved path.

Golden Gate Park features a number of landscaped gardens, including the Japanese Tea Garden. The garden features azaleas, pines, Japanese maples, and cherry trees, which come alive with pink and white blossoms in early spring.

In contrast to the majority of the park, which is more landscaped, the Oak Woodlands Natural Area offers a glimpse of the historic oak woodlands that once made their home at the eastern edge of the area's sand dunes.

Chapultepec Park

Location: Mexico City, Mexico
Best time to visit: March–May

In Mexico City, the sprawling 1,600-acre (647-hectare) Chapultepec Park has been a public space since 1530, making it the oldest urban park in Latin America. Packed with various trees, it is known as the city's "lungs." It surrounds the rocky Chapultepec Hill (meaning "grasshopper hill"), which reaches 200 ft (60 m) above Mexico City and was once a residence of Aztec rulers. Construction of the castle that now sits on the hill began in 1785. It later became the national military academy before being rebuilt in 1864 by Emperor Maximilian, who also rejuvenated the forested area that surrounded the castle. Mexican presidents continued to live in this castle until 1940, when it became a museum. Chapultepec Park is now home

to a forest; paths; lakes; fountains; a zoo; botanical gardens; and several museums, including the world-famous Museum of Anthropology. The park is split into three sections: the castle and museums are found within the first; the second houses an amusement park and a children's museum; and the third is a magnificent area of dense forest filled with wildlife and trees, including cedars, redwoods, and poplars. The Montezuma cypress (*Taxodium mucronatum*), the national tree of Mexico, stands out as one of the park's most spectacular tree species because of its broad spreading crown.

Ibirapuera Park

Location: São Paulo, Brazil
Best time to visit: June–October

Set in the middle of São Paulo and spanning 390 acres (158 hectares), Ibirapuera Park was opened in 1954 to celebrate the fourth centenary of the city. It provides residents and visitors with spaces to participate in the city's vibrant cultural scene, including several museums and galleries. São Paulo Fashion Week is held in the Biennial Pavilion each July. The park also provides ample

CHAPULTEPEC PARK, MEXICO CITY, MEXICO

JARDIN DU LUXEMBOURG, PARIS, FRANCE

opportunity for health and leisure activities, with its skate park, bike paths, and jogging track that leads runners through the wooded perimeter of the park.

Ibirapuera Park is home to more than 500 species of tree, both native and exotic. It boasts a range of ipê trees (*Handroanthus* spp.), which are native to Brazil. Each spring around June, these trees bear flowers in a variety of colors—purple, yellow, pink, and white—followed by the brilliant purple blossoms of jacaranda trees (*Jacaranda mimosifolia*) in October. Monkey puzzle trees (*Araucaria araucana*) can be observed in the Bosque das Araucárias. Also notable are the jabuticaba trees (*Plinia cauliflora*) found across the park, which produce dark purple, spherical fruit that grow directly on the trunk. Non-native trees include several banyan trees (*Ficus benghalensis*), whose trunks and branches attractively fan out, and a large number of Australian eucalyptus trees.

Jardin du Luxembourg

Location: Paris, France
Best time to visit: June–August, September–October

Situated between the Latin Quarter and Saint-Germain-des-Prés is Paris's most popular park: Jardin du Luxembourg. The picturesque park is named after the Duke of Luxembourg, who sold it to queen consort of France Marie de Medici in 1612, though it has changed a lot since she acquired it. It is particularly popular among chess players (and spectators) who come to play friendly games in the dappled shade of the park's many trees and Parisians who come to stroll along the tree-lined, gravel paths or relax in one of the park's little green chairs.

Perhaps most iconic is the park's octagonal pond, the Grand Bassin, that sits elegantly in front of the Luxembourg Palace, with the Medici Fountain to the side. The 57-acre (23-hectare) manicured gardens are split into French

gardens and English gardens and feature an orchard with numerous ancient apple varieties, a world-famous orchid collection, an orangery, an apiary, and more than 100 sculptures.

In spring, along with its apple trees, the gardens come alive with the pink blooms of the rare Judas tree (*Cercis siliquastrum*) and the white bracts of handkerchief tree (*Davidia involucrata*). The garden's extensive grove of horse chestnuts are meticulously planted in mesmerizing rows, offering a sea of lush green through summer, warming to rusty orange as fall arrives.

Table Mountain National Park

Location: Cape Town, South Africa
Best time to visit: March–May, September–November

This sprawling national park is situated on the border of the city of Cape Town. A popular hiking

destination, it covers an area of 85 sq miles (221 sq km) and has diverse natural features, including Table Mountain itself (known for its distinctive flat-topped appearance) the Cape of Good Hope, and extensive forest areas, as well as beaches and varied animals. The area has hugely diverse flora and a number of endemic plant species. Part of the park includes the Afromontane Forest, on the eastern side of Table Mountain. A and a few notable local tree species include silver tree (*Leucadendron argenteum*), found only on this peninsula; black ironwood (*Olea capensis*); and cape beech (*Rapanea melanophloeos*). The area also features the fynbos landscape, a shrubby bushland unique to the area, with high biodiversity.

Hong Kong Park

Location: Hong Kong
Best time to visit: February–April, September–December

Since it opened in 1991, Hong Kong Park has provided a place of calm and tranquility amid the chaos of one of the world's busiest cities. Spread over 20.16 acres (8.16 hectares), the park was created on part of the site of the Victoria Barracks and has preserved several of the original buildings, which date back to 1842 and 1910.

Flowing water is central to the park's landscape, with a lake and waterfall sitting near the middle of the park, surrounded by its central garden, fountains, tai chi garden, conservatory of plants, and aviary. Visitors can stroll along a walkway through the tree canopy to observe the 80 different species of bird that make their home in the Edward Youde Aviary.

A number of large and old trees have been preserved in the park. These include several Chinese banyan trees (*Ficus microcarpa*) with crown spreads of 46–98 ft

(14–30 m). Particularly notable is the Hong Kong Park's 75 ft (23 m) tall cotton tree (*Bombax ceiba*), which flowers from February to March, wowing park visitors with its red blooms.

Lumpini Park

Location: Bangkok, Thailand
Best time to visit: November–May

Central Bangkok's first public park is also its largest. Spanning 143 acres (58 hectares), it is home to a public library, a vast lake, lawns, woodlands, and plenty of wildlife—most notably the monitor lizards that made the news in 2016, when they reached 400 in number. Named after the Buddha's birthplace, the park originally belonged to King Rama VI before he donated it to the public in 1925. A memorial statue of the king sits at the entrance to the park.

Now, locals and visitors alike make use of the space for walking, jogging, practicing tai chi, and paddleboating. The park is at its most pleasant in the morning or evening, when the temperature and

humidity are lower, but the trees, including towering palms, that fill the park offer respite from the rigors of life and the whims of the weather at all times of the day.

Native to parts of southeast Asia, the spectacular golden shower tree (*Cassia fistula*)—the national tree of Thailand—can also be found in this park. Its long racemes of bright yellow flowers create a beautiful hanging display between March and May.

Sanjay Gandhi National Park

Location: Mumbai, India
Best time to visit: September–January

Sanjay Gandhi National Park is a protected wild forest area in the densely populated city of Mumbai. It dates as far back as the 4th century BCE, when part of the land route between two nearby ports in ancient India ran through the forest. This wilderness covers an extraordinary 25,450 acres (10,300 hectares). Spread over hills and valleys, it varies in elevation

KINGS PARK, PERTH, AUSTRALIA

from 98 ft (30 m) to 1,575 ft (480 m) and makes up about 20 percent of Mumbai's area.

In the park's center lie the magnificent Kanheri Caves. Numbering more than 100, these were carved out of the black rock by Buddhist monks between the 1st century BCE and 11th century CE. The national park's two lakes, Vihar and Tulsi, were constructed in the 1860s to supply water to Mumbai in response to shortages. They now house a population of mugger crocodiles (*Crocodylus palustris*) and offer scenic vistas for tourists. Park fauna also includes leopards, porcupines, rhesus macaques (*Macaca mulatta*), and Atlas moths (*Attacus atlas*).

Sanjay Gandhi National Park provides a home for roughly 40 species of mammal, 78 species of reptile and amphibian, 150 species of butterfly, 254 species of bird, and 1,300 species of plant. Lush forest dominates the landscape, with mostly mixed-deciduous plants, including plenty of bamboo; silk trees; figs; and several small patches of true Ashoka trees (*Saraca asoca*), which exhibit dense bundles of orange-red flowers from around February to April. Evergreen and semievergreen plants and trees can be found within some narrow valleys.

Kings Park

Location: Perth, Australia
Best time to visit: September–November

A mix of natural bushland and sculpted gardens over 400 acres (160 hectares), Kings Park and Botanic Garden sits atop Mount Eliza, with views of Perth's skyline and Swan River. The Botanic Gardens and Park Authority is committed to preserving these gardens to honor the Aboriginal culture that holds this area sacred.

A 750-year-old, 39.6-ton (36-tonne) giant boab tree (*Adansonia gregorii*) called "Gija Jumulu" can be seen in the park. In 2008, this mature tree was transported over 1,988 miles (3,200 km) from Warmun, Western Australia, to Kings Park as a gift from the local indigenous Gija people to Western Australians. The Botanic Garden has more than 3,000 species of wildflower native to Western Australia.

A 2,034-ft (620-m) path called the Lotterywest Federation Walkway leads visitors across a bridge of glass and steel and through the treetops to showcase the best of the region's fauna, from zamia cycads and grass trees below, to jarrah (*Eucalyptus marginate*), tingle (*E. jacksonii*), and sheoak in the canopy.

HONG KONG PARK, HONG KONG

Famous Trees

Some tree species are so remarkable that any specimen is worthy of note, while other individual trees are so celebrated that they have entered popular, religious, or ethnic culture, or even been named by the people who revere them.

Trees of 40 Fruits

Location: Various, US
Species: multiple, Prunus family
Access: varies with location

Found in New York, Arkansas, and other states, these trees came from 40 buds from different members of the genus *Prunus*, grafted onto a root stock. As a result, different branches bear different fruit.

Methuselah

Location: Inyo National Forest, US
Species: Bristlecone pine
Access: location undisclosed

Named after the oldest person in the Bible, this dense, resinous pine was aged as more than 4,789 years old after samples from its core were taken in 1957. Its precise location is kept secret to protect it.

Lone Cypress

Location: Monterey, California
Species Monterey cypress
Access: observable from a public viewpoint

Described as one of the most photographed trees in the world, this rare, wind-whipped Monterey cypress is a prominent landmark on the 17-Mile Drive coastal road of northern California.

Arbol del Tule

Location: Oaxaca, Mexico
Species: Montezuma cypress
Access: open to the public

Found in a churchyard in the town of Santa Maria del Tule, this immense Montezuma cypress measures 46 ft 1 in (14.05 m) in diameter and 116 ft (35.4 m) in height. Its heavily buttressed trunk makes it the widest tree in the world— DNA testing was required to prove that it is a single specimen rather than several conjoined trunks.

Cajueiro de Pirangi

Location: Pirangi do Norte, Brazil
Species: Cashew
Access: open to the public

This tree has a canopy that extends over an area of around 91,500 sq ft (8,500 sq m), making it larger than a soccer field. Four of this single specimen's five radiating branches have taken root, effectively creating clones of the original tree. It yields 60,000 cashew nuts each year.

Newton's Apple Tree

Location: Lincolnshire, UK
Species: Apple
Access: open to the public

Located at Woolsthorpe Manor in England, this apple tree is the scene of scientist Isaac Newton's 1666 observation of the force of gravity, which he realized had caused an apple to fall to the ground. The rare "Flower of Kent" variety that grows there today is the only apple tree recorded to have grown at the site.

Bridegroom's Oak

Location: Eutin, Germany
Species: Oak
Access: open to the public

A hole in the trunk of this oak tree 10 ft (3 m) off the ground acts as a public mailbox where lovers leave their letters, a practice that began in the late 19th century. The tree has its own postal address—local postal workers deliver letters from around the world that may be read by members of the public.

Chapel Tree

Location: Seine-Maritime, France
Species: Oak
Access: open to the public

Since 1696, this ancient oak has contained two chapels within its trunk, which was partially hollowed out after a lightning strike. An external spiral staircase allows visitors to climb the outside of the still-living tree, which is thought to be the oldest in France.

CHAPEL TREE, FRANCE

DEADVLEI SKELETON TREES, NAMIBIA

Deadvlei skeleton trees

Location: Namib-Naukluft Park, Namibia
Species: Camel thorn (acacia)
Access: open to the public

These desiccated trees perished around 700 years ago. The dry desert conditions preserved the once-thriving trees after their water source was blocked by encroaching dunes, which also turned the marshy ground to solid clay.

Sunland baobab

Location: Limpopo, South Africa
Species: African baobab
Access: open to the public

Like many baobabs that reach an old age, the Sunland baobab, more than 1,000 years old, has an immense trunk that has hollowed over time. Its owners installed a bar that is open to the public, although part of this tree collapsed in 2016.

Jaya Sri Maha Bodhi

Location: Sri Lanka
Species: Bodhi
Access: open to the public

Thought to be the oldest tree, with a documented date of planting—249 BCE—this sacred *Ficus religiosa* tree is revered for having grown from the branch of the fig tree under which Buddha gained enlightenment. The branch was taken from Bodhgaya, India, to Sri Lanka and planted in the Mahamevnāwa Gardens, where it can be visited to this day.

Dragon's Blood trees

Location: Soqotra island, Yemen
Species: Dragon's blood tree
Access: varies with location

Growing only on the island of Soqotra, this extraordinary evergreen tree has an umbrella-shaped canopy supported by inverted, rootlike branches. Once widespread on the island, it is now only found in numbers at higher altitudes. The species is named after its ruby-red resin, which was known for its medicinal properties.

Tree of Life

Location: Bahrain
Species: Ghaf
Access: open to the public

This lone ghaf tree—thought to be more than 400 years old—grows in the desert. Its crown is 32 ft (9.75 m) high and its spread is around twice that, with trailing branches that lie prostrate on the sand. The trunk is protected by railings, but the branches are freely accessible.

Abraham's Oak

Location: West Bank, Israel
Species: Tabor oak
Access: viewing by arrangement

Also known as the "Oak of Mamre," this tabor oak may be up to 5,000 years old. Located in the grounds of the Russian Orthodox Monastery in Hebron, it is one of several sites linked to the prophet Abraham. The main stem was thought to be dead since 1996, but a new shoot sprouted nearby two years later.

Baobab Prison Tree

Location: Australia
Species: Baobab
Access: open to the public

This hollow baobab tree is thought to be 1,500 years old and was reputed to have been used as a holding cell for prisoners by colonial officials. Anecdotal evidence suggests it is more likely to have been used by Aboriginal peoples as an occasional shelter, while human bones found by 20th-century settlers indicate it also served as an ossuary.

Sacred Kauri trees

Location: Waipoua Forest, North Island, New Zealand
Species: Kauri
Access: open to the public

More than 2,300 years old, Tane Mahuta ("Lord of the Forest") and Te Matua Ngahere ("Father of the Forest") are the tallest and broadest of the kauri trees—a slow-growing coniferous species that once proliferated in New Zealand—in Waipoua Forest. According to Maori belief, the ancestor of the kauri tree created all of life, and the species is seen as *taonga*—a natural treasure.

Dave Evans Bicentennial Tree

Location: Warren National Park, Western Australia
Species: Karri
Access: open to the public

Named after a local politician, this much-loved and immense eucalyptus tree features a spiral stairway pegged to the trunk, which was added in 1988 to mark Australia's bicentenary. Towering to 246 ft (75 m), the steps can be climbed by visitors, but they also have a practical application, allowing the tree-top viewpoint to be used as a lookout during wildfire season.

LONE CYPRESS, CALIFORNIA

Habit and Leaves

Trees have a number of features that can be used to determine their species. A tree's habit and its leaves can offer plenty of identifying information; some examples of common characteristics are illustrated here.

Narrow, spirelike shape with uniform branches

Habit

A tree's overall shape, known as its habit, can be used to help distinguish its species. Age, location, and other external factors can lead to variation across species.

Multiple woody stems

SHRUBLIKE

Usually large, with wide, horizontal branches

SPREADING

Wider at the base than the top

CONICAL

COLUMNAR

Leaf type

The blade of a leaf can be whole or fully divided into individual leaflets. Sometimes the blades are like needles or scales. As the name suggests, broadleaf trees possess broad leaves rather than the needles or scales typical of conifers.

Individual, undivided leaf

SIMPLE

Leaf divided into leaflets

COMPOUND

May taper to a sharp point

NEEDLELIKE

Tiny, flattened leaves

SCALELIKE

Leaf arrangement

This refers to the positioning of leaves, or, in compound leaves, the leaflets relative to one another. Tree species may share similar leaf shapes, but their arrangement may be completely different.

Leaves arranged in pairs

OPPOSITE

Leaves positioned alternately along stem

ALTERNATE

Leaflets radiate from a central point

PALMATE

Leaflets arranged along a central stem

PINNATE

Leaf shapes

Trees display a remarkable range of leaf shapes and sizes. Broadleaf trees exhibit the greatest variety of shapes, while conifers are mainly scalelike or needlelike. Some of the most commonly found leaf shapes are shown here.

Leaves overlap one another

SCALELIKE

Leaves may have a sharp or blunt tip

NEEDLELIKE

Barely widening along length

LINEAR

Heart-shaped

CORDATE

Egg-shaped, with wider base

OVATE

Egg-shaped, with narrower base

OBOVATE

Long and lance-shaped, tapering toward the tip

LANCEOLATE

Widest near the middle

ELLIPTIC

Almost circular in shape

ORBICULAR

Almost triangular in shape

DELTOID

Long, with nearly parallel sides

OBLONG

Hand-shaped, with lobes radiating from base

PALMATE

Feathery leaves made up of tiny leaflets

FERNLIKE

Leaflets are twice-divided

BIPINNATE

Consists of three leaflets

TRIFOLIATE

Leaf margins

The margins of leaves may be smooth or indented, and indentations can range from deep lobes to jagged teeth. Margins can be a useful tool in tree identification, particularly when looked at alongside leaf shape.

Smooth edge with no indentations

ENTIRE

Undulating (sinuous) edge

SINUATE

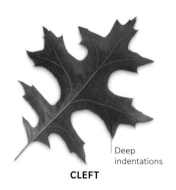

Deep indentations

CLEFT

Forward-pointing, sawlike teeth

SERRATE

Very fine, forward-pointing teeth

SERRULATE

Each serration is subserrated

DOUBLE SERRATE

Outward-pointing teeth

DENTATE

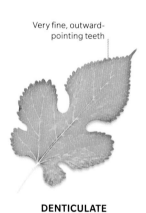

Very fine, outward-pointing teeth

DENTICULATE

Rounded indentations

LOBATE

Rounded scallops, known as crenations

CRENATE

Smaller scallops than those on crenate leaves

CRENULATE

Fine hairs called cilia along margin

CILIATE

Sharp spines at tip of each tooth

SPINOUS

Margin forms waves

UNDULATE

Irregular indentations

INCISED

Leaf color, markings, texture, and venation

Looking beyond the more obvious shape and arrangement, a leaf can have various textures, from hairy to glossy, and can exhibit a variety of colors, which can be permanent, seasonal, or related to the age of the leaves. The patterns the veins make can also be diagnostic.

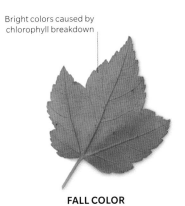

Bright colors caused by chlorophyll breakdown

FALL COLOR

More than one color

VARIEGATED

Color changes as the leaf matures

BRONZE

Paler underside to each leaf

WHITE MARKING

Covering of tiny hairs

HAIRY

Prominent veins create wrinkled texture

WRINKLED

Hairless, shiny surface

SMOOTH

Highly shiny surface

GLOSSY

Matte surface

MATTE

Veins radiate from single point at base of leaf

PALMATE VEINS

Irregular venation

WEBLIKE VEINS

Parallel secondary veins arise from a central midvein

PINNATE VEINS

Bark, Twigs, Flowers, and Fruits

Tree bark offers a variety of colors, textures, and shapes. Fruits and flowers present obvious—and often beautiful—visual characteristics, while twigs can reward careful inspection.

Bark

Many trees can be identified by their bark alone, as most have a characteristic bark structure, pattern, or texture—particularly useful in winter, when many trees are leafless. The protective layer may stay the same throughout a tree's life or change as it matures.

RIDGED

LENTICELLATE

SCALY

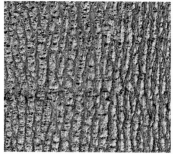

FISSURED

FLAKING

PEELING

SPINY

Twigs and buds

Looking closely at the twigs and the buds that broadleaf trees exhibit in the winter months can offer clues to a tree's species. Buds vary greatly in number and arrangement around a twig, and their protective bud scales may vary in color or be sticky, hairy, or furry.

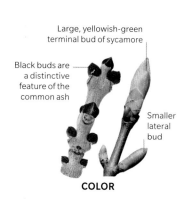

Large, yellowish-green terminal bud of sycamore

Black buds are a distinctive feature of the common ash

Smaller lateral bud

COLOR

Furry coating on birch bud

TEXTURE

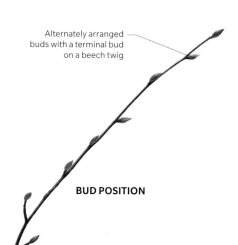

Alternately arranged buds with a terminal bud on a beech twig

BUD POSITION

Flowers

As well as size, color, and form, the position of flowers may offer clues to a tree's species. The flowers may be arranged in clusters or alone at the end of a stem. Some species have both male and female flowers on one tree, while in other species, they may be found on separate trees.

Many stalks grow from a single point

UMBEL

Outer flowers have longer stalks than the central flowers

CORYMB

Short stalks of equal length

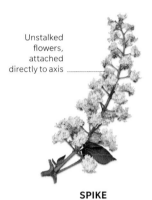

Unstalked flowers, attached directly to axis

SPIKE

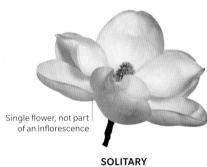

Single flower, not part of an inflorescence

SOLITARY

Cluster of single-sex flowers, often petalless, arranged around one stem

CATKIN

Many flowers along one axis

RACEME

Fruits

As the bearer of the seeds from which a new tree will grow, a tree's fruit is a vital part of its life cycle. In order to guarantee success in spreading seeds, fruits have evolved into many different shapes, sizes, and forms, from woody cones to sweet, juicy berries.

Winged fruit containing seed

SAMARA

Seed pod will split to release seeds

SEED POD

Seed is found within a hard shell

NUT

Outer, fleshy part encases a single seed

DRUPE

Flesh surrounds multiple seeds

BERRY

Seeds encased in a hard, woody cone

CONE

Record-breaking Trees

Although they are a common sight, some trees have uncommon characteristics—whether growing to great heights, surviving for millennia, or exuding deadly poisons. This is a selection of some of these extraordinary trees from around the world.

Oldest living trees

- Quaking aspen (*Populus tremuloides*), Utah: estimated at 14,000 years old. While its age is much debated, this tree colony, known as Pando, is the oldest clonal colony of an individual tree.

- Palmer oak (*Quercus palmeri*), California: 13,000 years old. A clonal colony in the Jurupa Mountains called the Jurupa Oak.

- Norway spruce (*Picea abies*), Dalarna Province, Sweden: 9,550 years old. Named Old Tjikko, this 16 ft (5 m) tall tree is another example of vegetative cloning.

- Bristlecone pine (*Pinus longaeva*), California: around 5,070 years old. The oldest known living, nonclonal, individual tree. It is unnamed and its location is kept secret.

- Mediterranean cypress (*Cupressus sempervirens*), Yazd Province, Iran: over 4,000 years old. The oldest cypress in the world and the oldest tree in Asia, known as the Cypress of Abarkuh or *Sarv-e Abarkuh*.

Tallest trees

- Coast redwood (*Sequoia sempervirens*), California: 380 ft 9 in (116.07 m). Nicknamed Hyperion, this tree's location is kept secret. There are many redwoods that exceed 330 ft (100 m) in height.

- Yellow meranti (*Shorea faguetiana*), Sabah, Malaysia: 330 ft 9 in (100.8 m). Named Menara, this highly endangered tree is the tallest tropical tree and the tallest flowering plant.

- Mountain ash eucalyptus (*Eucalyptus regnans*), Tasmania, Australia: 327 ft 6 in (99.82 m). Named Centurion, it is the tallest tree in Oceania.

- Coast Douglas-fir (*Pseudotsuga menziesii*), Oregon: 327 ft (99.7 m). Named the Doerner Fir, this tree is 11 ft 6 in (3.5 m) in diameter.

- Sitka spruce (*Picea sitchensis*), California: 317 ft 3 in (96.7 m). The location of this tree, called Raven's Tower, is undisclosed.

- Giant sequoia (*Sequoiadendron giganteum*), California: 316 ft (96.3 m). Sequoias like this one are the largest trees in the world by volume.

- Bhutan weeping cypress cashmeriana), Wangdue Phodrang, Bhutan: 310 ft 4 in (94.6 m). It is said the hollow trunk of this tree contains relic items.

- Tasmanian blue gum (*Eucalyptus globulus*), Tasmania, Australia:

GIANT SITKA SPRUCE AND PERSON, BRITISH COLUMBIA, CANADA

WOLLEMI PINE TREE, KEW, UK

310 ft 10 in (92 m). Its name, Neeminah Loggorale Meena, means "mother and daughter."

- Manna gum (*Eucalyptus viminalis*), Tasmania, Australia: 292 ft (89 m). Nicknamed Sir Vim, this is one of a group of three manna gums known as the White Knights.

- Angelim vermelho (*Dinizia excelsa*), Para, Brazil: 290 ft 4 in (88.5 m). Thought to be the tallest in the Amazon rainforest.

Smallest tree species

- Dwarf willow (*Salix herbacea*): ³⁄₈–2¼ in (1–6 cm). This tree's size helps it survive arctic and subantarctic environments.

Largest trees by diameter

- Montezuma cypress (*Taxodium mucronatum*), Oaxaca, Mexico: 37 ft 10 in (11.52 m). This

1,400-year-old tree is named El Árbol del Tule and has a height of 116 ft 2 in (35.4 m).

- Baobab (*Adansonia digitata*), Limpopo, South Africa: 35 ft 7 in (10.85 m). Also known as the Sunland Baobab, this tree is so large that a bar was opened inside it by the landowners.

- Giant sequoia (*Sequoiadendron giganteum*), California: 29 ft (8.85 m). This tree, named General Grant, is also the second-largest tree in the world by volume, after General Sherman, also in California.

- Chinese camphor tree (*Cinnamomum camphora*), Kagoshima, Japan: 25 ft 4 in (7.71 m). Nicknamed the Great Camphor of Kamō, this tree's circumference is 79 ft 6 in (24.22 m).

- Za (*Adansonia za*), Madagascar: 23 ft 3 in (7.08 m). This baobab,

known as the Ampanihy Baobab, has a circumference of 73 ft (22.25 m).

Heaviest tree

- Quaking aspen (*Populus tremuloides*), Utah: 6,614 tons (6,000 tonnes). This clonal colony contains 47,000 stems and is the world's heaviest organism.

Highest-altitude tree

- *Polylepis tomentella* (formerly *Polylepis tarapacana*). These trees live at 13,100–17,000 ft (4,000–5,200 m) above sea level in Bolivia, the highest elevation for any tree in the world.

Largest tree-borne fruit

- Jackfruit (*Artocarpus heterophyllus*): up to 35½ in (90 cm) long and up to 75 lb (34 kg). In 2020, the largest fruit was 38 in (97 cm) long and 113 lb (51.4 kg). Native to the Indo-Malay region of Asia.

Most poisonous trees

- Manchineel (*Hippomane mancinella*). Native to Caribbean coasts and nicknamed "little apple of death," the sap of this tree is so poisonous that it can blister human skin or cause blindness on contact, and eating its fruit can be fatal.

- Suicide tree (*Cerbera odollam*). Native to India; ingestion of its seeds is highly deadly to humans.

- Strychnine tree (*Strychnos nux-vomica*). The bark and seeds of this tree are poisonous and are sometimes used in pest control.

Highly endangered trees

- Wollemi Pine (*Wollemia nobilis*). Discovered near Sydney, Australia, there are fewer than 100 known trees in the wild.

- Three Kings Kaikōmako (*Pennantia baylisiana*). There is just one known tree remaining in the wild in New Zealand.

JACKFRUIT TREE, INDIA

Tree Calendar

Trees, woodlands, and forests continue to hold an important place in a range of religious, cultural, and seasonal events that are held throughout the year. A selection of these is listed below.

JANUARY

January–March Millions of Monarch butterflies overwinter in oyamel firs in central Mexico's Monarch Butterfly Biosphere Reserve. Their combined weight famously bends the branches of the host trees.

FEBRUARY

February First held in 1959, Vietnam's Tree Planting Festival aims to counteract loss of green space by planting 1 billion trees by 2025.

Early February The Jewish new year festival for trees, *Tu Bishvat* marks the beginning of the agricultural year and features tree-planting and feasts of fruit. The date varies between late January and early February.

MARCH

March 12 In China, National Tree Planting Day involves millions of citizens joining in with tree-planting activities.

March 21 The United Nation's International Day of Forests is observed around the world, with local and international events to celebrate forests and raise awareness of their importance.

Late March–early May *Hanami* is the cherry-blossom (*sakura*) viewing season in Japan. People gather to admire and celebrate the spectacular sight of cherry trees in bloom.

March–June In Jharkhand, India, the tribal festival of *Sarhul* marks the beginning of the new year with *sal*-tree worship, a banquet, and dancing.

JULY

First week of July In India, *Van Mahotsav* is a week-long tree-planting festival held each year to celebrate the importance of trees and counter the effects of deforestation.

Around July 4 In Michigan, the five-day-long celebration of Manistee National Forest Festival is held around the country's Independence Day.

Last weekend of July With around 300,000 people taking part each year, Australia's National Tree Day encourages schools and community groups to plant trees and protect nature.

AUGUST

August 3 Arbor Day is held in Niger to celebrate the country's national tree-planting day. Citizens can plant a tree to fight desertification.

First weekend of August The Olive and Olive Oil Festival in Sellasia, Greece, celebrates the abundant olive trees in the area. It promotes the region's olive oil and olives.

SEPTEMBER

September 5 On Amazon Day, people around the world take action to protect the Amazon Rainforest. The day is observed in Brazil with celebrations and, more recently, protests.

September–October Visitors flock to the US for peak "leaf peeping" season to see the warm colors of fall foliage transforming the country. Vermont, New Hampshire, and Colorado offer particularly striking scenes.

September 26–October 3 Spring in New Zealand marks the start of cherry blossom season. Festivals and other events take place across the country to celebrate the confettilike blooms.

Trees continue to hold significance for people across many different cultures and religions. They have often been venerated to promote health, wealth, fertility, and success and are still relied upon not only for shelter, materials, and food, but also for medicine, light, and warmth. They also play an important role in many cultural and religious ceremonies—both as tools and as offerings—and are often given great meaning within stories and myths. In an increasingly urbanized world, where deforestation and climate change threaten the ecological balance of the planet, many people are seeking greater connection with nature—listed below are some of the events that take place around the world to do just that, by celebrating the tree.

APRIL

Early April The *Qingming* Festival in China involves people commemorating their ancestors by sweeping tombs, making offerings, and placing willow branches on gates and doors.

April In the US, National Park Week involves events in all 423 national parks to encourage people to celebrate and connect with their natural heritage.

Last Friday in April Celebrated across the US, the Arbor Day holiday encourages people across the country to plant trees.

April–May In the UK, spring sees the blooming of bright bluebells, creating a carpet of color throughout the country's woodlands.

MAY

May 1 Each year on May Day, many towns in Bavaria, Germany, celebrate the return of spring by erecting a towering *Maibaum* (May tree). Neighboring communities seek to steal each other's Maibaum and demand a ransom of beer and food for its safe return.

May–June In late spring and early summer, visitors to South Korea are rewarded with the blooming of the country's national flower, *Magnolia sieboldii*.

JUNE

June The Hindu celebration *Vat Purnima* is observed over three days in northern and western India. As part of the festival, married women pray for their husband's health, chant, and tie threads around a banyan tree's trunk.

June 5 Timed to coincide with World Environment Day, New Zealand's Arbor Day is celebrated with community tree-planting events.

June 22 On World Rainforest Day, people around the globe celebrate rainforests and take action to preserve and protect them.

OCTOBER

Late September–early December In Scotland, the annual Scottish Tree Festival celebrates the country's trees, gardens, and woodlands.

October Across Japan, visitors appreciate the fiery colors of fall with the ancient tradition of maple leaf hunting (*Momijigari*).

October In Palestine's Olive Harvest Festival in Manger Square, Bethlehem, the olive tree is celebrated through traditional dances, music, crafts, and olive-based produce.

Mid-October–November Each spring, the vibrant purple blooms of jacaranda trees burst to life in Sydney, Australia, attracting tourists and locals alike.

NOVEMBER

November European Forest Week is celebrated with events including workshops, lectures, and exhibitions to raise awareness across the continent.

Mid-November–early December The Jingu Gaien Ginkgo Festival in Tokyo, Japan, marks the ginkgo as they turn golden yellow for fall.

Mid-November–early January Spectacular lights illuminate the trees of Kew Gardens in London, UK, at an annual nighttime display to mark the coming of the festive season.

Late November–early December The UK's largest annual tree event, National Tree Week involves tree planting in locations across the country.

DECEMBER

Wednesday after Thanksgiving At the Rockefeller Center in New York, a soaring Christmas tree is lit up for the coming festive season.

December 8 On Bodhi Day, Buddhists celebrate Siddhartha Gautama's enlightenment beneath a bodhi tree (*Ficus religiosa*) by meditating and decorating a bodhi tree with lights. The date varies, but many celebrate it on December 8.

December Similar to Christmas trees, *yolkas* (New Year's trees) can be seen across Russia, such as the spectacular decorated *yolka* displayed at the Kremlin in Moscow.

Conservation and Rewilding

Trees play a stabilizing role in the ecological balance of our planet. The biodiversity they provide, livelihoods they support, and carbon they store are vital for the flourishing of life in all its many forms.

The human impact

For much of their long existence on Earth, the sprawling forests that once covered much of the planet's surface were threatened only by fire—caused by natural phenomena such as lightning, heatwaves, and volcanic activity—and the "bulldozing" activity of large mammals. These herbivorous animals stimulated a varied mix of tree, shrub, and herb species by grazing and foraging among the forest understory.

As human populations gradually migrated and spread across the globe, trees were cut down—or cleared with the controlled use of fire—in small numbers. But despite this small-scale destruction of trees to obtain wood as a resource, create clearings that would attract prey animals, and encourage the natural growth of plants as a food source, human activity barely had an impact on the virgin forests. This began to change when humans started to abandon a hunter-gatherer existence in favor of a more settled, pastoral way of life. The adoption of farming at different times among different people across the world entailed the intentional clearance of forest cover in order to cultivate plants and crops and tend animals for human consumption.

Modern-day deforestation

The most dramatic increase in the pace of deforestation came during the industrial revolution of the 18th century. Beginning in Britain and quickly spreading across Europe and North America, the age of mechanized production transformed wood into an economic commodity that could be rapidly used to make a host of products. Mechanized tree-felling and timber-processing methods occurred alongside colonial acquisition of Indigenous lands containing vast virgin forests, which were rapidly exploited.

Today, ecologists estimate that one-third of the world's original forest cover—an area of 4.9 billion acres (2 billion hectares), equivalent to twice the size of the US—has been destroyed in the last 10,000 years. A staggering 2.4 billion acres (1 billion hectares) of this forest loss occurred during the last 100 years, demonstrating that without determined conservation and action, humanity's need for farmland, timber as a building and fuel resource, and living and working space for a burgeoning human population threatens to destroy the green heart and lungs of life on our planet.

Endangering environments

From the boreal forests of the subpolar regions to the humid rainforests of the tropics, deforestation has had a profound effect on the natural world. Few areas have been completely untouched—usually the most inaccessible and least economically viable pockets of natural habitat are the last intact areas to remain.

Since the 1960s, half the world's tropical rainforests have been destroyed entirely or degraded to the extent that they can no longer support native wildlife or sustain the livelihoods of the Indigenous people who live there. This can take the form of soil degradation due to the loss of tree roots that bind the earth together—meaning that fertility is lost and food crops can no longer be grown—or the complete absence of tree species upon which local people rely for food, hunting, shelter, and natural medicines.

Deforestation does not just threaten the forests themselves and the life that they support—it can also endanger other environments. For instance, trees act as a buffer in cases of coastal flooding and help regulate water flows in rivers and estuaries. Removing trees from these natural systems makes them far more vulnerable to extreme weather events, posing risks to human life and destabilizing economic and social cohesion.

TIMBER PRODUCTION, CANADA

AMAZON RAINFOREST, ECUADOR

ENDANGERED QUETZAL, COSTA RICA

The increased likelihood of extreme weather—from high temperatures and drought to intense, prolonged rainfall and flooding—due to global heating makes the mitigating effects of protected forest landscapes more important than ever.

Trees also have a vital role to play in the planet's changing climate, which is being fueled by increasing amounts of greenhouse gases, including carbon dioxide (CO_2). Cutting down trees releases CO_2 into the atmosphere— estimated, at the latest levels of deforestation, to be around one-eighth of current global CO_2 emissions—while healthy forests are one of the Earth's proven natural methods for absorbing CO_2. Around 2.9 billion tons (2.6 billion tonnes) of CO_2—one-third the amount released by burning fossil fuels— is absorbed by forests every year. Although not solely caused by deforestation, loss of natural habitats—such as tree cover—also brings wild animals and humans into closer contact with each other, increasing the risk of transmission of unknown pathogens. The dangers posed by this have been seen during the COVID-19 global pandemic, which is thought to have originated from an animal host.

Wildlife under threat

Around the world, the populations of a sample of animal species were found to have fallen by an average of 60 percent since 1970. This dwindling in wildlife numbers means that globally, 41 percent of all amphibians, 26 percent of all mammals, and 14 percent of all birds are threatened with extinction. More than 80 percent of the world's terrestrial biodiversity resides within forest environments, so the destruction and degradation of our trees threatens the very existence of a huge range of species. The biggest single cause of species becoming near-threatened or threatened with extinction (as reported by the International Union for Conservation of Nature [IUCN]), aside from crop farming, is logging—cited as a threat in 47 percent of studied species.

Statistics are only beginning to reveal the true losses hidden beneath the planet's leafy canopy. For instance, rainforest destruction and fragmentation on the island of Borneo led to the loss of more than 100,000 Bornean orangutans between 1999 and 2015, largely driven by palm-oil production, timber exploitation, and illegal hunting for meat and as pets. In Central and South America, the population of jaguars has fallen by up to 25 percent since 2000 and is now severely fragmented due to the destruction of the jaguar's preferred rainforest habitat and illegal poaching for its fur.

Protecting trees

The world's forests encompass a myriad of trees and other plants, animals, and fungi interacting in complex ecosystems, all of which are at risk without some level of legal protection. While the most populated and developed countries in the world contain few truly untouched forests, their protected reserves and national parks nevertheless act to conserve any vulnerable or endangered species. In parts of the world where governance and infrastructure are less developed, forested areas can be in danger of overexploitation because they lack the necessary conservation measures and legal protections to ensure their survival.

One of the world's most critically endangered trees is the Wollemi pine, a prehistoric species that was thought to be extinct until a small population was discovered in Australia in 1994. Around 100 wild specimens grow in a remote gorge within Wollemi National Park and were saved in 2020 by the bravery of firefighters during the devastating forest fires that swept Australia.

A close relative of the Wollemi pine is the monkey puzzle tree, a long-lived, slow-growing conifer native to the temperate zones of Chile and Argentina. Prized as timber for its durability and resistance to fungal decay, it is threatened by illegal logging, grazing, fire from volcanic activity, and its slow rate of regeneration.

Perrier's baobab tree is also on the IUCN's Red List of critically endangered species. Endemic to northern Madagascar, it has been subject to fire, felling for charcoal and timber, and clearance for mining activity to the extent that only around 250 mature adult specimens remain, mostly occurring outside the country's protected national parks.

Although it is a well-established tree across sub-Saharan Africa, African blackwood is a near-threatened species. Overharvesting due to its popularity as a high-quality timber for woodwind instruments, poor conservation practices, and a low germination rate have placed this commercial species under threat.

Encouraging biodiversity

Latin America and the Caribbean boast the highest biodiversity of any forested region, with a large number of endemic species. This is partly because the natural resources of the "New World" were among the last virgin areas to be exploited by Europeans. Many of the remaining endemic species are highly specialized and are unable to adapt well to changes in local conditions, so conservation and protection are vital.

One country in the region, Costa Rica, has pioneered the development of responsible ecotourism to boost its economy and protect its precious natural heritage. In the 1990s, it was an early adopter of tree planting to reverse decades of deforestation.

Among approaches to increasing biodiversity is the concept of "rewilding," which aims to rebuild ecosystems by reintroducing native plant and animal species to a landscape that has been modified by human intervention, sometimes over hundreds of years or more. Alongside the natural processes kick-started by the reintroduced species, support is provided to enable any nearby human activities to be conducted along sustainable principles. For example, livestock and farming infrastructure was removed from an area of 345 sq miles (890 sq km) in Chile. Native vegetation and wildlife were reintroduced, recreating Patagonian steppe and temperate beech forest systems capable of functioning without human intervention. Alongside this, the ranchers who farm nearby were encouraged to adopt a series of sustainable land-management practices.

Sustainable forests

Increasingly, responsible methods of forest management are being adopted that prioritize biodiversity and the rights of Indigenous people. Part-founded by the World Wide Fund for Nature (WWF), the Forest Stewardship Council (FSC) scheme provides accreditation for low-carbon, ethical, sustainable methods of timber production. WWF has also helped develop projects for a series of nontimber forest products, such as wild rubber and brazil nuts, which allow trees to be commercially grown and harvested without being cut down.

There can be significant economic benefits from adopting sustainable practice. In El Salvador, a forest landscape restoration project created around 50 jobs per $1 million invested—more than generated by a similar investment in manufacturing—that were located in rural, low-income areas. Similarly, a forest-restoration project in Rwanda created jobs that fell equally to women and men. However, the arguments for sustainable management of forests, whether for commercial activity or conservation, are not purely economic. The ecological balance of our planet and all its flora and fauna depend on our ability to protect, restore, and value the true worth of life-giving trees.

PROTECTED WILDERNESS, GRAND TETON, WYOMING

Glossary

ALTERNATE Describes leaves that form an ascending spiral, with one leaf per plant node and on alternate sides of the stem.

ANGIOSPERM A seed-producing plant that produces flowers and produces seeds enclosed within a carpel. This includes herbaceous plants, grasses, and most trees.

ANTHER The male part of the flower, found on the stamen, that contains the pollen. Usually borne on a stalk.

ARIL An extra coat that covers some seeds. This layer is often hairy or fleshy and brightly colored.

AXIL The upper angle formed by a leaf (or branch) and the stem (or trunk) bearing it.

BARK The protective outer layer or "skin" of the trunk, branches, and roots of a tree. This layer overlays the wood and protects the plant from water loss, cold, and other types of damage. The bark stretches as the plant grows.

BRACT Modified, usually small, leaflike structure typically found at the base of a flower or inflorescence or in the cone of a conifer. It can resemble normal foliage.

BUD A small swelling on a plant's stem that can develop into a flower, leaf, or shoot. This protuberance consists of immature leaves or petals protected by a layer of thick scales.

BURR A fruit, seed head, or flowerhead that has hooks or teeth. A burr is also a term for a woody outgrowth found on the trunk of some trees.

BUTTRESS Large and wide roots surrounding a tree with shallow roots. They help the tree maintain stability in shallow soil conditions.

CALYX (pl. CALYCES) The collective name for the usually green outer whorl of sepals.

CANOPY The layer of high-level foliage, continuous or discontinuous, found in a forest and made up of the crowns of the trees.

CATKIN A type of inflorescence, usually pendulous, in which scalelike bracts and tiny, stalkless, often petalless flowers are arranged on an unbranched axis.

CHLOROPHYLL The pigment that gives plants their green color. Chlorophyll traps sunlight as energy and uses it to produce sugars through photosynthesis.

CLONE A plant that is genetically identical to another plant. This can be achieved through taking a cutting from the mother plant and planting it.

COLUMNAR A tree shape that is taller than it is broad, thin, and with parallel sides.

COMPOUND Describes a leaf composed of two or more leaflets. Compound leaves grow from the same singular bud.

CONE The fruiting structure of conifers. Male cones are small and soft and bear pollen. Female cones are larger and woody and bear seeds when fertilized by pollen.

CONIFER A cone-bearing seed plant. It is usually evergreen, with small, needle- or scalelike leaves.

COPPICING The process of trimming back trees at ground level in a way that encourages them to grow new shoots from the stumps.

COTYLEDON The food-containing seed leaf situated within the embryo of a seed. Cotyledons aid the supply of nutrition that a plant embryo requires in order to germinate.

CROWN The rounded, topmost part of a tree made up of branches growing out from the main trunk.

CULTIVAR Contraction of "cultivated variety." A plant originally bred for a desired trait and subsequently maintained in cultivation.

DECIDUOUS A tree that is leafless for several months of the year. This is usually in winter (in the temperate zones) or the dry season (in the tropical zones).

DIOECIOUS A plant that carries male and female reproductive organs on separate plants. In dioecious species, only female plants bear seeds.

DISPERSAL The manner in which seeds are transported away from the parent plant that produces them. The main methods of dispersal are wind, water, animals, and mechanical (such as exploding seed capsules).

DOUBLE FLOWER A flower with more than one layer of petals. They are usually sterile and often have few or no stamens.

ELLIPTIC Describes a leaf that is oval in shape and broadest the center, tapering toward each end.

EMBRYO A young plant that is at a rudimentary stage of development. In seed plants, including seed trees, the embryo is encased in a seed until it grows into a seedling during germination.

EPIPHYTE A plant that relies on another plant for support and lives above the ground surface, with no roots in the soil.

EVERGREEN A tree that bears leaves all year round.

FASCICLE A tight bundle of leaves or stalked flowers that diverge very little. For example, the leaves of many pine trees form fascicles.

GENUS A term applied to a group of closely related species and denoted by the first part of the scientific name. For example, in *Pinus pinea* (stone pine), the genus is *Pinus*.

GERMINATION The sprouting of a seed, spore, or other reproductive body typically following a period of dormancy.

GRAFTING The process of attaching a shoot from one tree onto the cut stem of another tree.

GYMNOSPERM A seed-producing plant with seeds that are left unprotected by an enclosing ovary or fruit. Gymnosperms include conifers, cycads, and ginkgo.

HABIT The size, shape, and orientation of a plant. The characteristic form of a plant.

HARDY Plants that are capable of surviving adverse growing conditions. This usually pertains to climactic conditions, especially those of winter.

HEARTWOOD The dead, inner, central wood of a tree; strong and resistant to decay. Over time, layers of living sapwood cells are converted to heartwood.

HERMAPHRODITE An organism that has both male and female reproductive organs; in a tree, where the male and female reproductive organs are borne on the same flower.

HYBRID The result of cross-pollinating two distinct plants to form a new plant. A hybrid's name comprises the genus name, followed by ×, and the hybrid's specific name, for example, *Ilex × koehneana*.

INFLORESCENCE A cluster of flowers arranged around a single axis (stem). There are many different types, based on the way the flowers are arranged.

LANCEOLATE Describes a leaf shaped like a lance head—broadest below the center, narrow, and tapering to a point at each end.

LEAF SCAR The mark left by a leaf after it falls off of a twig or stem. Each tree species has a unique leaf scar.

LEAFLET A small leaf that makes up one part of a compound leaf. Also known as a pinna (plural: pinnae).

LENTICEL One of many raised pores found on the surface of bark or some fruits that allow air to access the plant's inner tissues.

LIGNIN An organic polymer central to the support tissues of most plants. Lignins are found in the cell walls of woody tissue and make a tree hard and rigid.

LOBE A protruding part of a leaf or a flower. A lobe is typically rounded or pointed.

MARGIN The edge of a leaf blade. There are many kinds of leaf margin, including smooth (entire), lobed, or serrated.

MIDRIB The main vein of a leaf or leaflet. Usually central, it runs from the stalk to the tip of a leaf or leaflet. Also called midvein.

MONOECIOUS Having separate male and female flowers on the same plant.

MUTATION A permanent alteration in the genetic makeup of an organism. Mutations can be passed on through generations.

NATURALIZED A non-native plant or species introduced to a foreign region by human activity that has adapted successfully and now forms self-sustaining populations in that region.

OVARY The lower, wide, vessel-like section of the female part of a flower that contains one or more ovules. After fertilization, the ovules become seeds and the ovary develops into a fruit.

OVULE Section of the flower that contains the egg cell. In flowering plants, ovules are encased in an ovary, but in gymnosperms, they are naked. After fertilization, the ovule develops into the seed.

PALMATE Describes the shape of a type of compound leaf that is lobed or divided into five parts like an open palm or a hand with fingers extended. The leaflets arise from a single basal point.

PANICLE An elongated flower cluster in which each flower has its own stalk (or pedicel) attached to the branch.

PERSISTENT In leaves, not falling, but remaining attached to the plant after the normal time of withering.

PHOTOSYNTHESIS The process by which a plant uses energy from sunlight to turn carbon dioxide and water into food and oxygen, fueling the plant's growth.

PINNATE A compound leaf arrangement in which the leaflets (pinnae) are arranged so as to resemble a feather. The leaflets are arranged either alternately or in opposite pairs on a central axis. Pinnately lobed leaves have lobes arranged in this fashion.

PISTIL The female reproductive organ of a flower.

POLLARDING A type of pruning in which the upper branches of a tree are removed; this reduces the size of large trees while promoting bushy growth of foliage and branches.

POLLEN A sticky or powdery mass of microspores produced by a flower's anthers. Pollen contains the plant's male gametes (sex cells) that are used to fertilize the female egg.

POLLINATE To fertilize a plant with pollen. This is often done by insects as they transfer pollen from the male anther of a flower to the female stigma.

RECEPTACLE The portion of the stem or axis that bears a single flower's organs or a flowerhead's florets. After pollination, the receptacle can swell to form the fruit.

ROOT The part of the plant usually underground that anchors the plant in the soil, absorbs water and minerals, and stores reserve foods.

SAP Watery fluid found in plants. In trees, sap contains dissolved minerals that are carried from the roots to the leaves in tiny pipelines through the sapwood—an inner layer of soft wood.

SAPLING A young tree. Specifically, a young tree that is no greater than about 4 in (10 cm) in diameter at breast height.

SEED The mature, fertilized ovule of a plant. Inside the seed case is the embryo and some stored food. Fruits, berries, nuts, pods, and cones all have different types of seeds. Given the appropriate conditions for growth, a seed will grow and become a plant.

SEEDLING The young tree that develops out of a plant embryo from a seed. Left to grow, it will later become a sapling.

SEMIEVERGREEN A tree that loses its leaves for only a short period during the year. This term can also refer to a tree that sheds a proportion of its leaves periodically—usually over fall and winter—but is never entirely leafless.

SEPAL One of the usually green, nonfertile leaflike parts that form the calyx of a flower. These parts protect the developing flower bud.

SPECIES (abbrev. SP.) A classification category used to group similar plants together that can interbreed with one another and reproduce.

SPORE A single reproductive cell that, unlike sex cells, is capable of developing without fusion with another reproductive cell. Spores, therefore, do not require fertilization. The only trees that reproduce by spores are tree ferns.

STAMEN The male reproductive part of a flower comprising an anther borne on a filament. In the vast majority of angiosperms, the stamen is a long, slender filament (stalk) with a two-lobed anther at its tip.

STIGMA The female part of the flower positioned at the tip of the pistil that receives the pollen. The stigma is usually elevated above the ovary on the style.

STIPULE A small leaflike or bractlike structure occurring on one or both sides of the base of a leafstalk (petiole) where the leafstalk arises from a stem.

STOMA (pl. STOMATA) A tiny pore on the surface of a plant leaf enclosed by a pair of guard cells that regulate its opening and closing. Stomata allow for the exchange of gases for photosynthesis and respiration.

STYLE The slender, sterile part of the ovary that bears the stigma so that it is presented in an effective location for pollination.

SUBSPECIES (abbrev. SUBSP.) A category of classification, below species, defining a distinct variant within a species, usually isolated based on geographical location. Subspecies can interbreed successfully with others of the same species.

SUCKERS A plant growth that usually develops from the roots of a plant or sometimes the lower part of the stem. Suckers arise from below the soil, some distance away from the main stem or trunk of the plant, and divert nourishment away from the plant.

TERMINAL Usually used to describe a bud or inflorescence growing at the end of a shoot, stem, branch, or other organ.

TRUNK The main stem of a tree and the tree's main organ. Made up of the bark, inner bark, cambium, sapwood, and hardwood. On most conifers, the trunk grows straight to the top of the tree. On most broadleaf trees, the trunk does not reach the top, but divides into branches.

VARIEGATED Usually used to describe leaves. Variegated leaves have more than one color, owing to a lack of chlorophyll in some of the leaf's cells. Variegated sections can appear as stripes, circles, borders, and other shapes. Variegation is a rare natural phenomenon.

VEIN A vascular bundle (bundle of transport vessels) at or near the surface of a leaf and running through a leaf. Veins provide support for a leaf and are used to transport both water and food.

WHORL A radial, vertical arrangement of three or more identical structural parts—such as petals, stamens, leaves—around a stem. For example, petals make up the whorl of the corolla.

Index

Locators in **bold** relate to pages with the most information. Locators in *italics* relate to photographs and illustrations.

Acknowledgments

DK would like to thank the following:

Additional text: Richard Gilbert, Sarah MacLeod

Editorial assistance: Shari Black, Polly Boyd, Michael Clark, Richard Gilbert, Janet Mohun, Priyanjali Narain

Design assistance: Nobina Chakravorty, Clarisse Hassan, Mahua Mandal

Technical assistance: Vijay Kandwal, Ashok Kumar, Mrinmoy Mazumdar, Mohd Rizwan, Jagtar Singh, Anita Yadav

Illustrations: Dan Crisp, Dominic Clifford, Mike Garland

Proofreading: Joy Evatt, Katie John

Indexing: Elizabeth Wise

Original photography: Gary Ombler

Senior Jackets Designer: Suhita Dharamjit

Smithsonian Enterprises:
Kealy Gordon, Product Development Manager
Jill Corcoran, Director, Licensed Publishing Sales
Brigid Ferraro, Vice President, Business Development & Licensing
Carol LeBlanc, President

British Museum. All rights reserved: (ca). 98-99 Getty Images / iStock: Ilbusca (Background). 100 Dreamstime.com: Simona Pavan (bl); Visa Sergeiev (2/clb). 100-101 Shutterstock.com: Olga Korneeva (background). 101 Alamy Stock Photo: Vladyslav Yushynov (br). Getty Images: Heritage Images (ca). 102-103 Dreamstime. com: Patrick Guenette (background). 102 Getty Images / iStock: Whiteway (clb). 103 © The Metropolitan Museum of Art: Girolamo dai Libri (Italian, Verona 1474–1555 Verona). 104 Alamy Stock Photo: Noel Bennett (br). Dreamstime.com: Patrick Guenette (background). Getty Images / iStock: w1d (tl). 105 Alamy Stock Photo: The Print Collector / © CM Dixon / Heritage Images (br). Getty Images / iStock: Gilmanshin (clb); Natali22206 (tr). 106 Alamy Stock Photo: Album. 106-107 Getty Images / iStock: Nastasic (background). 107 Alamy Stock Photo: Jose Mathew (c). Dreamstime.com: Dinesh Gamage (1/cra, 2/cra). 108 Getty Images / iStock: MahirAtes (crb). Getty Images: Universal Images Group / Hulton Fine Art / Contributor (tl). 108-109 Getty Images / iStock: Nastasic (background). 109 Alamy Stock Photo: Robertharding (br). Dreamstime.com: Anat Chantrakool (cr). © The Metropolitan Museum of Art: Gift of Irwin Untermyer, 1968 (ca). Shutterstock. com: Av Tukaram.Karve (tr). 110 Alamy Stock Photo: flowerphotos (2/crb). Dreamstime.com: Vladimir Melnik (1/crb, 3/crb). 110-111 Dreamstime.com: Aisha Nuraini (background). Kristina @ hobopeeba Makeeva: (t). 111 Alamy Stock Photo: Jurate Buiviene (crb); World History Archive (tc). 112-113 Dreamstime.com: Aisha Nuraini (background). 112 Dreamstime.com: Alex7370 (tc). 113 123RF.com: Natalie Ruffing (r). Shutterstock.com: Av Bennekom (cb). 114 Alamy Stock Photo: Robertharding (c). Dreamstime.com: David Steele (2/cra). Shutterstock.com: FLPA / Shutterstock (1/cra). 115 Alamy Stock Photo: GFC Collection (bl); Anette Mossbacher (tr). 116 Dreamstime.com: Ogonkova (crb). Getty Images / iStock: Catshila (l). Shutterstock. com: pixbox77 (2/crb). 116-17 Getty Images / iStock: ilbusca (background). 117 Alamy Stock Photo: Nature Picture Library (cb). © The Metropolitan Museum of Art: Gift of The Salgo Trust for Education, New York, in memory of Nicolas M. Salgo, 2010 (cra). 118-119 Science Photo Library: Alex Hyde. 120 Bridgeman Images: Bridgeman Images (tl). Dreamstime.com: Chernetskaya (1/cra); Rinchumrus2528 (2/cra); Lars Ove Jonsson (cr); Sisyphus Zirix (crb). 121 Alamy Stock Photo: Dennis Frates. 122-123 Dreamstime.com: Foxyliam (background). 122 Getty Images: Eric Lafforgue / Art in All of Us / Contributor (c). 123 Alamy Stock Photo: Artokoloro (br). Getty Images / iStock: Antonel (r). 124 Dorling Kindersley: Gary

Ombler / Westonbirt, The National Arboretum (2/cla, 3/cla). 125 Alamy Stock Photo: agefotostock (br). Getty Images / iStock: Duncan1890 (background). Getty Images: Heritage Images (tr). 126-127 Lorraine Devon Wilke: (t). 126 Alamy Stock Photo: Sandra Standbridge (cl). Getty Images / iStock: Duncan1890 (background). 127 Look and Learn: Valerie Jackson Harris Collection (bc). 128 Shutterstock.com: Martina Birnbaum. 129 Alamy Stock Photo: Marcus Harrison—botanicals (background). Dreamstime.com: Bat09mar (2/cla). Science Photo Library: Gustoimages (ca). 130 Alamy Stock Photo: Marcus Harrison—botanicals (background); Anna Poltoratskaya (ca). Dreamstime.com: Karayuschij (2/cra); Alfio Scisetti (1/cra); Pancaketom (3/cra). 131 Jack Brauer (www. MountainPhotography.com). 132 Alamy Stock Photo: Peter Horree (tl). 132-133 Alamy Stock Photo: Marcus Harrison—botanicals (background). 133 Alamy Stock Photo: Minden Pictures (br). Dreamstime.com: Amelia Martin (cl). 134 Alamy Stock Photo: Duncan Usher. 135 Alamy Stock Photo: Richard Tadman (r). Dreamstime.com: Foxyliam (Background). 137 Alamy Stock Photo: Album (bc); Uber Bilder (tc). Dreamstime.com: Foxyliam (Background). 138 Alamy Stock Photo: Agefotostock / Terrance Klassen (t). 139 123RF.com: Morphart (Background). Alamy Stock Photo: Artokoloro (bc). Getty Images: Sepia Times / Contributor / Universal Images Group (tc). 140 Dreamstime.com: Vvoevale (cl). 140-141 Getty Images / iStock: Ilbusca (Background). 141 Alamy Stock Photo: Nature Picture Library / Sandra Bartocha (tr); Nature Picture Library (br). 142 Alamy Stock Photo: Arterra Picture Library / Clement Philippe (bc); Painting (tl). Getty Images / iStock: Ilbusca (Background). naturepl.com: Philippe Clement (br). 143 Alamy Stock Photo: Arterra Picture Library / Clement Philippe (bl); Minden Pictures / Wil Meinderts / Buiten-beeld (br). 144-145 Steven Palmer. 146-147 Image courtesy Rick Worrell. 146 Alamy Stock Photo: Marcus Harrison—botanicals (Background). Dorling Kindersley: Royal Botanic Gardens, Kew (bl). 148 Alamy Stock Photo: Chronicle (tl); George Reszeter (bc). 148-149 Alamy Stock Photo: Marcus Harrison—botanicals (Background). 149 Shutterstock.com: iPostnikov (cr). 150-151 Alamy Stock Photo: Jacky Parker (t). 151 Alamy Stock Photo: Artokoloro (tr). Dreamstime.com: Patrick Guenette (Background). 152 Getty Images: Popperfoto (tr). © The Metropolitan Museum of Art: Mary Griggs Burke Collection, Gift of the Mary and Jackson Burke Foundation, 2015 (cr). 153 Dreamstime.com: Patrick Guenette (Background). Image courtesy mokuhankan.com. 154 Getty Images: swim ink 2 llc / Contributor / Corbis

Historical (tl). 154-155 Alamy Stock Photo: Crystite RF. 156 Alamy Stock Photo: The History Collection (tl). naturepl.com: Klein & Hubert (crb). 157 Getty Images / iStock: U. J. Alexander (cra); Ilbusca (Background). Science Photo Library: Cordelia Molloy (c). 158 Alamy Stock Photo: Carolyn Jenkins (bl). Getty Images / iStock: Ilbusca (Background). Library of Congress, Washington, D.C.: LC-USZC4-11920 (tl). 159 Bridgeman Images: Photo © Christie's Images (tr). Dreamstime.com: Stephan Bock (br). Getty Images / iStock: Ilbusca (Background). 160 Dreamstime.com: Hellmann1 (cla). Wellcome Collection: (bc). 160-161 Alamy Stock Photo: Jacky Parker (c). Getty Images / iStock: Ilbusca (Background). 161 Alamy Stock Photo: Hamza Khan (tr). 162-163 Dreamstime.com: Patrick Guenette (background). 162 Alamy Stock Photo: Tom Joslyn (br). Dreamstime.com: Volodymyr Kucherenko (l). 163 Getty Images: Hulton Archive (br). 164 Dreamstime.com: Hellmann1 (3/cla). 164-165 Alamy Stock Photo: Marcus Harrison—botanicals (background). 165 Bridgeman Images: Lebrecht History / Bridgeman Images (tr). 166-167 Alamy Stock Photo: Patrick Guenette (background). Getty Images: Matt Anderson Photography (c). 166 Dorling Kindersley: Gary Ombler / Batsford Garden Centre and Arboretum (1/crb, 3/crb). Getty Images / iStock: Andrea_Hill (2/crb). 168-169 Alamy Stock Photo: Patrick Guenette (background). 169 Bridgeman Images: Kallir Research Institute / © Grandma Moses Properties Co. / Bridgeman Images (crb). Getty Images: Transcendental Graphics / Contributor (tr). 170-171 Dreamstime.com: Patrick Guenette (background). 170 Alamy Stock Photo: Album (cr). Dreamstime.com: Alessandrozocc (2/cla); Fotokon (3/cla). 171 Brent Mooers: (cb). 172-173 Courtesy Longwood Gardens . 174-175 Dreamstime. com: Info718087 (background). 175 Alamy Stock Photo: Peter Horree (tr). Dreamstime.com: John Biglin (br). 176-177 Dreamstime.com: Info718087 (background). 177 Alamy Stock Photo: Nigel Cattlin (cb). Rebecca Allen: (tr). 178 Alamy Stock Photo: Nature Picture Library. 179 Bridgeman Images: Purix Verlag Volker Christen / Bridgeman Images (crb). Dorling Kindersley: Gary Ombler: Centre for Wildlife Gardening / London (2/cla). Dreamstime.com: Tetiana Kovalenko (3/cla). Getty Images / iStock: Nastasic (background). 180-181 Getty Images / iStock: Nastasic (background). 180 Alamy Stock Photo: Robertharding (bl). 181 Science Photo Library: Bildagentur-Online / Mcphoto-Rolfes (tc). 182 Alamy Stock Photo: Lamax (c). 182-183 Getty Images / iStock: ilbusca (background). 183 Christianne Muusers: RIJKMuseum / adapted by Christianne Muusers (tc). 184 123RF.com: Denis Barbulat (Background).

Bridgeman Images: Alinari (tl); Photo © Heini Schneebeli (crb). Dreamstime.com: Simona Pavan (cra). 185 Alamy Stock Photo: Mauritius Images GmbH / Andreas Vitting. 186-187 123RF.com: Denis Barbulat (Background). 186 Alamy Stock Photo: The Picture Art Collection (br). 187 Bridgeman Images: © Holburne Museum (tc). Dennis Greenwood: (c). 188-189 123RF.com: Denis Barbulat (Background). 189 Getty Images: Print Collector / Contributor / Hulton Archive (bl). 190 Dreamstime.com: Metacynth (crb); Sdbower (crb/Bark). Lana Gramlich: (t). 190-191 Shutterstock.com: Foxyliam. 191 Shutterstock.com: Kent Weakley (tr). 192 Alamy Stock Photo: The Natural History Museum (ca). 192-193 Dreamstime.com: Patrick Guenette (background). 193 Alamy Stock Photo: Jürgen Feuerer (r); World History Archive (tr). 194-195 Dreamstime.com: Patrick Guenette (background). Getty Images / iStock: PeskyMonkey (t). 194 Alamy Stock Photo: Album (br); Zoonar GmbH (crb). Dreamstime.com: Iva Villi (2/cla); Simona Pavan (3/cla). 196 Alamy Stock Photo: Heritage Image Partnership Ltd. (tl). 196-197 Getty Images / iStock: Mammuth (b). 197 Getty Images: Paul Popper / Popperfoto (c). 198-199 Getty Images: Emil Von Maltitz / Photodisc. 200-201 Alamy Stock Photo: Marcus Harrison—botanicals (background). 200 Alamy Stock Photo: Marcus Harrison—plants (r). Bridgeman Images: Marcus Harrison—botanicals (tl). Dreamstime. com: Vasiliybokov (cra). 202-203 Alamy Stock Photo: Marcus Harrison—botanicals (background). 203 Bridgeman Images: Bridgeman Images (cr). Getty Images: Marcus Harrison—botanicals (tr). 204 Bridgeman Images: William Salt Library / Bridgeman Images (tr). Dorling Kindersley: Gary Ombler / Westonbirt, The National Arboretum (bl). 204-205 Dreamstime. com: Patrick Guenette (background). 205 Getty Images: Heritage Images (tc). 206 Tomas Munita. 207 Alamy Stock Photo: Suwannee Suwanchwee (Background). Dreamstime.com: Elise Pearlstine (cla); Songwuth Suwannawong (fcla); Shariqkhan (cla/Fruit). Jafeth Moiane: (tr). 208-209 Alamy Stock Photo: Suwannee Suwanchwee (Background). Dreamstime. com: Le Thuy Do. 208 Haarlem House: (bc). 209 Alamy Stock Photo: Minden Pictures / Steve Gettle (bc). 210 Cheryl Bigman. 210-211 Alamy Stock Photo: Suwannee Suwanchwee (Background). 211 Alamy Stock Photo: Agefotostock / Christian Goupi (tr); Agefotostock / Emilio Ereza (bl). 212 Dreamstime.com: Lucy Brown (crb); Iliukhina Olga (background). Wellcome Collection: Kapok or silk cotton tree (Ceiba pentandra) growing by a village in Surinam. Colored lithograph by P. Lauters, c. 1839, after P. J. Benoit. (cr). 213 Alamy Stock Photo: The Book Worm (background). Dreamstime.com: Verastuchelova (br). Getty Images:

Bildagentur-online / Contributor (tr). **214-215 Getty Images / iStock:** ilbusca (background). **214 Alamy Stock Photo:** Firn. **215 Alamy Stock Photo:** Heritage Image Partnership Ltd. (cra). **Dorling Kindersley:** Gary Ombler / Royal Botanic Gardens, Kew (cla). **216 Alamy Stock Photo:** Minden Pictures (cb). **Dreamstime.com:** Ericsch (fclb); Fjmolina65 (fcla); Sweet Hour Photography (fcl). **217 Bridgeman Images:** Luisa Ricciarini / Bridgeman Images. **Getty Images:** ilbusca (background). **218 Dreamstime.com:** Ecophoto (c); Oleksandr Tkachenko (1/cra). **Shutterstock.com:** Estelle R (2/cra). **219 Alamy Stock Photo:** Minden Pictures (cb). **Dreamstime.com:** Czuber (1/crb); Brian Scantlebury (2/crb). **Getty Images:** Education Images (tr). **220 Alamy Stock Photo:** FLPA (br). **Getty Images / iStock:** Olga Gont (l). **221 Alamy Stock Photo:** Patrick Guenette (background); Mikehoward 2 (bl); Historic Collection (br). **222 Alamy Stock Photo:** Roberto Colino (tc). **Dorling Kindersley:** Neil Fletcher (crb). **223 Getty Images / iStock:** Jani_Autio. **224-225 Dreamstime.com:** Patrick Guenette (background). **225 Alamy Stock Photo:** AB Historic (bc); Elizabeth Wake (tr). **226-227 Daniel Kordan (c). 228 Dreamstime.com:** Toby Gibson (br). **229 Alamy Stock Photo:** Emmanuel Lattes (c). **Getty Images / iStock:** ilbusca (background). **Getty Images:** Paul Popper / Popperfoto (bl). **230 Alamy Stock Photo:** Universal Images Group North America LLC (c). **Getty Images / iStock:** ilbusca (background). **231 Alamy Stock Photo:** FLPA (bl). **Shutterstock.com:** Gianpiero Ferrari / Flpa / imageBROKER (cr). **232 123RF.com:** eshved (background). **Alamy Stock Photo:** agefotostock (br). **Dreamstime.com:** Matyas Rehak (3/cra). **Getty Images:** Yannick Tylle (tl). **naturepl.com:** Hanne & Jens Eriksen (2/cra). **233 Dreamstime.com:** Junko Barker. **234 Alamy Stock Photo:** The Natural History Museum. **235 akg-images:** akg-images / VISIOARS (tr). **Dreamstime.com:** Jeneses Imre (background); Pran Yadee (3/cla). **Muséum de Toulouse:** Roger Culos / "CC-BY-SA" (br). **236 Alamy Stock Photo:** Niday Picture Library (tl). **236-237 Weerapong Chaipuck:** (b). **Dreamstime.com:** Jeneses Imre (background). **237 Getty Images:** Ipsumpix / Contributor (bc). **238 Bridgeman Images:** Giancarlo Costa. **239 Shutterstock.com:** Morphart Creation (backgrounund). **240-241 Shutterstock.com:** Morphart Creation (background). **240 Alamy Stock Photo:** The Granger Collection (br); Richard Grange (bl). **242 Alamy Stock Photo:** Marc Anderson. **242-243 Getty Images / iStock:** ilbusca (background). **243 Alamy Stock Photo:** Dmytro Synelnychenko (br). **Dreamstime.com:** Oskanov (tr). **244 Science Photo Library:** Natural History Museum, London (c). **244-245 Getty Images / iStock:** ilbusca (background). **245 Alamy Stock Photo:**

www.pqpictures.co.uk (br). **Getty Images / iStock:** MykolaIvashchenko (t). **246 Getty Images / iStock:** ilbusca (background). **Ilkin Kangarli.:** (tc). **247 Hagströmer Medico-Historical Library, Karolinska Institutet. 248-249 Dreamstime.com:** Thanu Garapakdee (t/(All)). **Getty Images / iStock:** ilbusca (background). **248 Getty Images:** George Rinhart (bl). **249 Getty Images:** Historical / Contributor (cb). **250 © The Trustees of the British Museum. All rights reserved:** (c). **Dreamstime.com:** Anuroop Khandelwal (2/cra). **251 Alamy Stock Photo:** Scott Biales (tc). **252-253 Dreamstime.com:** Athapet Piruksa (background). **Ryosho Shimizu:** (t). **252 Getty Images:** Sepia Times / Contributor (bl). **254-255 Kallol Mukherjee. 256 Getty Images:** Sadik Demiroz (cra); Arun Roisri (br). **257 Dreamstime.com:** Betta0147 (bl); Irina Iarovaia (Background). **Getty Images:** Peter Unger / Stone (r). **258 Dreamstime.com:** Ksena2009 (1/cla, 2/cla); Tamara Kulikova (3/cla); Ashley Whitworth (tr). **259 Getty Images:** Auscape. **260 Getty Images / iStock:** ilbusca (bc); tamara_kulikova (tc). **260-261 Getty Images:** De Agostini Picture Library / Contributor (background). **261 Alamy Stock Photo:** FLPA (tr). **262-263 Getty Images / iStock:** Alhontess (background); Phaelnogueira (t). **263 Alamy Stock Photo:** Diego Grandi (br). **Bridgeman Images:** Purix Verlag Volker Christen (cra). **264 akg-images:** Roland & Sabrina Michaud. **265 Alamy Stock Photo:** Imagebroker / Sohns (r). **Dorling Kindersley:** Royal Botanic Gardens, Kew (cla). **Dreamstime.com:** Engin Korkmaz (Background). **266 akg-images:** Fototeca Gilardi (tc). **Dreamstime.com:** Adhitya Ramadhan (bc). **Getty Images / iStock:** Changphoto (br). **Eric Royer Stoner:** (clb). **266-267 Dreamstime.com:** Engin Korkmaz (Background). **267 Trevor Cole. 268-269 Dreamstime.com:** Patrick Guenette (Background). **268 Dreamstime.com:** Thongchai Nakim (cra). **Shutterstock.com:** Koifish (c). **269 Alamy Stock Photo:** Martin Bond (bc); Lanmas (tr). **270 Dreamstime.com:** Snowwhiteimages (1/cra); Thana Ram (2/cra, 3/cra). **Dr. Poonam Singh:** (l). **270-271 Dreamstime.com:** Patrick Guenette (backgrouond). **271 Bridgeman Images:** Chester Beatty Library (cra). **Dreamstime.com:** Tetiana Kovalenko (br). **272 Rijksmuseum, Amsterdam:** (bc). **272-273 123RF.com:** anisimovfedor (background). **Dreamstime.com:** Jesse Kraft (c). **273 Dreamstime.com:** David Pillow (cra). **274 Alamy Stock Photo:** CPA Media Pte Ltd. (tl). **274-275 123RF.com:** anisimovfedor (background). **Getty Images / iStock:** Eivaisla (cb). **275 Dreamstime.com:** Ekaterina Simonova (br). **Shutterstock.com:** Everett Collection (tr). **276-277 Dreamstime.com:** Mariia Sultanova (background). **276 Alamy Stock Photo:** Album. **277 Dorling Kindersley:** Colin Keates / Natural History Museum,

London (cra). **Getty Images:** Science & Society Picture Library / Contributor (ca). **Science Photo Library:** Sheila Terry (br). **278-279 Alamy Stock Photo:** Mauritius Images GmbH / Stefan Hefele. **280-281 Dreamstime.com:** Geraria (Background). **280 Getty Images / iStock:** Edsongrandisoli. **281 Ardea:** Nick Gordon (tr). **282-283 Dreamstime.com:** Geraria (Background). **282 Shutterstock.com:** Guentermanaus. **283 Image courtesy of liveauctioneers.com and (the auction house):** (bl). **284-285 Getty Images / iStock:** Bokasana (Background). **284 Dreamstime.com:** Irina Magrelo. **285 Dreamstime.com:** Tetiana Kovalenko (tl, br); Simona Pavan (cla). **Getty Images / iStock:** Jez_Bennett (tr). **286 Alamy Stock Photo:** Martin Harvey (tl). **286-287 Alamy Stock Photo:** Decha Somparn (t). **Getty Images / iStock:** Bokasana (Background). **287 Dreamstime.com:** Sarot Chamnankit (cra). **Getty Images / iStock:** PeterEtchells (fcrb); YoriHirokawa (crb). **Shutterstock.com:** Pedro Helder Pinheiro (cr). **288-289 Alamy Stock Photo:** Quagga Media (Background). **288 Alamy Stock Photo:** Florilegius (tr). **Dreamstime.com:** Kschua (cla); Likit Supasai (tl). **289 Getty Images:** Thierry Falise / Contributor / LightRocket (t); Arun Roisri / Moment (br). **290 Getty Images:** Somnuk Krobkum / Moment. **291 Dreamstime.com:** Foxyliam (Background); Kreatifiani Maulana (tl); Saengdao Srisupha (cla). **Getty Images / iStock:** Boonsom (cr). **292 Plantaholic Sheila!:** (bl). **292-293 Dreamstime.com:** Foxyliam (Background). **293 Mary Evans Picture Library:** Onslow Auctions Limited (t). **Photo Scala, Florence:** Digital image, The Museum of Modern Art, New York (br). **294 Dreamstime.com:** Boonchuay Iamsumang (cl); Alf Ribeiro (clb). **Getty Images / iStock:** Chitaya (r). **294-295 Shutterstock.com:** Lubov Chipurko (Background). **295 Dreamstime.com:** Peter Zijlstra (crb). **Getty Images:** Bloomberg (t). **Getty Images / iStock:** Mashuk (bc); Luis Echeverri Urrea (br). **296 Alamy Stock Photo:** Lordprice Collection (bl). **296-297 Alamy Stock Photo:** Ivan Vdovin (background). **Getty Images:** Jose A. Bernat Bacete (c). **298 Bridgeman Images:** Look and Learn / Illustrated Papers Collection (tl). **naturepl.com:** Heather Angel (crb). **298-299 Alamy Stock Photo:** Ivan Vdovin (background). **299 Dreamstime.com:** Igor Abramovych (br); Pipa100 (tl). **Shutterstock.com:** Nataly Studio (tc); SOMMAI (tr). **300-301 Alamy Stock Photo:** Stephen Bridger (b). **Dreamstime.com:** Patrick Guenette (Background). **300 123RF.com:** Wirojsid (cra). **Dorling Kindersley:** Thomas Marent (fcra). **Dreamstime.com:** 7active Studio (tr). **301 Getty Images:** Ed Reschke / Stone (tr). **302-303 Dreamstime.com:** Patrick Guenette (Background). **302 Phil's 1stPix. 303 Alamy Stock Photo:** Bob Gibbons (clb). **Plantaholic Sheila!:** (cra). **Shutterstock.**

com: Candrafirman (cla). **304-305 Doron Talmi. 306-307 Dreamstime.com:** Patrick Guenette (Background). **309 Getty Images / iStock:** Jaboo2foto (br). **310 Getty Images / iStock:** Avi_Cohen_Nehemia / E+ (bl). **311 Getty Images:** John Elk III / The Image Bank (tl); Sebastián Crespo Photography / Moment Open (br). **312 Getty Images:** Avalon / Contributor / Universal Images Group (br); Oliver Gerhard (tl). **313 Getty Images:** Fhm / Moment (tr). **314 Getty Images:** Education Images / Contributor / Universal Images Group. **315 Getty Images:** Education Images / Contributor / Universal Images Group (t); Juergen Ritterbach / Photodisc (br). **316 Getty Images:** Newton Kakadia / EyeEm (br); Tuul & Bruno Morandi / The Image Bank (t). **317 Getty Images:** Andrew Merry / Moment. **318 Alamy Stock Photo:** Francois Roux. **319 Alamy Stock Photo:** Angus McComiskey (tl); J.Enrique Molina (br). **320 Getty Images:** Atlantide Phototravel / Corbis Documentary. **321 Alamy Stock Photo:** Rafael Ben Ari (tr). **Getty Images:** Casarsa / E+ (bl). **322 Getty Images:** Christophe Kiciak / Contributor / Moment. **323 Getty Images:** Martin Harvey / The Image Bank (tl); Prisma by Dukas / Contributor / Universal Images Group (br). **324 Dorling Kindersley:** Royal Botanic Gardens, Kew (bc). **325 Dorling Kindersley:** Will Heap / Mike Rose (tc). **Dreamstime.com:** Somkid Manowong (bc). **326 Dorling Kindersley:** Batsford Garden Centre and Arboretum (fcra, fcrb); Westonbirt, The National Arboretum (crb); Centre for Wildlife Gardening / London Wildlife Trust (bc). **Getty Images / iStock:** ByMPhotos (fclb); Joakimbkk / E+ (clb). **327 Dreamstime.com:** Anitasstudio (cra); Qpicimages (bl). **328 123RF.com:** Nvelichko (cra). **Alamy Stock Photo:** Joe Blossom (cla). **Dorling Kindersley:** Neil Fletcher (crb). **Dreamstime.com:** Georgesixth (bc); Michal Paulus (br). **330 Alamy Stock Photo:** All Canada Photos / Graham Osborne. **331 Getty Images:** Kilito Chan / Moment (br); Prisma by Dukas / Contributor / Universal Images Group (tl). **332-333 Dreamstime.com:** Geraria (Background). **334 Getty Images:** Cavan Images. **335 Alamy Stock Photo:** Mark Fox. **336 Getty Images:** © Juan Carlos Vindas / Moment. **337 Getty Images:** Jeff R Clow / Moment

All other images © Dorling Kindersley

DK would especially like to thank: Matthew Hall, Head Gardener for permission to photograph tree species and all of his help at the **Batsford Arboretum and Garden Centre**, Moreton In Marsh, Gloucestershire, UK. www.batsarb.co.uk